Investment in Innovation

Investment in Innovation

An Historical Appraisal
of the Fund
for the Advancement
of Education

PAUL WOODRING

Little, Brown and Company
Boston—Toronto

LIBRARY OF CONGRESS CATALOG CARD NO. 76-128361

01345 W0541 T10/70

FIRST EDITION

The author gratefully acknowledges permission to quote from the following sources:

Learning to Read: The Great Debate, by Jeanne S. Chall. Copyright ©
1967 by McGraw-Hill, Inc. Used by permission of the author and Mc-
Graw-Hill Book Company.

"The Care and Feeding of Institutions" by Clarence H. Faust from *Saturday Review,* March 30, 1968. Copyright © 1968 by Saturday Review, Inc.
Used by permission.

"Editorial Policy for the Education Supplement" by Paul Woodring from
Saturday Review, September 17, 1960. Copyright © 1960 by Saturday
Review, Inc. Used by permission.

*Published simultaneously in Canada
by Little, Brown & Company (Canada) Limited*

The Right Agenda

Foreword by Roy E. Larsen

In the pages of this book and elsewhere, a great many thoughtful individuals have expressed their judgments about the Fund for the Advancement of Education and its works. If I were to choose just one person to make such an evaluation, I could hardly do better than to single out Francis Keppel.

During the sixteen-year existence of the Fund from 1951 to 1967, Keppel was successively dean of the Harvard Graduate School of Education, U.S. Commissioner of education, assistant secretary for education of the Department of Health, Education and Welfare, and chairman and president of General Learning Corporation. So while he was anything but a detached witness to what was going on in the world of education, he nevertheless had the broadest kind of background from which to assess the Fund's operations.

Here, in a nutshell, is his appraisal: "When you look back at what was happening in education at the time, as well as what was about to happen, and when you examine the record of the Fund, I think you will see that it had the right agenda."

This thought is not only reassuring, but it strikes me as a rare insight into the meaning of the Fund. The programs that the Fund had decided to explore — most of them chosen almost twenty years ago, and many of them moving into virtual vacuums at the time — did indeed constitute the right agenda, for then and much of it also for now. These were the major undertakings:

1. An examination of the needs for improved teacher training, for better use of teacher time and talent, and for clearer articulation between high schools and colleges.
2. The recognition of the importance of citizen interest in education.
3. A look at new technologies, especially classroom TV, at curricular updating and reform, and perhaps at the learning process itself.
4. An examination of civil rights in education, and of the means of converting the fiction of equal educational opportunity into fact.
5. A hard look — and this came late in the Fund's life — at national educational assessment and accountability.

In this superb history of the Fund, Paul Woodring discusses these programs, and poses the question whether the Fund should or should not have continued beyond its termination in 1967. Regardless of how one may seek to resolve that rather imponderable question, it becomes quite clear that the Fund was a highly appropriate creation of its time.

The Fund for the Advancement of Education began just after the midcentury point, and those days, like the present, were far from subdued and complacent, particularly in the world of education. There were mounting cries of protest over teaching methods, over progressive education, about whether our children could or could not read, or indeed whether they were learning any useful arts other than the means of making the proper social adjustments. The debate was joined by a great many people who understood it only imperfectly, if at all. Unhappily, it also opened the gates to witch-hunters and book-burners, whose professed fear of subversion was exceeded only by their own efforts to subvert all of American education.

It was in this period of dissatisfactions and suspicions that Paul Woodring first invited me to write a foreword to a book. The year was 1952, and his book was *Let's Talk Sense About Our Schools*. In the intellectual climate that then prevailed, I welcomed Paul Woodring's work as a breath of fresh air, with its hard facts cutting through popular misconception and its incisive thinking replacing widespread prejudice. But I had to turn down his request with regret, because I was then chairman of the National Citizens Commission for the Public Schools. The commission's primary purpose was to promote citizen support of their local schools and to develop a high degree of citizen interest in the programs and problems of the schools — but without taking positions on such professional matters as curriculum and approaches to teaching. As its chairman, I felt it would be out of the question for me to prejudice the commission or place it in the position of supporting any point of view in controversial matters — and curriculum and teaching methods were certainly controversial in those days.

Professor Woodring's book was undoubtedly contributory to the fact that a large measure of sanity soon returned to most of public education. In any event, most of these problems were already being submerged under the unprecedented floodtide of youngsters, products of the wartime and postwar baby boom, who were descending on our schools and would continue to arrive in increasing numbers. In the sixteen years of the Fund's existence, from 1951 to 1967, as Mr. Woodring has pointed out, the number of students in our schools and colleges grew from 32 million to 57 million, reaching almost a third of the total population.

What no one could have honestly foreseen, however, or would have dared to predict in those early postwar years was the staggering increase in expenditures for education — from $11 billion in 1951 to $29 billion in 1961, or from 3.4 per cent of the gross national product to 5.6 per cent. To me this stands out in retrospect as the magnificent triumph of an aroused public over the always considerable forces of apathy and short-sightedness.

But even while this was taking place, there was another and equally important challenge to the schools — that of maintaining and upgrading the level of educational quality. Whereas the Citizens Commission had taken as its major assignment that of helping provide for the larger number of students, the Fund for the Advancement of Education focused its efforts primarily on areas closely related to quality — in teaching, in learning and in administration — and in pursuing what John Gardner was subsequently to describe as the quest for excellence.

To me it is remarkable how many of the right people appeared to rise to this occasion. The initial salutes must be made, of course, to such perceptive and foresighted thinkers as James Conant from the academic world, John Gardner and Devereux Josephs from the foundations, and Paul Hoffman and others from the business world. For its administrative leadership, the Fund struck a rich vein when it was able to recruit both Clarence Faust and Alvin Eurich. The first board chairman was Frank Abrams, who might well be deemed the father of modern corporate support for higher education, and working with him were a group of men and women whose dedication, whose credentials and whose talents would have done credit to any boardroom in the nation (see pages 43–49). Almost all of them remained on the board during the full sixteen years of the Fund's existence.

All of this begs the question, however, of how well the Fund did with its "right" agenda. The answer would probably have to be that the results ranged from questionable to spectacularly good. What is still remarkable is how much the Fund was able to accomplish with expenditures that averaged just over $4 million a year. The lasting consequences of the Fund's activities would be all but impossible to weigh or evaluate, but one knows intuitively that its contributions were both substantial and unique. Many of the things that moved, almost imperceptibly, into the mainstream of our teaching and learning were first initiated — often with doubts and misgivings — by the Fund.

That the face of American education has changed since 1950, few would question. Perhaps fewer still are aware of what the Fund did to help bring this about.

The contribution to the Master of Arts in Teaching program is pointed out in some detail in the chapters of this book. There were other programs, too. Teacher aides, now taken so very much for granted in our classrooms, represented one of the bold experimental programs the Fund developed. A teacher-aide project in Bay City, Michigan, was one of the Fund's earliest undertakings. Paul Briggs, who was superintendent of schools there, was in charge of that experiment. Subsequently as school superintendent in Cleveland, he used some three thousand volunteer teacher aides in that system.

Recognizing the need for a strong underpinning of citizen understanding and support of public education, the Fund made grants of almost $2 million for the National Citizens Commission for the Public Schools. The value realized here was not alone in the work of the commission, but perhaps equally important, in the lingering effects of a long-term commitment to education on the part of a great many of our most able and intelligent citizens.

Some other consequences of the Fund's initiatives are perhaps less visible, or are yet to have their full impact on American education. The encouragement of curricular reform, for example, was receiving its impetus from other quarters as well, but its effects become increasingly obvious. Many of us can remember when it was not unusual for new educational content programs to take forty or fifty years to get from the idea stage to acceptance for the country's classrooms. Now, discoveries which won Nobel awards in the mid-1950's have found their way into high school textbooks by the early 1960's. A recent study by the Educational Testing Service, covering 38,000 students from 7,500 high schools, disclosed that there have been more important changes in high school teaching and curricula in this country during the past ten years than in any previous decade. Educational television experiments have been among the more frequently criticized of the Fund's projects; if there was indeed a miscalculation by the Fund in this area, it was one of timing, rather than of substance. It is now becoming increasingly obvious that an important contribution was made by the Fund.

Yet this was merely a microcosm of the much larger efforts made by the parent Ford Foundation in keeping alive the important concept of educational television during the long dry spell when it had no other major source of support. This applies not alone to the use of television in the schools, but perhaps even more importantly to the tremendous educational potential of noncommercial "public television."

In the area of civil rights, the Fund was far ahead of most agencies, public or private. Very early, as Professor Woodring points out, it sponsored Harry Ashmore's study of segregation in the schools, published the day before the Supreme Court's landmark decision in 1954 that struck down the "separate but equal" doctrine with regard to education. Thereafter the Fund underwrote *Southern School News* which not only recorded the languorous progress of integration but became a kind of guide to those school districts that seriously sought to do something about it.

Such matters were a continuing concern of the Fund throughout its brief history. The next to the last grant made by the Fund was for seeking out, in the highways and byways of the North and South, among black and white, local people who could be trained as leaders in sparking their own communities to greater educational progress.

In the last two years of the Fund's existence, it made grants of $1,336,000 to support a program of national assessment of education. Although this project was new, it was probably long overdue. Back during the earlier period of attacks on American education, when a book called *Why Johnny Can't Read* fed the flames of criticism and discussion, there was almost no real knowledge of how many Johnnies could or could not read, and at what level. One assumes that this would have been fundamental to our knowledge of what is happening in public education, and that it would be a vital prerequisite to proper curriculum design and development. But the fact is that we did not have the answers or the evidence then, and we still do not have them today.

The idea of developing an educational census that would yield this information was first suggested by Francis Keppel when he was U.S. commissioner of education. The Carnegie Corporation, soon joined by the Fund, underwrote the preliminary investigation of the idea. An exploratory committee was formed, and its final report was issued in 1968. Shortly thereafter the Compact of the States, through its Committee on Education, took on the responsibility for implementing the assessment program. While the National Assessment of Educational Progress has yet to prove its real value, it could become the basis of measuring for education the kind of broad progress that is measured by gross national product and employment statistics. The assessment hopes to record the present state of American education, but its basic purpose is to be able to detect the progress that is made from here on out. Such information, incidentally, would have been enormously helpful to the Fund itself, had it been available.

The right agenda for an organization like the Fund for the Advancement of Education could never be a static thing, of course, regardless of how prescient its original board and staff might have been. Not only was it necessary for the early projects to grow and develop, but a changing society always calls for new goals and new approaches to those goals.

If the Fund were in existence today, for example, it would undoubtedly be deeply involved in the subject of educating the very young. It may indeed have been remiss in not doing so earlier. There is surely far more still to be discovered about early learning than what is already known. One cannot help but wonder how many of those organizations now involved in the field have the needed know-how, the professional staffs, the materials, and the knowledge of what has been and is being done and discovered. The initial impetus for the federal government's Head Start program grew out of projects financed by the Taconic, Ford, and Carnegie foundations, but one wonders whether enough of the right resources and knowledge were marshaled to give Head Start a real chance to work — even though this was perhaps the most popular part of the entire antipoverty program.

Foundations, free of inhibiting pressures from many quarters, are often in a uniquely favorable position to evaluate real needs and the most promising ways of meeting those needs — before billions of dollars have been spent on less productive and less efficient avenues toward those goals. And yet foundations today are under fire and find themselves very much on the defensive. The irony is that this should take place at a time when foundations finally have the resources and the capabilities to help solve some of the major problems of society and eliminate some of the age-old afflictions of humankind. The Ford Foundation, the largest philanthropic body in history, has been outstanding in its courageous initiatives, in its high aims, and in its solid achievements. It might be noted here that Ford and other foundations have made larger strides than any other agencies toward a solution to the world's food problems by developing new high-yielding strains of wheat and rice. To have restrained them in this effort would have been a disservice to humanity.

Granted, a foundation is not a democratic institution, in the sense of basing its decisions on popular consensus. This is shown very clearly by Professor Woodring in this book. Some of the pioneering work of the Fund for the Advancement of Education, for example, brought it into abrasive contact with many of the established forces in education. Yet this did not keep its innovative successes from making their way into the schools. National assessment, once fiercely opposed by many school administrators and their organizations, is now becoming widely accepted as a promising approach to a basic need in education. Not everything that the Fund tried was a success, by any means. But its real contribution lay in the ability to finance those promising experiments whose value could only be conjectured, not demonstrated.

The larger point, perhaps, is that our society needs institutions that are free to underwrite and support unpopular experiments. Without such freedom, private philanthropy has very little meaning; there are too many other and easier ways to accomplish those things with which the public agrees at the moment. But there are not enough other ways to bring about all the changes for which our society has a real present or prospective need.

The Fund, if nothing more, was a major instrument of change. The Fifties and Sixties were decades of sweeping and pervasive change, of course, and no one individual agency or institution can take any large part of the credit for making them so. Nevertheless, in the field of education, the Fund was clearly both a catalyst and a kind of control mechanism for promoting change and for channeling it into the most desirable directions.

If we have learned anything of lasting value from our experiences over the past two decades, it must surely be that progress is an inevitable precursor to new problems, and that, in education at least, the best solutions to old problems invariably beget new ones. Success is a dynamic, not a static quality; it is never sufficient unto itself. Having tasted success in any field, we learn to savor its potential, to catch a glimmering of much greater successes still possible.

From that viewpoint, and on the basis of the dissatisfactions being felt and expressed today, the record of what happened in education from 1950 to 1970 must have been a successful one. This book is an important part of that record.

Preface

WHEN the officers and directors asked me to prepare a history and appraisal of the work of the Fund for the Advancement of Education they made it clear that what was wanted was not a conventional institutional history but rather an objective evaluation that would include an analysis of mistakes and failures as well as a report of achievements. They asked also that the record be placed in its historical setting of the changing educational scene of the Fifties and Sixties. Beyond that, they gave me a free hand to approach the task in whatever way seemed most appropriate. I have had access to Fund correspondence, records of board meetings, and confidential files.

In addition to the documented factual record, a history of the Fund must include an account of the many controversies which resulted from the Fund's activities, for it was these that made the Fund a distinctive philanthropic organization. Had the officers and directors of the Fund been content to support existing educational institutions and practices without attempting to change them, much of the controversy might have been avoided, but the Fund was committed by its name and its charter to the *advancement* of education and interpreted advancement to be not merely an expansion of educational institutions but also an improvement of educational quality. A judgment of quality must rest upon decisions regarding the goals of education which have been a subject of debate throughout the centuries. "All men do not agree," said Aristotle, "in those things they would have the child learn. From the present mode of education we cannot determine with certainty to which men incline, whether to instruct a child in what will be useful to him in life, or what tends to virtue, or what is excellent, for all these things have their separate defenders."*

The disagreements observed by Aristotle were no less acute when the Fund undertook its task of contributing to the advancement of education in the 1950's. The educational controversies of the time reflected fundamental differences in educational philosophy. In reporting these controversies I have tried, in addition to giving the facts, to give some indication of the emotional intensity of the conflicts among intelligent and educated people who were striving toward different goals. Since much that is significant cannot be documented because it did not appear in print, I have relied heavily on the memories of men and women with whom I have talked at length, and also on my own long experience as a consultant to the Fund. The possibility of errors resulting from the distortions of memory are obvious but a history based exclusively on the written record, in addition to being dull, would be incomplete.

My sources of information have included officers and directors of the Fund, officers and former officers of the Ford Foundation, educators who were the recipients of grants and other educators who were critical of the Fund's activities. All have

* Aristotle, *Politics* 8.2.1.

provided valuable background information though some have preferred not to be quoted directly.

I have talked with Robert Maynard Hutchins and Paul Hoffman, who were the Ford Foundation officers responsible for establishing the Fund for the Advancement of Education, with Dyke Brown, Champion Ward, and Joseph McDaniel, of the Foundation, and with Henry Heald who was president of the Foundation at the time the Fund staff was taken over by the Foundation. I have had extended conversations with Clarence Faust and Alvin C. Eurich, who were the senior officers and major policy makers of the Fund during the major part of its history, and with other officers, including Lester Nelson, Frank Bowles, O. Meredith Wilson, and John Scanlon as well as with Paul Rehmus, a longtime consultant to the Fund. G. H. Griffiths, who has been secretary-treasurer of the Fund during its terminal phase, has been most helpful, not only in providing background information but also in giving me access to the records and providing office space and secretarial assistance. Renata von Stoephasius has assisted me in compiling data and conducting interviews.

I have talked at some length with a number of members of the Fund board: Frank Abrams, Ralph Bunche, C. Scott Fletcher, Mrs. Douglas Horton, and Roy E. Larsen. I am particularly grateful to Mr. Larsen who, after reading the manuscript, agreed to write a foreword to the book.

I am deeply indebted to all those whom I have interviewed for their time and their willingness to contribute to this appraisal of the Fund's contribution to American education. Though my report reflects their views, the responsibility for opinions and judgments expressed in the pages to follow is, of course, my own.

P. W.

Contents

Foreword   *v*

"The Right Agenda" by Roy E. Larsen   *v*

Preface   *xv*

Prologue   *3*

1.   Origins: Fund and Foundation   *10*

   Sources of Philanthropic Policy   *12*
   The Ford Foundation Study Report   *15*
   Origin of the Fund   *26*

2.   The Policy Makers   *31*

   Faust and Eurich   *33*
   The Board of Directors   *43*

Other Officers and Staff   *52*
The Role of Robert Maynard Hutchins   *62*
Evolution of Fund Policy and Program   *65*
The Fund Within the Foundation   *72*

3. The Educational Milieu   *79*

The Great Debate   *81*
Teaching Johnny to Read   *90*
Other Issues   *94*
Pupils and Teachers   *99*
The Persisting Problem   *106*

4. The Fund as a Grant-making Agency   *114*

The Improvement of Teaching   *117*
The Arkansas Program   *125*
Other Programs   *130*
Educational Television   *137*
Better Use of Teacher Time and Talents   *146*
Early Admission and Advanced Standing   *152*
Equalizing Educational Opportunity   *156*
Other Grants   *159*

5. The Fund as an Operating Agency   *172*

The Ashmore Report and SERS   *174*
The Education Supplement   *178*
Statistics and Projections   *185*
Fund Publications   *190*
Sponsored Publications   *196*
Conferences and Committees   *199*

6. Judging the Results   202

    What Did the Fund Hope to Achieve?   205
    Where Did the Money Go?   211
    Controversy and Criticism: An Analysis   218
    The Judgment of Educators   242
    Overview   258

7. A Look Ahead   267

    Appendices   285

    Board Members of the Fund   285
    Officers of the Fund   286
    News Release, April 30, 1967   287
    Program Highlights, 1951–67   287

    Bibliography   300

    Publications of the Fund   300
    A Selected List of Fund-supported Publications   302

Investment
in Innovation

Prologue

THE Fund for the Advancement of Education was in operation during a time of national affluence, population expansion, international tension, growing social unrest, educational turmoil, rapid social change, and the adventure into space. Its policy evolved, and its activities took new directions, in response to changes in the world around it.

In 1951, when the Fund was established, the Korean War dominated the headlines. In 1967, when the Fund terminated its activities, the Vietnam conflict was dividing the nation into hawks and doves. But between these two frustrating and unpopular military excursions the nation enjoyed a decade of relative peace even though the cold war remained a disquieting threat. To most of the people, most of the time, external threats to the nation seemed less than immediate — we were preoccupied with other things.

One major concern was the "population explosion." Though a high birthrate is characteristic of postwar periods, no one expected the one that followed World War II to last for more than a few years. But the rate of births per thousand population, which had risen from seventeen in the Thirties to twenty-five in the Fifties, remained high throughout the decade. During the Fifties, some forty million babies were born into American homes and it was obvious that most of these babies would soon be in the schools. But the schools were not prepared for them and the taxpayers were not prepared for the shock of having to pay for their education.

The population growth was accompanied by significant shifts of population from east to west and from the north to Florida and Arizona. Though there was much loose talk about "urban growth," it was not the large cities that grew most rapidly. Indeed many of them actually *decreased* in population. The growth was in the suburbs, which expanded at a phenomenal rate. One reason for moving to the suburbs was that they provided a better life for the children, and one reason for the strong opposition to the incorporation of suburbs into the parent cities was the conviction that suburban schools were superior to big-city schools.

While upper-middle-class white families moved out of the cities to the suburbs, families of lower socioeconomic level and more meager educational background moved into the inner cities. Of these, an estimated two million were Negroes from the rural South who moved into the cities of the North and West in search of a better life, more freedom, and greater economic opportunities. For many the move led to bitter disappointment because the northern cities did not offer the kinds of jobs for which they were prepared. And though there was no *de jure* segregation in the North, Negroes who lacked formal education and job skills were forced by economic circumstances to live in areas which soon came to be called "ghettos," areas in which housing was abominable, jobs unavailable, and the police no more sympathetic than police in the South. Even highly skilled Negroes discovered that in the northern cities the skilled trades were controlled by unions that were reluctant to admit outsiders, particularly those whose skin was not white.

The arrival of these migrants from the South, and also, in some cities, the influx of Puerto Ricans, most of whom did not speak English, created problems for which the big cities were unprepared. Among the least well prepared were the educators who had developed city school systems for children from different backgrounds and with different problems.

The plight of those living in the urban ghettos was made all the more poignant by the unprecedented prosperity of other Americans. During the Fifties and Sixties the gross national product rose from $300 billion annually to $800 billion and the median income of American families doubled, growing from approximately $3,500 a year to more than $7,000. Although a part of this gain was wiped out by inflation, the increase in real income was substantial. While half the world remained hungry, and though pockets of poverty continued to exist in the United States, the great majority of Americans enjoyed more material things than had been known to any nation at any time in history. The standard of living was so high that any child living in a home without a bathroom, electric lights, automatic washing machine and dishwasher, and a television set, could be termed "disadvantaged."

The Fifties saw the emergence of a new teen-age subculture complete with its own clothing styles, its own music, its own literature, its own mores, and its own concept of the good life. This was something different from the adolescent culture of a previous day, when boys and girls who thought of themselves as adolescents had been eager to grow up and consequently had taken adults of conspicuous achievement for their models. But teen-agers of the Fifties, who were scornful of adults and contemptuous of "the establishment," had no wish to grow up. For their models they chose other teen-agers or young adults acting like teen-agers, who had gained publicity by playing the guitar while swaying their hips or by playing adolescent roles in motion pictures. This subculture was nourished by advertisers promoting phonograph records, motion pictures, sports equipment and specialized clothing for young people with money to spend as they wished. New magazines for teen-agers gained rapidly in circulation. And high school teachers soon discovered that instructing the new breed was a task greatly different from that of teaching the previous generation of adolescents.

During the Fifties, television replaced radio and motion pictures as the chief source of entertainment. While defenders of the new medium pointed to the fact that many television programs were instructive and some were of a high cultural level, critics of "the tube" charged that a child, by selecting his programs, could spend all his hours after school and until bedtime watching scenes of violence in which women were threatened and abused and men were maimed and slaughtered. Many children did just that and though there was disagreement among psychologists and psychiatrists as to the long-range effect on the child's mental health, it seemed obvious to parents that the emotional impact of violence on the screen was much greater than that of violence in the books read by earlier generations.

Televised news programs contributed to the impression of the younger generation that this is an evil and violent world. Perhaps it has always been, but the generation of the Fifties and Sixties — because it had grown up in front of the television set — was the first that was never allowed to forget human conflict. A picture of crime, war, or racial violence, seen on television while it happens, is far more anxiety-producing than a written account read days or weeks later.

To the surprise of many, the popularity of television did not result in a decline in reading. Although several popular magazines were forced to suspend publication (in most cases because of loss of advertising to television rather than because of loss of readers) the number of new book titles published annually rose from 11,000 in 1950 to 30,000 in 1966. The number of copies sold annually doubled between 1950 and 1960 and continued to rise in the Sixties. By far the most rapid increase was in paperback editions, and though a large percentage of the total was of dubious literary quality, most of the great literature of the Western world also appeared in paperback during the Fifties. And it sold: paperback editions of *The Iliad* and *The Odyssey* sold a combined total of more than a million copies during the decade.

Toward the end of the decade of the Fifties, college professors were pleased to discover that, as a result of improvements in secondary education, college freshmen had become more literate and better prepared for college work. Because these were years of comparative calm on college campuses, many educators were led to believe that no substantive reforms were necessary at the higher levels of education — that an expansion of existing programs of college work was all that was needed.

It was not until well into the Sixties — when the Fund was nearing the end of its history — that colleges rather than the public elementary and secondary schools became the focus of public interest and concern. The student uprisings that began at Berkeley in 1964 and later spread to many other campuses were variously diagnosed as the result of the Vietnam war, the draft, excessive prosperity, and permissiveness in home and school. But the demand of college students for a role in policy making, better teaching, a more relevant curriculum, and elimination of parietal rules on the campus, and an "open enrollment policy" for the disadvantaged, made it clear that colleges and universities must now be as concerned about reform as the elementary and secondary schools had been in the Fifties.

Throughout the period of the Fund's history, but particularly in the Sixties, it was apparent that the generation gap was widening. Millions of young Americans from the affluent middle and upper-middle classes turned their backs on the society that had nourished and overprotected them, rejecting the life styles and middle-class strivings of their parents' generation. Some became society's dropouts, joining one or another of the subcultures of the day — beatniks of the Fifties, hippies or flower children of the Sixties — refusing regular employment, scorning the status symbols in which their parents took pride, choosing to live a simple but often parasitic life in a crowded city pad or a rustic rural retreat while occasionally joining the demonstrators of the day in protest movements. To these groups, psychedelic drugs offered an escape from a reality that they found unbearable and became a part of a new way of life.

Though all these social problems had their roots deep within our society, they were related in one way or another to the quality of the nation's education. Consequently, the schools and colleges took their share of the blame and new demands were made upon our educational institutions.

The Fund played its role against the backdrop of these social changes and demands upon the schools that resulted from them. But, in 1951 when the Fund was established, many of the problems had not yet become apparent and some were not yet foreseen. Though the public schools were under sharp attack in the early Fifties, criticism of the colleges was yet to come. The time of student unrest and campus disorders was still a decade ahead. Many of the students of the early Fifties were veterans, attending college under the GI Bill, and instead of wanting to overthrow the establishment they were eager to become a part of it. They were criticized for their conventionality and for having no goals more imaginative than a split-level home in the suburbs with two cars in the garage and four or five children in the nursery. The word "hippies" had not yet entered the vocabulary, few people had heard of LSD, and marijuana was something used only by criminals and a few jazz musicians.

In 1951 the major preoccupation of those concerned about education was the quality of instruction in the public schools. It seemed clear to many that reforms were necessary, not only in the schools but also in the education of teachers for those schools, but there was sharp disagreement about the directions these reforms should take. Because educational institutions are by their very nature conservative and resistant to change, those who saw a need for innovations needed the encouragement and support of outside agencies. The Fund for the Advancement of Education was one such agency.

The Fund responded vigorously to the problems of the Fifties, particularly to the demand for greater intellectual rigor in the schools and better liberal education for teachers. It foresaw and took steps for dealing with the problems that would result from population growth, problems that would include the teacher shortage and new approaches to instruction. It anticipated the necessity for racial desegregation in southern schools.

When new problems arose in the Sixties, the Fund had much smaller resources at its command. Its staff had become the Education Division of the Ford Foundation, which was gradually taking over the responsibilities that had once been those of the Fund. Consequently, though this report covers the period from 1951 to 1967, the major emphasis is given to the educational reforms of the 1950's and to the Fund's contributions to those reforms.

1

Origins:
Fund and Foundation

THE Ford Foundation, a conspicuous institution known throughout the nation and the world as the largest of all philanthropic organizations, was established in "optional perpetuity" for the comprehensive purpose of advancing human welfare throughout the world. Unless the trustees decide to terminate its existence, and provided that neither our civilization nor our economic structure collapses, it will exist indefinitely, making grants out of income while retaining the major portion of its capital.

The Fund for the Advancement of Education, a much smaller philanthropy with a more restrictive purpose and a shorter life, was established by the Ford Foundation to advance and improve formal or institutionalized education in North America. Though it was legally an independent organization with its own board of directors, its work was often confused with that of the parent foundation. The confusion is understandable because the relationship between the two was an involved and perplexing one that changed with the years.

For the first three years after its establishment in April 1951, the Fund operated with a high degree of independence. The fact that its independence was less than total became apparent in 1955 when it returned to the Ford Foundation with a request for additional money with which to continue its work. At this time the Foundation saw fit to exercise its right to review the work of the Fund before granting the request, and after a time gave the Fund a "terminal grant" of $25 million with the express stipulation that the Foundation would henceforward have a right to exercise a veto power over any future addition to the Fund's board of directors. The parental authority had been clearly established, whatever the Fund's charter might say about its legal independence.

In 1957, the trustees of the Foundation, deciding that the work of the two organizations should be more closely related, invited the staff of the Fund to become the Education Division of the Foundation. The president of the Fund became a vice-president of the Foundation and the chairman of the Fund's board of directors became a trustee of the Foundation. Other staff members were also given Foundation titles and the entire group moved into Foundation offices.

From that date onward the Fund was looked upon as the experimental arm of the Foundation. The staff wore two hats, making small grants for innovative projects in the name of the Fund and larger, follow-up grants out of the much larger Foundation resources, while struggling valiantly to satisfy the wishes of two very different boards. Gradually the Fund lost its separate identity until, in 1967, the officers of the Foundation decided to terminate its separate program.

Because of the complex interrelationship of the two organizations, it is obvious that a history and appraisal of the Fund must include some attention to the history of the Ford Foundation and the changing philosophies of those who directed its course. The Fund was established by men who were convinced that a relatively small, independent philanthropic organization, with a board and staff which was able to focus its entire attention upon one area of philanthropy, could make a greater contribution to the advancement of education than could be made by a larger foundation whose board and officers were concerned with so many aspects of human welfare that they could give only passing attention to education. Its work was terminated by men who believed either that the Fund had outlived its usefulness or that its work could be done better by a staff division of the larger institution, working under the board and president of the Ford Foundation. The conflict between these two points of view is a significant part of the Fund's history.

SOURCES OF PHILANTHROPIC POLICY

Although philanthropy in one form or another has a long history, dating from the dawn of civilization, the contemporary approach to large-scale giving is of recent origin. The major philanthropic foundations, which are both larger and more numerous in the United States than elsewhere, were made possible by the enormous profits that accrued to entrepreneurs under the free enterprise system as it operated in the late nineteenth and early twentieth centuries when cheap labor was available, raw material was abundant, taxes were low, and there were few governmental restrictions on individual initiative. Under this system, a fortunate few, who surpassed their rivals in energy, imagination, foresight, and intelligence — or perhaps in competitiveness and good luck — accumulated wealth far beyond that which could be used for personal needs. Many built fantastically expensive mansions patterned after European palaces, others constructed yachts that rivaled warships in size and cost, and some supported expensive mistresses or accepted the financial burden of marrying their daughters to impecunious dukes and counts. But the wealth continued to accumulate.

Andrew Carnegie, one of the richest men of this time, had less hedonistic tastes and a different view of his responsibilities. Although he seems never to have questioned the system that had made it possible for him to amass his fortune, he became convinced that having amassed it he should devote the remainder of his life to using his money for the benefit of mankind. In an article published in 1889, he said, "A wealthy man dies disgraced if the talents he has employed to acquire wealth are not used to distribute the wealth for the public good."

John D. Rockefeller read the article and agreed. He wrote to Carnegie: "I would that more men of wealth were doing as you are doing with your money, but, be assured, your example will bear fruits, and the time will come when men of wealth will more generally be willing to use it for the good of others." And his prediction proved sound. Other wealthy men did follow the examples of Carnegie and Rockefeller in establishing foundations that outlived them and eventually became largely independent of family control.

It seems not to have occurred to Carnegie, Rockefeller, or other nineteenth-century industrialists that they might best contribute to the welfare of mankind by returning a larger share of the profits of industry to the workers in the form of higher wages. In the ethos of their day it was considered sound business practice to pay the lowest wages that workers would accept, just as it was sound to buy raw material at the lowest possible cost and sell the products of industry at the highest price that the consumers could be persuaded to pay. But early in the twentieth century Henry Ford came to a different conclusion — he decided that it would be good business to raise wages, both to motivate the workers and in order that they might be better able to purchase the products of industry. In 1914, at a time when an ample supply of labor was available at a much lower figure, he startled the public, delighted his employees, and angered other industrialists by establishing a minimum wage of five dollars a day in his factories. When it became evident that the policy was sound, other industrialists were forced to follow Ford's example. The economic status of industrial workers improved rapidly and industry prospered.

Though Henry Ford was an austere man who refused to devote his wealth to riotous living, he did not accept Carnegie's doctrine that a wealthy man ought to distribute his wealth for the public good. During his lifetime the Ford Foundation, which he and his son Edsel established in 1936, remained a small, local charity in Detroit, contributing money at the rate of about one million dollars a year to the Detroit Symphony, the Henry Ford Hospital, and the Henry Ford Museum, which collects American artifacts of a bygone day such as buggies, sleighs, lamps, and trolley cars. The Foundation also supported the development of Greenfield Village, which houses such historic structures as Edison's laboratory and the birthplaces of Noah Webster, Luther Burbank, the Wright Brothers, and William McGuffey. It is doubtful that Henry Ford ever anticipated the dimensions or the directions that his foundation would take after his death in 1947. The decisions that led to the expansion of the Ford Foundation into a major international philanthropy were those of the heirs: Mrs. Henry Ford, Mrs. Edsel Ford, Henry II, Benson, William, and Mrs. Josephine Ford.

Historians and social commentators have offered various interpretations of the motivations of philanthropists, suggesting that men of great wealth may be motivated by the desire to save their souls, to expiate guilt feelings resulting from their ruthlessness in accumulating wealth, and to perpetuate their names. But there seems no good reason to doubt that whatever their supplementary motivations may have been, Carnegie, Rockefeller, and many other wealthy men, in their twilight years, were sincere in their desire to see their surplus used for the betterment of mankind.

Because Henry Ford did not share the enthusiasm of his predecessors for philanthropy — he once said "I have no patience with professional charity" — historians and social commentators have made much of the fact that the Ford Foundation in its present dimensions is a product of the tax laws. It is true that with the settlement of the estates of Henry and Edsel Ford the family would have lost the control of the Ford Motor Company if it had sold enough stock to pay inheritance taxes. The family retained control by giving a major portion of these estates to the Foundation in the form of nonvoting stock. But because human motives are always complex, and frequently unclear even to the individuals concerned, it would be presumptuous to assume that tax avoidance was the only reason for the expansion of the Ford Foundation to its present size. The younger generations of the Ford family had grown up in a different world from that which molded the character of Ford the elder. By giving some 90 per cent of the family's stock to the Foundation, the Ford family was able to retain control of the company, to assure that the name Ford would have an honored place in history, and at the same time to contribute in very large measure to the betterment of the human condition. Such a combination of motives would seem overwhelming to any family, and particularly to one that already had more wealth than it could possibly use for personal satisfactions.

THE FORD FOUNDATION STUDY REPORT

When the Ford family made its decision to contribute the major portion of the stock of the Ford Motor Company to philanthropic purposes, it immediately became apparent that the Ford Foundation was destined to become the largest institution of its kind in the history of the world. The trustees of the Foundation, seeing the need for the best advice they could get and for a new statement of policy consistent with their enlarged responsibilities, called upon Rowan Gaither to reorganize and direct a planning study of policy and program. Gaither, a San Francisco lawyer who had a considerable amount of experience as an intermediary between brains and capital, had come to the attention of the trustees through Karl Compton, a Foundation trustee who was also chairman of the board of the Massachusetts Institute of Technology.

On November 22, 1948, Henry Ford II, chairman of the trustees, gave Gaither his instructions in a letter that reads as follows:

The Foundation was established for the general purpose of advancing human welfare, but the manner of realizing this objective was left to the Trustees. Now that the time is near when the Foundation can initiate an active program, I think that its aims should be more specifically defined.

The people of this country and mankind in general are confronted with problems which are vast in number and exceedingly disturbing in significance. While important efforts to solve these problems are being made by government, industry, foundations, and other institutions, it is evident that new resources, such as those of this Foundation, if properly employed, can result in significant contributions.

We want to take stock of our existing knowledge, institutions and techniques in order to locate the areas where the problems are most important and where additional efforts toward their solution are most needed.

You are to have complete authority and responsibility in this undertaking, and you are to have a high degree of discretion, subject, of course, to general policy approval of the Trustees in the means you employ and in the choice of consultants and other personnel. We want the best thought available in the United States as to how this Foundation can most effectively and intelligently put its resources to work for human welfare.

The Study Committee appointed by the trustees to work with Mr. Gaither was made up of widely known and respected men: Thomas H. Carroll, T. Duckett Jones, Donald Marquis, William C. DeVane, Charles C. Lauristsen, Peter H. Odegard, and Francis T. Spaulding. The staff of the committee included William McPeak, Dyke Brown, Paul Bixler, and Don K. Price, three of whom were later to become officers of the Foundation.

In November 1949, after one of the most thorough, painstaking, and significant inquiries ever made into the whole broad question of public welfare and human needs, the Study Committee submitted its conclusions and recommendations to the trustees in an internal document for the use of the officers titled, "Report of the Study for the Ford Foundation on Policy and Program." This report, which was accepted unanimously by the trustees, became the basic policy statement of the Foundation. Since it also substantially influenced the policy and program of the Fund for the Advancement of Education, it seems appropriate to present it here in some detail.

The committee agreed at the outset that the purpose of the study was not to accumulate a comprehensive catalogue of projects which the Foundation might undertake, but to block out in general terms those critical areas where problems were most serious and where the Foundation might make the most significant contributions to human welfare. The committee's conception of human welfare as stated in the first chapter of the report was in large measure synonymous with a declaration of democratic ideals. It said, "It is the consensus of men of judgment today that the real hope for the advancement of

human welfare lies in the reaffirmation in practice of democratic principles." [1]

It was the considered judgment of the committee that the
most critical problems of the day were those which are social
rather than physical in character — those which arise in man's
relation to man rather than in his relation to nature.

The committee commented on the changing philosophy of
philanthropy which had resulted from the emergence of large
foundations:

The history of philanthropy is a record of a continuous evolving
philosophy of giving. At one time the gifts of individuals and of bene-
volent organizations were intended largely to relieve the suffering of
"the weak, the poor and the unfortunate." Philanthropy was thought
of merely as a temporary relief for evil conditions which would always
exist and about which nothing fundamental could be done. With the
establishment of the modern foundation a much greater concept came
into being. The aim is no longer merely to treat symptoms and temporarily to alleviate distress, but rather to eradicate the causes of suffering. Nor is the modern foundation content to concern itself only
with man's obvious physical needs; it seeks rather to help man achieve
his entire well-being — to satisfy his mental, emotional, and spiritual
needs as well as his physical wants. It addresses itself to the whole man
and to the well-being of mankind. [2]

Because the needs and problems of human welfare far exceed the total of all available foundation funds, the committee
recommended that the Foundation concentrate its support
upon those problems which are at once the most important
and which obstruct progress in the most directions. It recommended five program areas for the advancement of human
welfare: 1. The Establishment of Peace. 2. The Strengthening of Democracy. 3. The Strengthening of the Economy.

[1] Report of the Study for the Ford Foundation on Policy and Program,"
1949, p. 14.   [2] Ibid., p. 22.

4. Education in a Democratic Society. 5. Individual Behavior and Human Relations.

In expanding on the fourth of these areas — education — the committee offered the following commentary:

It is impossible to conceive of a true democracy with restricted opportunities for education or with educational institutions which are not geared to the needs and goals of society as a whole. It has been said that "No society can long remain free unless its members are freemen, and men are not free where ignorance prevails."

The Committee has received from its advisers evidence of an unusual degree of dissatisfaction with educational institutions and influences which now operate in our society. This evidence covered not only our formal educational system, but also the whole range of informal educational agencies, such as the home and the church, and especially the mass media which have become so influential — the newspaper, the inexpensive book, the magazine, the moving picture, the radio, and television.

In considering the functions of formal education, the Committee recognized that democratic objectives require three things of our educational system: first, that it apply in action the principle of equality of opportunity; second, that it train citizens and leaders in coping with society's problems; and, third, that it assist all men to employ their native capacities not only to make a living but to carry on satisfying and purposeful lives. In all three respects our educational system is thought to exhibit serious deficiencies.

In practice education should accord equal opportunity to all. This is not only a fundamental democratic principle; it is a prerequisite to the social mobility and fluidity which are basic to democracy. Without equal educational opportunity, equality of economic opportunity cannot exist. The effects of unequal opportunity in education are aggravated as industry, business, and the professions become more complex, requiring lengthier and more specialized training.

Prejudice and discrimination abridge the educational opportunities of the members of our minority groups. Persons of all races and colors do not have equal access to education. The advantages of education are also walled off behind economic barriers, which are even more prevalent though perhaps less well publicized. Free tuition alone does not guarantee all children a chance to attend primary and secondary schools. Some are barred by such things as the cost of books, clothing, and supplies; others must drop out because their families need the money they can earn when kept out of school. The poorer families, and those composed of members of our minority groups, are the ones which urgently require educational opportunity to improve their economic and cultural status. Yet they are the very ones to whom these educational barriers are most real, and in consequence their cultural and economic inequalities tend automatically to be inherited.

The high cost of college and of higher education in general means that real equality of opportunity is far from being realized. The veterans' program following World War II temporarily lessened this inequality. Our colleges now face, however, a serious situation resulting from rapidly rising costs, the decreasing proportion of the national income going into higher education, and the decline in gifts and income from endowments. More and more of the financial burden is being thrust upon the student in the form of higher tuition fees. In consequence, higher education threatens to become the prerogative of the well-to-do. This trend is already evident in advanced education, especially in professional schools, and will become more pronounced unless suitable measures are taken to reverse it.

Permitting education to depend so largely on individual economic status presents grave dangers to democracy. We not only deny to millions of young people an equal chance to make the most of their native abilities; we also deprive society of a vast number of potential leaders and of citizens prepared to assume their adult responsibilities — personal, civic, and social. Without question one of the most important jobs of education today is to train well-balanced citizens and leaders able to participate intelligently and constructively in the society in which we live. Only through our schools can youth learn to interpret life's problems as men face them, to acquire a sense of participating in the common culture, and to assimilate the knowledge needed to meet the demands of the contemporary world.

An important function of our schools which is largely disregarded is education for the adult population. Institutional thinking customarily interests itself less in adult education than in the education of youth —

even to the extent of assuming that graduates will, in the remaining forty or fifty years of their lives, acquire by themselves all the further learning they will need. Experience shows this assumption is unfounded. Moreover, as many of society's most crucial decisions will be made in the years immediately ahead, we cannot with safety neglect the very people upon whom we must depend for the shaping of democracy's destiny.

The education of youth for balanced, productive, and socially useful lives must, of course, go forward immediately with all the energy at our command. The deficiencies are numerous; they will require our uninterrupted efforts if education is to sustain democratic modes of living.

Perhaps the greatest single shortcoming of our school system is its tendency to concern itself almost exclusively with the dissemination of information. Schools should be the most important influence outside of the home for the molding of whole persons. The function of the school is the broad training of mind and intellect. Yet individual purpose, character, and values, the bases of which are laid in the home, are often inadequately developed by the institutions which could, by precept and deeper teaching, assume a major share in supporting them most successfully. To concentrate on the absorption of information seems unrealistic when one realizes that students retain only a small portion of such information. Education must meet the needs of the human spirit. It must assist persons to achieve a satisfactory personal philosophy and sense of values, to acquire tastes for literature, music, and the arts, and to develop the ability to analyze problems and to arrive at conclusions on the basis of rigorous thinking. Only thus will graduates of our schools and colleges attain the balance necessary to live integrated and purposeful lives . . . .

If we are to train youth for effective citizenship, and particularly if we are to prepare those suited by interest and capabilities to assume roles of expertness and leadership, we must bring about a satisfactory relationship between general and special knowledge. While specialization is to be encouraged as a proven technique for the acquisition of knowledge and for its application in our complex society, we must strive to educate as many persons as possible to understand how specialized knowledges fit together for the constructive interests of society as a whole. This means more than graduating adequate numbers of specialists and generalists; it will require the development in both of an understanding of their relations one to the other and of the relations of both to society. We are today turning out too many specialists who lack a sense of the meaning of what they learn for our society as a whole.

Even in general or liberal education the tendency is to break the curriculum into fragments and to overspecialize in teaching. There is an excessive emphasis on scholasticism as an end in itself, and a notable failure to keep abreast of both social development and social needs.

Thus the student lacks the knowledge, attitudes, and values needed to live well and constructively in a complex free society, and to enable him to participate with breadth of understanding in the world community in which we live.

The training offered by our graduate schools has been justly criticized as too narrow and as too exclusively directed toward proficiency in research. Most young Ph.D.'s proceed immediately to relatively unspecialized teaching in undergraduate colleges. Here, at least in the first few years, their highly specialized training as graduate students often proves not only of little use but even a positive obstruction in teaching general subjects, in which the ability broadly to integrate and interpret knowledge is of basic importance. These facts present a problem for serious consideration.

Our educational system faces numerous other problems, such as the great shortage and often poor quality of teaching personnel at the primary and secondary levels; the pressure of enrollment upon physical plant during the growth of the post-war school population; the apathy of parents and other citizen groups toward school requirements; the difficulties of obtaining adequate financing, particularly in regions of low economic potential; and the slowness with which schools adopt new procedures and aids for teaching. Many of these problems would remain substantial even if mitigated by federal aid or by other sources of financial assistance.

The functioning units in primary and secondary education are the thousands of local school boards and authorities throughout the nation. While to maintain our historical democracy in school affairs we must retain a high level of local autonomy in education, it is at the same time necessary to overcome the deficiencies inherent in such a wide scattering of policy planning and administrative functions. How to attain coordination of the many local school systems, how to provide the planning and guidance for continuity of progress, and how to achieve a basic unity of purpose among them — these are problems of extreme difficulty. How to solve these problems in the interest of society as a whole, and how to do so without at the same time undermining freedom of education itself, constitutes a problem of a still higher order in the application of democratic principles.[3]

The Study Committee offered a number of recommendations concerning the administration of a philanthropic organization which, though intended for the Ford Foundation, were applicable also to the Fund for the Advancement of Education (FAE) and seem to have been accepted by the FAE as a part of its policy. Concerning the responsibilities of the board, the committee advised:

Individual members of the Board of Trustees should not seek to decide the technical questions involved in particular applications and projects. Nothing would more certainly destroy the effectiveness of a foundation. On the contrary, the Trustees will be most surely able to control the main lines of policy of the Foundation, and the contribution it will make to human welfare, if they give the President and the officers considerable freedom in developing the program, while they avoid influencing (even by indirection) the conduct of projects to which the Foundation has granted funds. . . . the function of the Trustees should be to supply the general judgment of the Foundation. They should, in a sense, speak for the general interests and needs of mankind. They should decide what goals the Foundation may desirably seek and, with their staff, should decide which are attainable. And they should con-

[3] Ibid., pp. 37–43. Although the various sections of the "Study Report" are not individually signed it seems clear that they were written by different individuals. This section on education probably reflects the views of Francis T. Spaulding, a widely respected educator and administrator who had been dean of the Harvard School of Education and chief of the Education Branch of the Information and Education Division of the U.S. Army during World War II; at the time of the study he was president of the University of the State of New York and commissioner of education in that state.

tinually stimulate their officers by reminding them of the problems which cry for solution but are untouched by any of the techniques of understanding or control yet developed.[4]

Concerning the responsibilities of the officers, the Study Committee recommended,

The President . . . should have full responsibility for presenting recommendations on programs to the Board, and full authority to appoint and remove all other officers and employees of the Foundation. The Foundation is not an institution to be administered autocratically, and the President will do well to consult freely with his principal subordinates, as well as the Trustees, on all major aspects. But he can help the Board keep a high degree of coherence in the total program only if his responsibility for the administration is quite clear.[5]

The recommendations of the Study Committee concerning the selection and appointment of officers and staff members also provided guidelines for the Fund as well as for the Foundation: "Salaries . . . should be high enough to let the Foundation recruit the best men from universities, government, and non-profit institutions, without being so high as to block entirely any possibility of movement in the opposite direction." [6] And one recommendation of the committee was followed by the Fund, even though it was sometimes ignored by the Foundation to which it was addressed: "The principal officers . . . should be given titles corresponding to their status . . . which will not commit them to interest in any particular phase of the Foundation program, or lead to the general development of divisions or departments according to subject matter." [7] One recommendation was followed by the Fund as a matter of necessity:

The principal officer of the Foundation will probably find one working rule extremely important if the experience of other foundation officers

[4] Ibid., pp. 127–128.   [5] Ibid., p. 132.   [6] Ibid., p. 135.   [7] Ibid., p. 134.

can be taken as a guide: they must travel. Only by frequent travel, by visiting people in all phases of government, in business, in labor, and in the universities can foundation officers dig beneath the mechanics of official and semi-official committees and councils and get realistic impressions of the work that needs doing and the people competent to do it.[8]

The committee asked itself whether foundation officers should passively wait for applications or should take the initiative in suggesting projects. Its conclusion was that the passive role was inadequate: "Since the work of a foundation officer gives him a more comprehensive view of the whole field than any single scholar is likely to have, he ought to have enough originality to produce many fruitful ideas." [9]

The Study Committee took the position that the Foundation should be a grant-making rather than an operating agency: "Since the proposed program is too broad to be encompassed by a single operating agency, and since it must be adjusted to meet new social problems, the Ford Foundation should avoid direct operations unless no other way can be found to accomplish a particular objective." [10] It does not appear, however, that this advice against becoming in part an operating agency was intended to apply to separate funds established by the Foundation for specific purposes.

Finally the Study Committee offered a word of advice which the officers of the Fund as well as those of the Foundation sometimes found difficult to follow:

. . . they must sacrifice a considerable degree of their freedom of self-expression. They cannot themselves be crusaders, or even take sides strongly in public on the issues involved in the work they support. They will have the satisfaction of making the resources of the Foundation available to persons in strategic positions to benefit society as a whole. In return, they, like the Foundation itself, must give up the luxury of taking credit for their accomplishments.[11]

[8] Ibid., pp. 135–136.   [9] Ibid., p. 112.   [10] Ibid., p. 103.   [11] Ibid., p. 136.

ORIGIN OF THE FUND

A major philanthropic foundation usually disperses the major part of the income through intermediary organizations. Unless a huge professional staff is maintained, this is a necessity because if a foundation with $200 million to disperse annually were to make grants averaging $8,000 or $10,000 each, it would be necessary for its officers to make final decisions regarding nearly one hundred grants each working day of the year. Consequently a large foundation becomes a wholesale rather than a retail operation.

The intermediaries which receive most of the grants include institutes, academies or councils of learned societies, departments of government here and abroad, universities, and "centers" of various kinds. But when no appropriate intermediary is available a foundation sometimes establishes a special fund to work within some clearly defined area.

The report of the Study Committee anticipated the possible need for the establishment of separate funds such as the FAE.

If the Foundation . . . finds that no existing institution can accomplish its purpose, it should entrust such a special fund to a new intermediary organization to be established according to the following principles:

1. Its Board of Trustees would not include any member who is a trustee of the Foundation, or personally connected in any way with the Foundation or its Trustees or principal officers. Its name should not suggest any connection with the Ford Foundation.

2. Its Board of Trustees should include men who have general interest in the proposed field but who are not specialists or technicians in it. They would thus be something of a bridge between the comprehensive interest of the Foundation Trustees, and the narrower technical interests of the operating agencies through which the program would be carried out. They would also be men who by reputation and status would take full public responsibility for their operations.

3. It would be set up with a single grant of money, not to be re-

newed or replenished, and with an obligation in its charter to go out of existence at the end of a certain period of years.

4. Its offices would be separate and distinct from the offices of the Foundation, preferably not near enough to invite frequent and informal association between the staffs of the two.

5. It should, if practicable, be headed by a president or executive director who would not be embarrassed by being out of a job at the end of its existence. It might be possible to make the term of the intermediary organization coincide with the remainder of a mature leader's active career, or to find someone who could return to an assured position in some university, corporation, or public agency at the end of the intermediary organization's existence. The staff should be recruited similarly so as to minimize continuing obligations to personnel. The organization would then be free to function not only as a grant-making foundation, but if necessary as an operating agency to accomplish directly the purposes in its charter. The president, trustees and staff of the organization should be able to render a broad national service as consultants in their fields of interest, in addition to their function of making grants or operating directly.

At the end of the term of the intermediary, the Foundation could then review its work in complete detachment and objectivity, without being harried by public criticism or committed by continuing relationships. The Ford Foundation Trustees could decide on merit whether the work of an intermediary organization and the importance of its field would justify its reconstitution, or its renewal under another name and with different personnel, or the amalgamation of its program, wholly, or partly, in another activity.[12]

Although this document provided the basis for the establishment of the Fund for the Advancement of Education, several of the principles laid down by the Study Committee were later ignored by Foundation officials. Instead of "a single definite grant of money, not to be renewed or replenished," the FAE was established with only a small initial grant and was

12 Ibid., pp. 120–121.

given to understand that it might return to the Foundation for more money when it was needed. Though the Fund had offices "separate and distinct from the offices of the Foundation" during the early years, the Foundation later asked the Fund staff to become the education staff of the parent foundation and to work within the offices of the Foundation under the direct control of Foundation officers, and subject to Foundation regulations. And some individuals did serve on both the board of the Fund and the board of the Foundation. Whether these deviations from the principles proposed by the Study Committee were necessary adaptations to changing conditions or tragic mistakes has been a subject of debate. The debate will be a necessary part of the effort to appraise the work of the Fund.

The decision to establish a fund for the advancement of education was made in 1950 by Paul Hoffman, president of the Ford Foundation, on the recommendation of Robert Maynard Hutchins, one of Hoffman's associate directors in the Foundation. At about the same time, Hoffman and Hutchins decided to establish a second organization, the Fund for Adult Education, to work in the field of informal and continuing education. Consequently it was decided that the work of the FAE would be restricted to formal or institutionalized education at all levels from kindergarten through the university. It was further decided that the FAE would work only within the United States and Canada, leaving the problem of education in other nations to the overseas divisions of the Foundation.

Early in 1951, President Hoffman sent a memorandum to the board of trustees of the Foundation for consideration at their meeting on January 29, 1951. One section of the memorandum, dealing with the proposed Fund for the Advancement of Education, reads as follows:

We can no longer afford the luxury of an unexamined educational system that grew up under different political, economic, and social conditions.

The crisis requires us to re-examine elementary education with a view to considering the number of years required for such education, its content, and the kind of institutions through which it should be administered. It calls for the reconsideration of the structure and content of secondary education. The colleges of liberal arts have for many years expanded their courses of study so that today they present an accumulation of courses, the reasons for which have not been thoroughly thought out. In advanced, as in specialized, and professional training, there are at least two important problems:

1. How can men and women needed for specialized services in the armed forces be expeditiously trained?

2. How can obsolete procedures in advanced, specialized and professional education be eliminated so that men and women returning from the services may have an opportunity to complete an advanced program without undue loss of time?

If all American males are to spend two or two-and-a-half years in the service of their country, some effort should be made to discover what educational opportunities should be available to them during that period.

Related to all these questions is the question of the education of teachers, since it is not likely that the present methods and institutions for this purpose will be adequate to meet the needs of a more efficient system and a revised curriculum.

The financial position of existing educational institutions will become acute within the immediate future. Emergency methods may have to be taken to tide over some colleges and universities. The whole question of the elimination of duplication and the promotion of cooperation among institutions, especially in the areas in which education is extremely expensive, will have to be seriously raised.

The Foundation will wish to consider resort to scholarship aid in order to promote equality of educational opportunity. To promote important new developments in education, it may be necessary to aid institutions in building up their faculties. The Foundation may wish to support activities that promise to educate and re-educate the teachers that the times demand. This may have to be done by exchanging teachers, by programs of in-service training, and by conferences, short and long. At some point the Foundation may wish to seek to clarify the basic ideas on which American education is founded; these ideas must be clarified if education is to serve its purpose in the contemporary conflict of ideologies.

In connection with these activities, it may be necessary to devise and carry through a variety of kinds of educational research. For example, it is often asserted that one type of education is better than another, that some students are too immature for certain kinds of education, and that some are not intellectually qualified for any kind or for some specific kind. Too often, little or inadequate evidence is offered in support of such assertions.

The range of experiments suggested covers almost the whole field of formal education. Since the officers believe that the Foundation requires the services of an outstanding man who will give direction to its program in this field and are thinking of recommending the establishment of a special institution to forward educational experimentation, they have asked Clarence H. Faust, Dean of Humanities and Sciences at Stanford University, to take charge of this work. He has accepted the post.

2

The Policy Makers

IT is one of the fictions of our highly structured society that in a properly run organization a board of directors makes policy, a president, assisted by other people called "officers," executes policy, while a much larger group of subordinates called the "staff" does the routine work. The fiction is perpetuated by organizational charts which show neat lines of authority flowing ever downward and outward.

In some large industries the fact may resemble the fiction but in nonprofit organizations the delegation of responsibility and of work is rarely so clear-cut. In government, policy is made by executive as well as legislative departments and is substantially altered by the judiciary. In military organizations the distinction between "line" and "staff" is not nearly so sharp as it appears to be on the charts. In universities and colleges, the faculty, which has always been a policy-making body, has in recent years taken over much of the responsibility for decisions that once were made by governing bodies or presidents and deans. Today the students, too, are demanding, and in some institutions are winning, the right to be policy makers.

The division of responsibility depends in part on the traditions of the individual institution, but at any point in time much depends on the talents and inclinations of those holding the various positions in the hierarchy. If the chief administrative officer is weak, a strong board may take much of his executive authority away from him and make administrative decisions in the guise of policy. But a strong executive, particularly one who is imaginative and intellectually vigorous, may take much of the policy making away from the board, to which he turns only for formal approval of decisions already made. A strong subordinate officer may take most of the administrative responsibility away from a weaker officer who holds a higher position on the organizational chart. Even a junior staff member may, by the force of his ideas, become an important policy maker. The wives of executives and board members sometimes play larger roles than are formally recognized. And an intelligent private secretary may greatly influence the decisions of the man who thinks he is her boss.

The answer to the question "Who made policy in the Fund for the Advancement of Education?" is so enormously complicated that a comprehensive answer would require close attention to the work and the personalities of dozens of individuals. The board was a remarkably able one, drawn from many facets of American life. It debated policy at great length and established boundaries for the Fund's activities as well as suggesting opportunities to be explored. The directors understood better than most boards the distinction between policy making and administration and, except in rare cases, restricted its activities to the former.

Some junior staff members and consultants substantially influenced policy through the force of their ideas. Grant applicants who came up with many stimulating ideas, had a distinct influence, as did some of the Fund's critics. Tradition played a role, but the determination of the officers and directors to break with tradition played a larger one.

But the policy of the Fund, as it developed and emerged, reflected many forces, some of which were beyond the control of the directors. It was responsive to social change, which was very rapid during the period of the Fund's existence. It was influenced by the high birthrate of the late Forties and the Fifties and the teacher shortage that resulted from it, by the cold war and threats of hotter wars, and by the emergence of new technologies, particularly television. And it was responsive to the ebb and flow of the great debate that preoccupied educators during the period.

But although the policy moved with the times, certain constants remained throughout the history of the Fund. These reflected the personalities, the philosophies, and the educational convictions of the men and women who held the ultimate responsibility for policy making.

FAUST AND EURICH

The major responsibilities for decision making in the Fund fell upon two men, Clarence Faust and Alvin Eurich, both of whom were members of the board of directors as well as the senior officers of the Fund. It was they who set the tone, interpreted the policy, and made most of the decisions concerning grants. They rarely failed to persuade other members of the board to accept decisions that they had made.

Although Faust was president while Eurich's title was vice-president, the two worked as a team of equals that operated effectively so long as the Fund was relatively independent of the Ford Foundation. Both men wrote policy statements for the annual reports and other publications, both proposed new programs, both interviewed applicants for grants, and both spent a considerable amount of time talking with other directors in advance of board meetings. Eurich accepted most of the responsibility for employing new staff members and assigning their duties, acting in this respect as executive officer.

The pattern, which seems to have been agreed upon at the time Eurich accepted this office, became firmly set during the first year of the Fund's operations, when Faust had his office in Pasadena while Eurich was in charge of the New York office, where he operated with a considerable degree of independence. The sharing of responsibility was acceptable to Faust and was essential for Eurich, whose temperament would have made it difficult for him to accept a subordinate position after having been a university president. "It was," says Faust, "a happy arrangement for both of us."

Although the appointments of the president and vice-president were not official until they were approved by the board of directors at its first meeting in April 1951, the approval was a mere formality. Before the board had come into existence, Faust had been selected by Robert Hutchins and Paul Hoffman to head the Fund, and Faust had assisted Hutchins in selecting the Fund board. Faust, with the approval of Hutchins, Hoffman, and Frank Abrams, had selected Eurich, and they, with the assistance of Abraham Flexner, had persuaded him to leave the presidency of the State University of New York to become vice-president of the Fund.

Clarence Faust and Alvin Eurich had been friends since their undergraduate days when both were students at North Central College in Naperville, Illinois. At the time, North Central was a very small institution affiliated with the Evangelical church — a religiously oriented college that required chapel attendance and Bible study. It seems a safe guess that Faust and Eurich were the brightest boys in their respective classes (Faust was a year ahead), that they received a considerable amount of attention from the faculty, and that they had many opportunities to develop their capacities for leadership.

Both, during their adolescent years, had strong religious convictions which undoubtedly influenced their choice of a college. In any case, scholarships to the more prestigious colleges were rarely available to boys from obscure families in the 1920's.

Clarence Faust who was born in Defiance, Iowa, March 11, 1901, spent his boyhood and attended public schools in various small towns of the middle west where his father served as a minister. Some of his earliest recollections are of debates between his father and ministerial colleagues concerning the perfectibility of man and of human institutions. As he grew older he became convinced of the possibility of social reform and assumed personal responsibility for doing whatever he could to bring it about.

After graduating from high school Faust attended Drake University for a time and then transferred to North Central College from which he graduated in 1923. He then took a year's work at the Evangelical Theological Seminary in Naperville and after receiving a B.D. degree served as a clergyman for four years. But the Evangelical church of the 1920's was far too orthodox and restrictive for a man of Faust's wideranging intellectual curiosity; he decided to become a teacher.

Commenting on his reasons for leaving the ministry for the academic world, Faust says:

Many young men of my generation who had been brought up in a narrow and anti-intellectual version of Christianity were as troubled as I was. Some of us were troubled by the triviality and irrelevance of the Puritan stress of the church on such matters of individual behavior as abstinence from an extended list of common pleasures. We were disturbed even more by matters more fundamental and perhaps more generally observable across denominational boundaries: the chasm between profession and performance as regards obedience to the basic Christian commandment enjoining love of one's fellows — the contradictions, for example, between the Christianity avowed by the church and the position taken in the 1920's of many of its members, lay and clerical (without protest from their churches) of earnest, often hysterical adherence to the Ku Klux Klan.

Above all, it was disturbing to find leaders of the church regarding the strength of the institution itself as the institution's chief purpose, on the assumption apparently that having been divinely instituted it enjoyed something akin to the divine right of monarchy in its claims to obedience and support." [1]

Faust confessed his unorthodoxy in doctrine and his discontent with the church's lack of interest in social justice to his superiors. Instead of defrocking him, as they might well have done, they offered him a more prominent post on the grounds that he had shown organizational and administrative capacity.

But Clarence Faust had had enough of the ministry. Instead of accepting the new post, he went to the University of Chicago to do graduate work in preparation for the teaching of English, the subject he had selected as an undergraduate major because it seemed to offer so broad and liberal a field for thought and reflection. As a graduate student his interests centered first on the Age of Reason and then on earlier periods when intellectual vigor and rigor were central to the culture. After receiving his M.A. in 1929 and teaching for a brief period at the University of Arkansas, Faust was appointed an instructor at the University of Chicago, where he earned the Ph.D. in 1935 and was promoted to assistant professor.

But he soon became dissatisfied with the higher learning as he found it in the universities of the Thirties. He says,

The university, generically, seemed less concerned with wisdom than with academic scholarship. It seemed to trivialize the rich material that is the subject of English studies by dealing with it in narrowly linguistic and historical ways, proudly eschewing judgments of value regarding either the literary art or the ideas literature records. It seemed

[1] Clarence Faust, "The Care and Feeding of Institutions," *Saturday Review,* March 30, 1968, pp. 12–13.

generally disinterested in all but the historical, even antiquarian, aspect of the humanities and preoccupied with learning in its academic form rather than with wisdom. So committed, it dampened hopes that institutional education would be any more effective in bringing intellect and reason to bear upon man's fundamental problems than the church was in replacing dogmatism and blind faith by the development of man's most important tool for advancement — his reason.[2]

Disenchanted with the narrowness of graduate-level scholarship, Faust, who now was rising through the faculty ranks at the University of Chicago, turned his attention to undergraduate teaching and to the development of programs in general or liberal education in the College of the University of Chicago where he was now a faculty member. Many of his faculty colleagues were astonished at his willingness to give up the status of teaching graduate students to "go down" to the undergraduate level. Some of them viewed with alarm the general courses being proposed for undergraduates, fearing that such courses would be superficial and wasteful of time that ought to be employed in taking the first steps toward scholarly specialization.

Had he been in some other university, Faust's decision might have been fatal to his career, but at Chicago his interest in undergraduate liberal education, and in wisdom rather than scholarship as a goal, brought him to the attention of Robert Maynard Hutchins who, as president of the University, was struggling valiantly, and against much faculty opposition, to reform liberal education in the undergraduate college. In 1941, at the age of forty, Faust became dean of the College of the University of Chicago.

In 1946, Faust became dean of the Graduate Library School at Chicago and a year later Eurich, who was then acting president of Stanford, persuaded him to come to Stanford as director of libraries and professor of English. When Eurich left

[2] Ibid., p. 13.

Stanford in 1949, Faust served as acting president of the University for a few months, and became dean of humanities and sciences, a position he held at the time he was invited to become head of the Fund for the Advancement of Education.

Commenting much later on his decision to accept the invitation, Faust wrote:

A certain degree of disenchantment with the church and a degree of disappointment in institutions of higher education may easily suggest to one who has worked in these institutions the attractiveness and promise of foundation work. Foundations, a characteristically and almost uniquely American phenomenon, have large resources, are independent, are free to operate with what wisdom they can muster. Foundation work is indeed fascinating and rewarding. It offers opportunities to see problems in their national or international scope and to learn to know a wide range of able and exciting people.[3]

As a foundation executive, Faust was courageous and independent. He was convinced that a foundation must expect and should welcome criticism but should not be too easily swayed by it, particularly when it took the form of mere abuse such as the Fund received from some quarters. Only when the criticism was intellectually persuasive did it alter his views or influence his actions. He says:

. . . it takes a great deal of persistence, even stubbornness, for a foundation to be selective in its grants rather than to yield to institutional and organized pressures and to fall in with what Abraham Flexner described as "scatteration giving!" Indeed, what nonprofit institutions need — and need the more when unaware of it — is sharp criticism from within and without. They need to be centers of controversy and debate, the very thing which is one of the merits of our pluralistic society to provide. Through debate or disciplined dialogue, reason may be brought to bear upon institutions and their practices to the end of making them effective agencies of needed reform instead

[3] Ibid.

of obstacles to it, and to make them wise contributors to the improvement of the lot of mankind. Institutions wisely reformed, and wisely stimulating reform, can be valuable agents in efforts to bring reason and justice into human affairs.[4]

Throughout his career, Faust has been a reformer, but one who places the emphasis on reason rather than revolution. Speaking of educational institutions he has said, "Given wise and courageous leadership, able to shake off the blinders and shackles of tradition, these institutions may reorganize and redirect themselves and come to adopt sounder educational goals and practices. Foundations, too, increasingly show on occasions an admirable willingness to stimulate controversy and to support righteous, though unpopular, causes.

"It is true that institutions change even more slowly than individuals. Spanning the generations, their commitments and policies do not so naturally and quickly expire. It can be convincingly argued, I feel as I grow older, that the rapid succession of generations is a wise provision for improving the human condition," and he adds, ". . . in our increasingly complex world — a world in which the pace of change constantly mounts (and our problems with it) — civilization is a race between the capacity of institutions to reform so as to stimulate reforms and the disappearance of our species, like that of earlier mighty ones, from the earth." [5]

As president of the Fund, Faust devoted most of his time to matters of basic policy and usually left the operating details to others. To staff members he was a kind and considerate leader who rarely criticized but was quick to indicate his approval when things were done well. Often he wrote notes to staff members and consultants expressing his admiration for their publications or other accomplishments. But officers in the Ford Foundation with whom he occasionally came into con-

[4] Ibid., p. 16.   [5] Ibid.

flict saw another side of his personality and discovered a toughness of fiber that enabled him to fight valiantly when causes to which he was committed were in danger.

Although the personalities of the two men differ greatly, Alvin Eurich, like Clarence Faust, believes deeply in the need for reform in educational institutions. An administrator of long experience, he understands the uses of ideas, power, authority, and money as a means of changing society and is eager to use whatever power is available to him to immeasurably improve the lot of mankind by bringing about changes in the educational system. He is also a prolific writer whose bibliography, including printed speeches, runs to several hundred titles and whose books on education — *Reforming American Education, Campus 1980, The Changing Educational World* — have been widely read.

Eurich was born in Bay City, Michigan, on June 14, 1902. After graduating from high school he entered North Central College where he met Clarence Faust. His undergraduate record was excellent and upon receiving his baccalaureate degree from North Central he was offered an instructorship at the University of Maine, where he also entered upon graduate work that led to the M.A. degree in 1926. He then continued his graduate studies at the University of Minnesota, again while serving as a part-time instructor, and was granted the Ph.D. in educational psychology by that university in 1929.

For eight years Eurich remained at Minnesota while rising through the ranks to a full professorship, and it was during this period that he gave evidence of his interest and talent in administration by becoming assistant to the president of the University. In 1937 he became a professor of education at Northwestern University, but after only a year moved to Stanford University in the same capacity.

During World War II Eurich was in charge of selection

and classification procedures for the Navy, with the rank of commander. He then returned to Stanford where he became vice-president, and in 1948, acting president of the University. In 1949 Eurich accepted an offer to become the first president of the State University of New York, a position that offered him an opportunity to build a scattered assortment of state colleges into a state university system. By 1951 his teaching and administrative experience in both public and private universities had given him a broad and comprehensive knowledge of American higher education and this was built upon the knowledge of elementary and secondary education that he had acquired during his years as an educational psychologist. Moreover, his professional experience had been gained in many sections of the nation, from Maine to California.

He had been president of the State University of New York for only two years when he was invited to join the staff of the Fund. Having so recently assumed the presidency, Eurich must have found the decision difficult but Faust made it clear that the responsibility for policy would be equally shared; Faust would remain in Pasadena while Eurich would have the full responsibility for setting up the New York office. It was also agreed that both Faust and Eurich would be members of the board of directors as well as the senior officers.

As an officer of the Fund, Eurich played the major role in developing educational television, new programs for teacher education, and programs for the better use of teacher time and talent. Although he had been a professor of education — or more likely because of it — he was convinced that the approach to teacher education that was standard in 1951 was totally inadequate and unsatisfactory. He believed that much of what was taught in professional courses for teachers was too obvious to require elaboration and that the teacher could learn many of the practical aspects of his work more effectively through a supervised internship than by means of college courses. He shared the conviction of many educators that many high school teachers at midcentury were inadequately prepared in the subjects they taught. And he shared with Faust the conviction that every teacher should be broadly and liberally educated before he undertook either specialization or professional training. The programs of teacher education which the Fund supported were consistent with these convictions.

Eurich saw a need for the better use of time, space, and personnel in the schools and for more effective use of the technologies such as television and teaching machines. He was convinced that teachers would be more effective if they were able to give more of their time to strictly professional duties, leaving other responsibilities to secretaries and teacher aides. Always willing to challenge the axioms that were deeply embedded in the conventional wisdom of the educational world, he sharply rejected the view, accepted as gospel by most professional educators, that class size must be reduced, holding instead that class size should vary with the nature of the class, the subject of instruction, and the quality of the teaching.

A restless and energetic man, Eurich is an enormously hard worker whose normal working day begins with a business conference at an early breakfast and continues throughout the day and often far into the evening. Impatient of stuffiness and mediocrity, he is not prone to suffer fools gladly and was convinced that some of the men who in 1951 held high posts in the educational establishment fell within that category. His willingness to live dangerously and to brush aside opposition to programs which he considered essential gained him a reputation for ruthlessness on the part of those who stood in his way. But those who worked closely with him found him humane, generous, and compassionate. Many of the rising young men in education are indebted to him for giving them support when they needed it most.

Mr. Eurich has clearly stated his philosophy of reform:

The key to reforming American education is new ideas: new ideas to challenge educational dogmas; new ideas to stimulate change; new ideas to suggest lines of research and development. And back of these new ideas a total *imaginative approach* which asks constantly: Why? *Why* are we doing things this way rather than another, possibly better, way? *Why* do we assume that students learn in such and such a fashion? *Why* do we limit our learning resources to such a slim sliver of the available technology and materials? *Why* do we organize our schools and colleges into self-contained classrooms and uniform-size classes each taught by a single teacher? *Why*, in fact, do we build schools, staff them with teachers, and attempt to educate at all?

New ideas are the key to educational reform. But public policy for education in the United States has not developed in such a way as to support innovation and change. We have simply not organized our educational enterprise to encourage rapid progress.[6]

During his years with the Fund, Mr. Eurich probably did as much as any man alive to encourage educational reform and make it possible. Although his unorthodox views aroused the ire of more cautious educators, they provided a stimulus to the new reform movement that emerged during the Sixties.

THE BOARD OF DIRECTORS

When Clarence Faust accepted the responsibility for planning a new fund for the advancement of education, his first task was to assemble a board of directors. It was obvious that the prestige of the new organization, the directions it would take, and the success it would achieve, would depend in substantial part on the wisdom of the men and women selected for the board and on the educational views which they held.

After discussing the matter with Paul Hoffman and Robert Maynard Hutchins, and getting the suggestions of members of

[6] Alvin C. Eurich, *Reforming American Education* (New York: Harper & Row, 1969), p. 15.

the Ford Foundation board, Faust approached Frank Abrams
with a request that he become chairman of the Fund board.
Abrams, taken aback by the suggestion, protested that he
knew very little about education. But he was intrigued by the
opportunity to take on a new and, for him, totally different
kind of responsibility and he was impressed by Faust, whom
he found very persuasive. After a few days' deliberation, he
accepted.

Abrams, who was chairman of the board of Standard Oil of
New Jersey, had come to the attention of Ford Foundation
officers as a result of an address he had delivered on September
18, 1947, at the Waldorf Astoria Hotel in New York titled,
"The Stake of Business in American Education." In this
speech, Mr. Abrams had called upon the business and industrial community to accept greater responsibility for the support of American education, particularly higher education. "If
business and industry could not draw upon a large reservoir of
educated manpower," he said, "they would be handicapped in
every phase of their operations. American education does a
job for business and industry. If our hope of an advancing
American economy involves reducing costs, increasing individual productivity, and devising better ways of doing things,
we must consider that we have a major interest in helping
American education and educators in their work."

"If we let our educational system decay," he continued,
"we will gravely injure the foundation of our greatness as a
nation. By the same token, if we develop our educational system — expanding it and making it stronger — we will be cul-
tivating the greatest of our national resources, the people of
America. And no one has a greater stake in the future of
America than American businessmen."

Coming as it did from one of the nation's leading industrialists, this speech would have been significant even if Mr.
Abrams had said no more. But he was not content merely to

state a point of view. "Now, what can we do about it?" he
asked, and he offered answers:

The most obvious answer is that business can give money to aid the
cause of education. Of course, many corporations already underwrite
the expense of research projects in college and university laboratories
which they feel will be valuable to their operations. Others grant
scholarships. These activities are excellent so far as they go, but they
do not meet the basic situation which this meeting has been called to
consider. . . . I think the matter goes deeper than grants and scholarships. A basic trouble with American education is public indifference.
*Something has got to be done to educate ourselves regarding the prob-
lem.* All of us have got to understand it better, because the job which
must be done will not be done by me or you or all of us in this room,
but by the American people.

And he concluded:

There is another thing that we as businessmen can do, we can give not
only our money and our advertising facilities [he was speaking to the
Advertising Council] but ourselves. If we hope to see this country
grow and develop under the democratic system, let us devote ourselves
personally to this task as one of our duties as citizens. Let us take part
in educational affairs both in our home communities and at the national level. Let us urge our associates to do the same. This is a very
important and very difficult problem. It deserves the best in all of us.

Mr. Abrams was almost overwhelmed by the response
which his remarks received from educators, particularly college and university presidents. As a result he found himself,
during the following fifteen years, giving a large portion of his
time to the problems of education.

Abrams, after serving as chairman for two years, resigned
from the Fund board in June 1953 to become a trustee of the
Ford Foundation. When he retired from the Foundation
board at the age of seventy in 1959, he was once again appointed to the Fund board and remained in that post until
1967.

Today, Abrams and Faust, two men of vastly different backgrounds and personalities, share a mutual admiration and respect that is not too common between board chairmen and their presidents after a period of years. The Fund opened up a new world to Mr. Abrams and his contributions to the work of the Fund were of a very high order.

Owen J. Roberts, a member of the original board who became chairman upon the resignation of Mr. Abrams, was a distinguished jurist who had been associate justice of the United States Supreme Court from 1930 until 1945. No stranger to the academic world, Justice Roberts had taught law at the University of Pennsylvania from 1898 until 1918 and after his retirement from the Supreme Court had returned to that university as dean of the Law School from 1948 to 1951. He became nationally known in 1924 as the prosecuting attorney in the Teapot Dome oil scandals. In 1942 he was appointed to investigate the Pearl Harbor disaster. Justice Roberts was chairman of the Fund board from 1953 until the onset of the illness which resulted in his death in 1955.

Roy E. Larsen, another member of the original board, who was chairman from 1955 to 1967, probably devoted more time to problems of education than any other board member. Larsen's concern for education predated the establishment of the Fund. The plight of the schools had been brought home to him in 1946 by James B. Conant and other educators in an exploratory meeting that led to the launching, in 1949, of the National Citizens Commission for the Public Schools. He became chairman of that organization and played a leading part in the work for many years.

Larsen was well known in business and publishing circles as the man who, as circulation manager of *Time*, had played a major role in building the Luce communications empire. In

1951 he was president of Time Inc. Explaining his concern for education in his foreword to *How to Get Better Schools*, Larsen said, "My personal gratitude to the American system of public education is boundless. As a first-generation American, I found the American ideal of equality of opportunity literally translated into reality by the public schools. Thus when I learned, a scant thirty years after graduating from the Boston Public Latin School, that our schools were in trouble, I felt that I must do what I could to help." [7]

Larsen's great personal charm, combined with his prestige and acumen, enabled him to make major contributions to the Citizens' movement. His own views on education were moderate and judicious; on most issues he took a middle-of-the-road position. His greatest concern was for better public support for the schools, moral as well as financial. He, like Frank Abrams, helped to persuade the business and industrial communities that increased financial aid to education was a necessary investment in the nation's future.

Though the board of directors included many famous names, Walter Lippmann's was probably the best known. Over a period of four decades he had established a distinguished reputation as an author of books on politics, the public philosophy, and international affairs, and by 1951 was considered the dean of American political columnists. He saw, far more clearly than most people, the relationship between educational quality and the quality of national life, and was convinced that the nation was doing far too little to improve its educational system. In 1954 he asked:

Can it be denied that the educational effort is inadequate? I think it cannot be denied. I do not mean that we are doing a little too little. I mean that we are doing much too little. We are entering upon an era

[7] David B. Dreiman, *How to Get Better Schools* (New York: Harper, 1956).

which will test to the utmost the capacity of our democracy to cope with the gravest problem of our modern times, and on a scale never yet attempted in the history of the world. We are entering upon this difficult and dangerous period with what I believe we must call a growing deficit in the quantity and the quality of American education. . . .

If we were not operating at a deficit level, our working ideal would be the fullest opportunity for all — each child according to its capacity. It is the deficit in our educational effort which compels us to deny to the children fitted for leadership of the nation the opportunity to become educated for that task.

So we have come to the point where we must lift ourselves as promptly as we can to a new and much higher level of interest, of attention, of hard work, of care, of concern, of expenditure, and of dedication to the education of the American people.

We have to do in the educational system something very like what we have done in the military establishment during the past fifteen years. We have to make a breakthrough to a radically higher and broader conception of what is needed and of what can be done.[8]

In addition to Abrams, Roberts, Larsen, and Lippmann, the original board of the Fund included Barry Bingham, Ralph Bunche, Charles D. Dickey, James H. Douglas, Jr., Mrs. Douglas Horton, Paul Mellon, Walter P. Paepcke, Philip D. Reed, James Webb Young, C. Scott Fletcher, Clarence Faust, and Alvin C. Eurich.

It was a remarkably able board, representing many facets of our national life. Bunche was well known for his distinguished service in the United Nations. Mrs. Horton, a former president of Wellesley, had been commander of the WAVES during World War II. Douglas was secretary of the Air Force under President Eisenhower. Mellon was thoroughly familiar with foundation work as a result of his experience with the

[8] Walter Lippmann, "The Shortage in Education," *Atlantic Monthly*, May 1954, pp. 37–38.

Mellon family foundations. Paepcke had been responsible for the restoration of Aspen, Colorado, as an intellectual as well as a cultural center. Bingham was publisher of the Louisville *Courier Journal*. Young was an author of books on a variety of subjects as well as an advertising executive. Reed and Dickey were leaders in the business and industrial world. Fletcher, who was president of the Fund for Adult Education, was made a member of the board, and Faust was made a member of the Fund for Adult Education board in order to assure proper coordination of the two institutions. Before becoming president of the Fund for Adult Education, Fletcher had been director of field development for the Committee on Economic Development and at the time of his appointment was president of Encyclopaedia Britannica Films. As a group these men and women brought to the FAE board a wide range of interests and an imaginative approach to educational problems.

Reed resigned in 1953 because of other commitments, and Bingham resigned in 1954 because of a possible conflict of interests when an associate became a member of the Foundation board. Justice Roberts died in 1955, and Paepcke died in 1960.

As resignations and deaths occurred, equally distinguished names were added to the board. Ralph McGill, who was elected in April 1954, brought to the board the point of view of a liberal southern editor whose reputation and interests were nationwide and worldwide. Other additions over the years included Walter Gifford, honorary chairman of the American Telephone and Telegraph Company; Arthur A. Houghton, Jr., president of Steuben Glass, Inc.; Frederick B. Adams, director of the Pierpont Morgan Library; Maurice Heckscher, a Philadelphia attorney; Joseph Charyk, president of the Communications Satellite Corporation; Arthur Howe; and Mrs. Everett Case. Each of the additions brought a new point of view and fresh ideas.

A criticism frequently made of the boards of philanthropic foundations is that they are overloaded with industrial and financial leaders, representatives of the "Eastern Establishment," who are indifferent to the fact that a substantial part of the United States lies to the west of the Alleghenies or south of the Mason-Dixon line. It has also been charged that too many of the members of such boards are graduates of exclusive preparatory schools and Ivy League colleges, who as a consequence of their own academic experiences are much more concerned with private schools and colleges than with the public institutions in which most Americans get their education.

The board of the Fund for the Advancement of Education was somewhat less vulnerable than most to such charges. All parts of the nation were well represented. McGill and Bingham knew the South and the border states as well as anyone alive. Young and Paepcke knew and loved the Mountain West. Faust, Eurich, and Bunche grew up in the Middle West and had lived on the West Coast before coming to New York. Other members of the board had spent their childhood years in such diverse areas as Kentucky, Missouri, New Mexico, Massachusetts, Iowa, Michigan, Tennessee, and Australia.

Though about half of the members of the board had achieved distinction as industrial or financial leaders, it was not for that reason that they were appointed to the board of the Fund — these were men of wide-ranging interest and broad sophistication who were known to be deeply concerned about social and educational problems. The others came from a wide variety of fields: law, journalism, publishing, government, and higher education. As a group the board held at least forty earned degrees — bachelor's, master's, and doctor's — as well as uncounted dozens of honorary degrees from universities that had chosen to recognize their achievements.

It is true, however, that many members of the board had

had no direct personal experience with publicly supported secondary or higher education. Thirteen of the twenty-four individuals who served on the board between 1951 and 1967 received their undergraduate education in Ivy League colleges (seven were from Harvard alone) or their feminine counterparts, while several of them attended private secondary schools. Only three had ever attended a state university and none had been enrolled in a state or municipal college, even though they were serving on the board at a time when more than half the nation's college graduates came from public colleges. It is hardly surprising that they were prone to look to private schools and colleges for their models.

But this board knew a great deal about education, particularly higher education; many of the members, including Roberts, Horton, Young, Bunche, Faust, and Eurich had at one time been college or university professors, and Mrs. Horton had also taught in elementary and secondary schools before becoming a college professor and president of Wellesley. Roberts and Faust had been deans, Eurich and Horton had been presidents of institutions of higher education. Several of the others had served on the governing boards of schools or colleges. Larsen, as national chairman of the Citizens Commission for the Public Schools, had close contacts with public schools throughout the nation and was thoroughly conversant with their problems. Bunche, who took his undergraduate work at UCLA, and was awarded his Ph.D. at Harvard, had also done postdoctoral work at the London School of Economics, Northwestern, and the University of Chicago, and had been a professor in several colleges and universities. Young had for a time been a professor of business history and advertising at the University of Chicago.

The board met three or four times each year, usually for a full day and on at least one occasion for two days. The agenda was prepared by the executive committee, which met in advance of the regular meeting. Each proposal for a major grant was described in some detail by an officer or staff member of the Fund, and then discussed and debated by the board before approval was granted or the request denied. The president was authorized to make small grants between board meetings within broad categories which had been approved by the board.

As is customary with such groups, the Fund board was self-perpetuating. When a vacancy occurred, a new appointment was made by the board itself. After 1954 the Ford Foundation claimed the right to exert a veto over new appointments but the record does not indicate that the right was ever exercised. The fact that the board membership included only two women, one Negro, and no representatives of labor or of the public schools has occasionally been offered as a criticism of the selective process. It has also been suggested that at least some members of each board of a philanthropic organization should be chosen in some way by the public. But a board member is not expected to represent a special interest group — his responsibility, however he is selected, is to the public at large. And it is difficult to conceive of a procedure of public selection with representation of various groups that would produce a board more intelligent, unselfish, and dedicated to the public interest than that which governed the Fund for the Advancement of Education.

OTHER OFFICERS AND STAFF

Clarence Faust was president of the Fund from its beginning in 1951 until his retirement in April 1966. Alvin Eurich held the office of vice-president from 1951 until April 1964, when he resigned to become president of the Aspen Institute for Humanistic Studies. But most of the officers and staff members had shorter tenure.

It is one of the hazards of philanthropic life that foundation officers seem always to be in great demand for presidencies of colleges and universities. Thomas A. Spragens, the first secretary and treasurer of the Fund, resigned after only a year to become president of Stephens College. O. Meredith Wilson, who followed him in office, resigned after two years to become president of the University of Oregon. Wilson has since had a distinguished career in administration. After six productive years at Oregon, he became president of the University of Minnesota and then, in 1967, president of the Center for Advanced Study in the Behavioral Sciences in Palo Alto.

Wilson was followed in office by Philip Coombs who had joined the Fund staff in 1952 as director of research. Coombs held the office of secretary (also serving as program director in the Education Division of the Ford Foundation after 1957) until 1961, when he left to become assistant secretary of state for Educational and Cultural Affairs.

Although he was only thirty at the time he joined the Fund staff, Coombs already had had a broad experience in higher education and public affairs. After graduating from Amherst in 1935, he entered upon graduate study in economics at the University of Chicago, taught economics at Williams College for two years, and then served in turn as an economist for the OPA, economic adviser to the director of the Office of Economic Stabilization, housing expediter in the Veterans Emergency Housing Program, professor of economics at Amherst College, economics adviser to the governor of Connecticut, and executive director of the President's Materials Policy Commission. During World War II he had served with the OSS and as adviser on strategic bombing targets for the U.S. Air Force.

In the Fund, Coombs's role was not sharply defined. The fact that he was the secretary meant that he had some responsibility for record keeping, but this was never his major responsibility, nor his favorite one. His activities included program planning and execution, serving as liaison between the Fund and various governmental agencies, and conferring with applicants for grants. Like other members of the staff he traveled a great deal, visiting colleges and universities and bringing back plans and proposals for consideration of the other officers. He was responsible, more than any other individual, for establishment of the Midwest Airborne Television program, having been one of the first to see the possibilities of transmitting education programs from an airplane.

Elizabeth Paschal, who followed Coombs as secretary, had been a member of the Fund staff since 1951, having served first as assistant to the president. An economist who had been a member of the faculties of New Jersey College for Women, the Brookings Institution, and the University of Utah, Miss Paschal had also served as chief of the program planning branch of the Bureau of Old Age and Survivors Insurance.

In the Fund, Miss Paschal carried a wide range of responsibilities, including program planning, preparing reports, and conferring with grant applicants. Mr. Faust greatly valued her advice and looked to her for criticism. In April 1963, she became treasurer as well as secretary and held both offices until her resignation, for family reasons, in August 1964.

The first treasurer of the Fund, after that office was split off from the secretaryship in 1953, was John K. Weiss, a brilliant young man whom Mr. Eurich had brought with him from the State University of New York, where he had been assistant to the president and secretary of the board of trustees. Mr. Weiss was assistant vice-president of the Fund before becoming treasurer, and then held both offices until his tragic and early death in 1958, in an airplane crash while he was traveling on Fund business.

After the death of Mr. Weiss, the office of treasurer was filled by Lester Nelson, who had come to the Fund in 1954 as a consultant. Mr. Nelson undoubtedly knew more about American secondary education than any other member of the Fund staff and had a wider acquaintance with secondary school people. He had for twenty years been the principal of one of the nation's great public high schools in Scarsdale, New York, and in 1951–52 had been president of the Middle States Association of Colleges and Secondary Schools. He was also a member of the board of Sarah Lawrence College.

While at Scarsdale, Nelson had been deeply involved in the "Battle of the Books," in which right-wing groups had attempted to remove from the school library all books by authors suspected of leftist tendencies, while he and other school authorities defended the principle of freedom of inquiry. After a long and painful struggle, extensively reported in the national press and during which the school received the support of numerous liberal organizations, Nelson won his fight. The books remained on the shelves. But, though his job was secure, he had become so weary of the battle that he decided to resign and if necessary to retire from school work, though he was only fifty-five at the time.

It was a measure of Mr. Nelson's modesty that he was surprised when he received a wide variety of job offers from people who knew of his fine reputation as an educator and who had heard of his courageous stand at Scarsdale. Turning down professorships and administrative posts, he chose to accept an offer from the Fund to become a full-time consultant. His title was changed to executive associate in 1957, and in 1958 he became an officer.

An administrator of exceptional imagination, vigor, and courage, Nelson was responsible for many of the programs supported by the Fund, particularly in the area of secondary education. His responsibilities and his influence within the Fund increased steadily over the years. Because he was widely known and accepted in professional educational circles, he was able to do much toward healing the breach between the Fund and professional educational organizations.

The years 1963 and 1964 saw many changes in the Fund staff. In April 1963, Lester Nelson retired as treasurer, though he was retained as a part-time consultant. Because the Fund was rapidly being absorbed into the Ford Foundation, the positions of secretary and treasurer were again combined and Elizabeth Paschal held both titles until she resigned in August 1964. She was replaced by John Scanlon, who had come to the Fund in 1953 as deputy director of research and had later become program associate. In 1960 Scanlon had joined Paul Woodring in making plans for the Education Supplement to the *Saturday Review* and from 1960 to 1964 was associate editor of the supplement while on loan from the Fund. In 1964 Scanlon returned to the Fund as secretary-treasurer and is now a program officer at the Ford Foundation.

In April 1964, when Mr. Eurich resigned from the Fund to become president of the Aspen Institute for Humanistic Studies, his resignation was followed by those of Sidney Tickton, Ronald Gross, Judith Murphy, and Joan Braucher, all of whom joined him in another of his new ventures, the Academy for Educational Development. Some of these resignations clearly were motivated by an awareness that the Fund's days were numbered and a conviction that a position within the Ford Foundation either would not be available or would not be an acceptable substitute.

Upon Eurich's resignation, Frank Bowles, former president of the College Entrance Examination Board and former director of admissions at Columbia University, became vice-president. When Mr. Faust retired two years later, Mr. Bowles became president of the Fund. G. H. Griffiths, who had been an officer in the Fund for Adult Education, joined the staff of the FAE in 1961 and has played a notable role in integrating the work of the two funds with that of the Ford Foundation, where he is now a program officer. Mr. Griffiths has been the secretary-treasurer of the FAE during its terminal phase.

Considering the size of the funds available and of the operations involved, the Fund operated throughout its history with a very small staff. The staff, counting the officers, grew from five members at the time of the first annual report to nine in 1957. After the staff became the Education Division of the Ford Foundation, the number was increased but never rose above thirteen. Some of the staff members felt that the staff was too small, that individuals were badly overworked, and that the Fund could have operated more effectively with a larger staff. But Faust and Eurich were reluctant to delegate to others decisions that might reflect policy or alter the direction of the Fund's activities, and the directors preferred to keep the staff small in order to keep overhead expenses at a minimum.

Though the first annual report lists an "executive staff" of only five members (which included the officers), a paragraph on "Organization" mentions that Mrs. Frances Cahn, Miss Elizabeth Paschal, and Mrs. Susan Spaulding were "also appointed to senior positions on the research and administrative staff." The second report (1952–54) lists four officers plus an "executive staff" consisting of Miss Paschal, Mr. Scanlon, and Arnold J. Kuesel, the assistant treasurer who handled accounting and payroll problems throughout the remainder of the Fund's history.

The report for 1954–56 lists two additional names on the executive staff: Lester Nelson and Jonathan King, who later became an officer in the Educational Facilities Laboratories. The report for 1957–59 includes only one new name, James W. Armsey, who had come to the Ford Foundation with Henry Heald when the latter became president and had chosen to work with the Fund as well as on the education staff of the Foundation. Armsey later became program director for both Fund and Foundation but his major responsibilities were for Foundation projects.

The name of Sidney Tickton first appears in the report for 1959–61 (as program associate), although Mr. Tickton had for a number of years been an important member of the staff and was the author of Fund publications dealing with statistical analyses and projections. Renata von Stoephasius, whose name first appears in the same report, remained with the Fund throughout its subsequent history as an editor and writer.

The report for 1961–62 lists two new names: Ronald Gross and Edward J. Meade, Jr. Gross, a writer and editor, later joined Eurich at the Academy for Educational Development where he is now vice-president. Meade, who was a graduate of Montclair State College and had received his doctorate in education from Harvard, came to the Fund as consultant to assist Lester Nelson on the School Improvement Program. His contribution was such that he became a permanent member of the staff and later program officer in charge of public education at the Ford Foundation.

Throughout its history, the Fund seemed to have difficulty deciding what titles to give the staff members who were not officers. One individual who worked for the Fund on a full-time basis for many years says he never knew what his title had been during the previous year until he read the annual report. In these reports he found himself listed at various times as consultant, educational advisor, educational writer, consultant to the general program, program associate, and then again as consultant, all without being told of any changes in his duties.

Even at the officer level the titles were misleading. Whether they were called vice-president, secretary, or treasurer, all were also program officers. After the staff moved into the

Foundation offices in 1957, Ford Foundation titles were given to most members of the executive staff. These, in descending order, were vice-president, executive director (a title held only by Eurich), program director, associate program director, program associate, and program assistant. The titles gave a rough indication of salaries but had little to do with duties which differed from one individual to another. The confusion was compounded by the fact that some individuals held one title in the Fund and another in the Foundation. When writing letters the secretary had to decide which letterhead to use and which title was to be used with it.

The Fund applied the title of consultant to a wide variety of individuals whose roles had little in common except that they did not fit into any conventional pattern. Some of those so listed had temporary, often part-time, assignments to work on specific projects. Others worked on a full-time basis for short periods. Some who rarely were seen in the Fund offices, were given the title because the officers were indebted to them in some way, or wished to have them available for consultation. But a few of those listed as consultants were full-time staff members — in some cases for as long as six or seven years — who were given this title because no one could think of anything better to call them.

Some of the full-time consultants came to the Fund for specific purposes and had clear-cut assignments from the outset. Others were placed on the payroll without specific assignments. These free-floating consultants enjoyed a degree of freedom rarely experienced by organization men, but theirs was not a role for one easily upset by uncertainty. Though the salary was generous — roughly that of a senior professor in a major university — the consultant might not know what it was to be until he received his first paycheck. Upon his arrival at Fund headquarters he would be provided with an office, a secretary, and an expense account — and then ignored. If he were the right man for the job he soon found a role for himself. He might investigate some educational problem and report his results or he might design a program dear to his heart and then get the job of directing it. Or he might write a critical evaluation of something the Fund had done.

After the Fund staff became the Education Division of the Ford Foundation such free-floating assignments became impossible. In the Foundation each man on the payroll was expected to be an executive — or at least to act like one. Just thinking and writing was not enough. But the use of consultants had much to recommend it. Most of the consultants did a prodigious amount of work and were productive in ways that executive officers cannot hope to be. The employment of individuals without definite assignment is risky, to be sure, but a foundation is better able than any other organization to take the risk.

The consultants came to the Fund from a wide variety of backgrounds. To name only a few, Burton Fowler was the former headmaster of the Germantown Friends School and a past president of the Progressive Education Association. Bernadette Giannini was a teacher in the Oakland, California, public schools. Paul Rehmus and Alexander Stoddard had been superintendents of schools in large cities. Sidney Tickton was an economist. Lester Nelson, who was a consultant before he became an officer, was a former high school principal. Oliver Carmichael had been chancellor of Vanderbilt University, president of the Carnegie Foundation, and then president of the University of Alabama. Several of these consultants became the authors of Fund publications to be discussed in a later chapter.

Paul Rehmus, who had been a high school classmate of Eurich's at Bay City, Michigan, was probably the most influential of all Fund consultants. After a heart attack made it necessary for him to resign from the superintendency of schools in Portland, Oregon, in 1953, Rehmus accepted an invitation from Eurich to travel around the country, visiting schools and colleges of education in search of new talent and places where new programs might be launched. Because of his ability to judge both men and institutions, he was able to identify a number of exceptionally able young professional educators, some of whom have since moved into positions of prominence and influence in education. His confidential reports to Fund officers had a substantial influence on grant-making decisions and on Fund policy.

Because secretarial and research positions in the Fund were highly attractive to young college graduates (they were once described as "glamour jobs" in *Mademoiselle,* perhaps because of the carpets on the floors and the original paintings on the walls as well as the academic and intellectual atmosphere), the Fund was able to employ a remarkable group of girls who had an excellent background of liberal education as well as secretarial skills. One consultant recalls a time when he was trying to document a quotation and looked into a room where a group of secretaries were having coffee. He read the line and asked if anyone could identify it. *Romeo and Juliet,* they chorused. "Act two, scene three," several added. The consultant, who had once been a professor of English, returned to his office somewhat chastened.

Marjorie Martus, who was a research assistant in the Fund, is now a program officer in the Foundation. Gladys Chang Hardy, another member of the research staff, was later associated with the National Endowment for the Humanities in Washington and is now an executive at Boston University. Dorothy Mitchell Dugdale, who began as a secretary, later became an administrative assistant. Thelma Coles and Eleanor Slaybaugh Krell became secretaries in the editorial offices of *Saturday Review*'s Education Supplement.

The only individual employed by the Fund throughout its

entire history was Janet Moreland McNeely, who as a recent graduate of Stanford became Mr. Faust's secretary in 1951, remained after his retirement, and is now with the Ford Foundation. Joan Braucher, who was Mr. Eurich's secretary during most of his time with the Fund, held a similarly responsible position. Other secretaries and members of the office staff who had long tenure — in some cases longer than the staff members with whom they worked — included Frances Sherman (who is now secretary to Mr. Eurich), Ronayne Huff, Natalie Braddon, Margaret Toulson, Roberta Lynch, Margery Thompson, Marjorie Harrison, Dorothy Soderlund, Patricia Norris Rae, Dorothy Thornton, Arlene Mensher Nance, Clifford Walsh, and Wendell Williams.

THE ROLE OF ROBERT MAYNARD HUTCHINS

In a discussion of the sources of Fund policy the role of Robert Maynard Hutchins cannot be ignored even though Hutchins was never an officer or director of the organization. Many educators — particularly those who were critical of the Fund — were inclined to see the shadow of Mr. Hutchins hanging over many of the Fund's programs, especially during the early years when the Fund was lending its support to programs of early admission to college and to programs emphasizing liberal education for teachers.

In part this impression reflected a confusion of the Fund with the Ford Foundation, where Hutchins was the chief education officer until 1954, and in part it was a natural result of Hutchins's high visibility. In 1951 he had been a conspicuous figure on the educational scene for more than two decades. As president of the University of Chicago he had fought valiantly to protect and defend liberal education at a time when the drift was toward ever greater specialization and vocationalization, even in the undergraduate colleges. For years he had insisted that liberal education should provide the focus for teacher education. He was the first president of a major university to have the courage to take a firm stand against big-time semiprofessionalized college football of a kind that provided entertainment for the public without contributing to the educational goals of the institution.

As a result of his charismatic personality, his unorthodox views, his vigorous prose style, and his towering self-confidence in the face of opposition, he had attracted devoted followers and made bitter enemies in approximately equal numbers. Every educator in the nation had heard of him and had some notion — though often a distorted one — of what he believed in and stood for. By comparison, the officers of the Fund for the Advancement of Education were relatively obscure in 1951, despite the important positions they had held in universities. Since many educators working on the elementary and secondary levels had never heard of Faust and Eurich, they found it easy to believe that Hutchins, whose name had become firmly tied to the Ford Foundation, was calling the tune for all the funds established by the Foundation.

Fund officers and directors are inclined to play down the Hutchins role — some even deny that he had any influence whatever on Fund policy or program. Perhaps they protest too much because it is apparent that many of the early programs supported by the Fund were far more harmonious with Hutchins's views of what education ought to be than they were with the thinking of the more orthodox educators of the day. In any case these facts are clear: Hutchins played a very large part — probably the determining part — in the decision to establish a separate fund for the advancement of formal education, and it was he who selected Clarence Faust to get it started. Hutchins and Faust had been friends since the Thirties. Hutchins had chosen Faust over a number of more senior faculty members to be dean of the College at the University of Chicago. Faust admired Hutchins and shared many of his convictions regarding the proper nature of liberal education and the importance of such education in a free nation.

But Clarence Faust, an inner-directed man who makes his own decisions, was by no means dependent upon Robert Hutchins or his views, and it is not at all clear that he was prone to ask for his advice. After Faust moved his office from Pasadena to New York, Hutchins rarely if ever was seen in the Fund offices and he had no occasion to attend meetings of the Fund board or the Fund staff. The other officers of the Fund were not nearly so well acquainted with him as Faust was and some of them did not share his views on education.

Hutchins's indirect influence on Fund policy during the early years when he was still a Ford Foundation executive was apparent in January 1952, when the boards of the Fund for the Advancement of Education and of the Fund for Adult Education met jointly in Philadelphia for a discussion of policy. Mortimer Adler, after presenting his own views, led a discussion which was interpreted by some board members as an effort to further expose the boards to the Hutchins-Adler philosophy, if not to indoctrinate them in it. A vigorous debate followed, involving confrontations between board members espousing elitism in education and those espousing egalitarianism, and also between the "Great Books" approach to liberal education and the belief that learning how to run a lathe can be taught in such a way as to make it a truly liberating activity. It became clear that the board intended to make its own decisions. And after the Fund staff became the Education Division of the Ford Foundation, in 1957, the Hutchins influence was negligible.

But three observations seem to be justified: Had it not been for Hutchins there might never have been a separate fund for the advancement of education. Had he not played the major role in selecting the president and the directors the Fund would have been a very different kind of organization, di-

rected toward different goals and with different programs.
(When in the summer of 1968 I asked Hutchins, "Who selected the first Fund Board?" his answer was unequivocal. "I
did," he said, and though there are those who disagree, it is my
impression that this comes very close to being the truth — and
it was a very good board.) And it is probable that if Hutchins
had retained his position in the Ford Foundation, the Fund
would have continued to this day to be an independent organization, separate from the Foundation.

EVOLUTION OF FUND POLICY AND PROGRAM

Any program of assistance to educational institutions must
rest, explicitly or implicitly, on certain assumptions about the
purposes of education, the nature of the educational process,
and the proper role of educational institutions. If these assumptions are explicitly stated and form a cohesive pattern
they may legitimately be called an educational philosophy.

The officers of the Fund recognized the need for such a philosophy. In the first annual report President Faust said:

Providing assistance for efforts to clarify the purposes and appropriate
processes of education is the cornerstone of the Fund's program. There
can be no advancement of education without some clarity about the
direction in which advancement lies. What is the role of education in a
modern, industrialized, democratic society? What are the functions of
educational institutions in relation to the function of other social institutions such as the home and the church? What kind of education
and what amount of it should every member of a democratic society
receive? Should the school confine its program to the three R's or
should it be concerned with all the child's activities during the twenty-
four hours of the day? How far should provision be made for the
development of exceptionally talented individuals? These questions
involve more basic ones concerning man and society, concerning the
nature of knowledge and how it is acquired, concerning individual and
social goodness or excellence. In short, the basic problems of education
are the basic problems of mankind and the clarification of educational

thought depends upon a general philosophical clarification as broad and deep as the whole sphere of fundamental ideas.

The advancement of education in America depends very largely upon the degree of clarification which can be achieved with respect to these and related questions. This is not to say that it depends upon the establishment of a single set of answers or a single system of thought. Differences in educational philosophy cannot and should not be eliminated. It is important, however, that they should be clearly understood. It is certain, moreover, that the resolution of conflicts between existing schools of educational philosophy by way of eclectic reduction to less common denominators will not provide the guidance education requires. What is needed is fundamental rethinking of the role of education in our time. Obviously this cannot be achieved overnight. Obviously, too, it must be the result of many minds. The Fund should not itself undertake to develop a philosophy of American education. It can best be useful by providing financial assistance for promising developments in this field.[9]

In accordance with this stated policy, the Fund never announced its own educational philosophy in any single document or even made it clear that it worked from a philosophy.

No doubt this was a sound decision because the educational philosophy for a democratic nation cannot be created by one man or by one organization, philanthropic or otherwise. It must emerge from the convictions of the people and must stem from their mores, their folkways, their ethical beliefs, and their concept of the good life. In a diverse nation it must allow for diversity; in a changing culture it must provide for change. Yet it must have sound moorings, it cannot be merely a reflection of the current tides or the whims of an uncertain people; it must have deep roots in the past and possess the stability provided by those roots.

Although the philosophy must come from the people, it

[9] *Annual Report,* 1951–52, p. 10.

cannot be articulated by the people as a whole. Although it must gain their acceptance in the long run, it cannot be discovered by asking the people to vote on separate issues, or it will be riddled with inconsistencies. It must be in the public interest and, in the words of Walter Lippmann, "The public interest may be presumed to be what men would choose if they saw clearly, thought rationally, acted disinterestedly and benevolently."

Though the Fund never stated its educational philosophy except in piecemeal form, it seems clear that any program of selective grant making must be based upon a set of assumptions, principles, and tenets. Obviously the officers and directors of the Fund had some firm convictions regarding education and the way it could best be advanced. Much of the controversy over the Fund's activities was based upon disagreement with the philosophy implicit in its decisions to accept some proposals and to reject others.

The Fund's philosophy must be inferred from the statements of its officers and directors and from the kinds of programs that they chose to support. But even before the Fund came into existence, its policy was to some extent set for it, or at least influenced by, the recommendations of the Ford Foundation's "Study Report" which, in its section on education, urged that economic, religious, and racial barriers to equality of educational opportunity be reduced at all levels, that the discovery, support, and use of talent and leadership be encouraged, and that ways be found for improving ths quality and ensuring an adequate supply of teachers for schools at all levels from the elementary school to the university. The Study Committee also stressed the need for liberal education: "The Foundation should find and assist programs of study in the schools and colleges which emphasize the breadth and richness of the student's educational experience and which direct the student's attention to life rather than to an immediate vocation and to his responsibility as a thinking and acting citizen in a democracy."

Soon after its establishment, the board of directors of the Fund adopted the following statement of general policy:

> The Trustees of the Ford Foundation in authorizing the establishment of the Fund for the Advancement of Education directed it to devote its attention to experiments and new developments in education. The Directors of the Fund are consequently concerned (1) with seeking, appraising, and supporting improvements and experiments in education which promise to have some general application and which are not being adequately supported by existing private or public funds, and (2) with providing aid which may be required for putting into effect practices which experimentation or other proven experience has demonstrated to be sound. Within these limits the operation of the Fund will be directed by the particular program of activities which the Board from time to time formulates on the basis of its judgment of the most critically important matters in the areas specified. In its initial program the Fund for the Advancement of Education will not make grants for building programs, the increase of endowments, or general operating expenses of institutions.[10]

The decision not to make grants for buildings, endowments, or general operating expenses was adhered to throughout the history of the Fund. But this early statement of policy left undefined the particular areas of opportunity to which the Fund should direct its attention. The number and variety of promising experiments in education were very great. To try to cover the whole range or even any large proportion of it, would inevitably have resulted in spreading the Fund's limited resources too thin. Merely to select projects without the framework of a program would have made the Fund's efforts haphazard and accidental, and, without adequate criteria for selection of projects, the net effect of years of grants might

[10] Ibid., pp. 7–8.

have been zero. Consequently a coherent program for the granting of funds was essential.

As the officers and directors studied the problems of education, and as they consulted experienced educators they came to the conclusion that it would be wise to concentrate on five problems: (1) clarification of educational philosophy; (2) clarification of the function of the various parts of the educational system and the improvement of the articulation of these parts; (3) improvement of the preparation of teachers at all levels of the educational system; (4) improvement of opportunities for education in the armed services of the country; and (5) development of financial support for educational institutions.

These categories were later revised in the light of the Fund's experience and in response to social pressures and social change. The second annual report (actually all but one of these annual reports cover two years rather than one) which covers the period from July 1, 1952, through June 30, 1954, indicates that the Fund has decided "to concentrate on assisting experiments designed to advance education along the following lines: (1) the improvement of teaching; (2) improvements in curricula; (3) clarification of the functions of educational institutions; (4) equalization of educational opportunity; and (5) improvement of educational management and financing." [11]

It will be noted that the improvement of teaching has been moved up to the first category. It is not clear that the listing of categories is in the order of priority but it was appropriate that the improvement of teaching should be listed first because the Fund was devoting more time and attention to this problem than to all others combined. "Clarification of educational philosophy" is no longer listed as a major goal although the Fund continued to give some attention to this problem. The

[11] *Annual Report*, 1952–54, p. 5.

disappearance of "improvement of opportunities for education in the armed services" as a category reflects the fact that the Korean War had ended, but this cannot be the full explanation because, in 1954, the nation still had between two and three million men and women in the armed forces where their opportunities for education remained a problem. More important was the fact that the Fund's efforts to work with the Department of Defense had not met with a high degree of success. "Improvements in curricula" was a new category which the Fund had decided it could not ignore. The other new category of interest, "equalization of educational opportunity," reflected a growing interest in the education of Negroes and other groups who had been denied equality of opportunity because of race, poverty, or place of residence.

The categories of interest listed in the annual report for 1954–56, published in June 1957, are much the same as those in the previous report except for a slight change of wording, but the next report, published in November 1959, indicates a decision to deal with the problems in a broader context which would reveal more clearly their dimensions and interrelationships. In view of the progress made and the experience gained the directors and officers thought it advantageous to redefine the Fund's program without basically changing its character or substance. In place of the five specific problems or objectives listed previously, three somewhat broader objectives were listed: (1) the improvement of educational personnel, (2) the improvement of educational programs, and (3) the improvement of the relationships between educational institutions and society. Among the advantages seen in this redefinition of program was the emphasis it gave to the fundamental requirements for a strong educational system: competent people, a clearly conceived and efficiently arranged program, and strong public support for both. But there were other advantages. "Educational personnel" was more appropriate than "teachers" in categorizing programs for the education of teacher aides, administrators, and various other kinds of specialists as well as teachers. The phrase "improvement of educational programs" could be used to describe efforts to relate curricular changes to improvements in teaching techniques, including approaches to the use of new technologies such as educational television and programmed learning. "Improvement of the relationships between educational instutions and society" covered both efforts to gain better public support (financial and moral) for the schools, and efforts to help the schools to explain their purposes and activities to the public.

The next two reports, for 1959–61 and for 1961–62, suggest little change in categories of interest but the last official report, for 1962–64 says, "In response to the changing needs of this country, the Fund has in the past several years shifted its emphasis from the improvement of teachers and administrators, which consumed the largest part of grant resources in the past, to a concern for the educational program and, to an even greater extent, to those improvements in education that promote greater equality of educational opportunity for minority groups." [12] The emphasis on equality of opportunity increased during the Sixties as the nation became increasingly aware of its past failures to provide such opportunity.

Throughout its history the Fund held to a number of other basic convictions which were not fully accepted by all American educators and were rejected by some. These convictions could be summarized in the Fund's implicit fundamental ends of education. One of them was that a broad, liberal education is the first essential of every citizen of a free and self-governing nation and particularly of every teacher, regardless of the subject or grade level which he is to teach. A second belief was that it is in no way undemocratic to seek out and nurture superior talent and that, in fact, the democratic way

[12] *Annual Report*, 1962–64, p. 13.

of life is bound to suffer if this is not done. A third was that American schools, if they are to produce any significant number of intellectually superior human beings, must reestablish the priority of the intellect. Consistently with this conviction, the Fund made a sharp distinction between *education* and *training* and gave priority to the former. It chose to use its resouces for the advancement of *education* and to leave the problem of improving vocational training and other kinds of training to others, including the Ford Foundation.

While the Fund had an ideological commitment to these basic *ends* of education, it had no similar commitment to any *means* of educational advancement. It sought always to find and encourage new approaches to the achievement of the ends. And although the ends chosen were a subject of debate during the years of the Fund's operation, the Fund officers and directors hoped and believed that their convictions eventually would become the core of a public philosophy to which a majority of Americans would subscribe.

THE FUND WITHIN THE FOUNDATION

In 1957 the Fund closed its offices at 655 Madison Avenue and moved its entire staff onto the seventeenth floor of the Ford Foundation building at 477 Madison Avenue. Although the distance traveled was only a few blocks, the move had profound consequences for the Fund and was traumatic for some individuals on the Fund staff.

It had been obvious for some time that the officers and directors of the Foundation had no intention of continuing to support the Fund in the style to which it had been accustomed. They had made no major grants to the Fund since 1955, and the money from the earlier appropriations was running low. Paul Hoffman and Robert Maynard Hutchins, the officers who had been responsible for the establishment of the Fund, had long since been eased out of the Foundation.

Rowan Gaither, who became president of the Foundation after Hoffman's resignation in 1953, was much less enthusiastic about independent funds even though they had been suggested in the "Study Report" which he signed. Henry Heald, who became president upon Gaither's resignation in 1956, preferred to keep the power and influence of the Ford Foundation concentrated under a single board and staff. Moreover (though there is some difference of opinion about this), it seems likely that the trustees of the Foundation had been troubled by the criticism which the Fund had received from many quarters, and that they were less willing than the directors of the Fund to accept the kind of criticism that was inevitable if the Fund were to make a courageous attack on the fundamental problems facing education.

Whatever the reasons, it seems clear that by the late Fifties the Foundation had become disenchanted with its "independent" funds and was ready to liquidate them. The Fund for Adult Education was given its terminal grant (to cover a five-year period) in December 1955. The Fund for the Republic already was what Hutchins had called it earlier — "a wholly disowned subsidiary of the Ford Foundation." But the Fund for the Advancement of Education received a different treatment.

In 1957 Mr. Heald invited Mr. Faust to become vice-president of the Ford Foundation with responsibility for the Foundation's education program. Mr. Faust accepted with the express understanding that he would bring the staff along to form the Education Division of the Foundation while it would continue to act as the staff of the Fund for the Advancement of Education. Mr. Eurich became executive director of the Education Division of the Foundation and other officers and staff members were offered positions on the Foundation staff. The Foundation agreed to continue, for an unspecified time, to make small annual appropriations of about two million dollars which the Fund board could use at its discretion for experimental projects, with the understanding that successful experiments would receive further support on a larger basis from the Foundation. The Fund board was also invited to act in an advisory capacity to the Foundation board on matters of education. But even with these concessions some Fund board members were far from enthusiastic about the decision and accepted it only because they saw no alternative, except slow starvation.

The Fund staff, too, was divided. Mr. Faust was convinced that the move was sound or at any rate that it was inevitable. Mr. Eurich was strongly opposed; at one point he threatened to resign if the Fund accepted the Foundation's offer. When other officers and staff members were informed of the decision (their opinions do not seem to have been invited prior to the decision), some were willing to give up their independence for the opportunity to work with the larger financial resources and to be a part of a more impressive-sounding organization, but others were convinced that the Fund would never again be able to operate as effectively and flexibly as it had in the past.

In their new offices in the Ford Foundation building, the education staff occupied an entire floor. It was somewhat cut off from other divisions of the Foundation and communication was minimal, except for the occasional informal meetings at lunch in the dining room on the twenty-first floor. Communication among staff members in different departments was discouraged by the clearly established hierarchy of the Foundation which made it necessary for everything to go through proper channels. The difference between the Fund for the Advancement of Education as it had previously been, and the Ford Foundation as it was in 1957, was something like the difference between a small informal liberal arts college and a massive multiversity. More than one staff member felt a nostalgic yearning for the easygoing ways of the smaller organization.

Under the new arrangement each officer and staff member wore two hats and had two titles — one in the Fund and another in the Foundation. Faust was president of the Fund and a vice-president of the Foundation. Eurich was vice-president of the Fund and an executive director of the Education Division of the Foundation. Other Fund officers were program directors in the Foundation. If a grant request seemed appropriate for the Fund, Mr. Faust could take it directly to the Fund board but if it seemed more appropriate for the Foundation (because of larger size or because it was not experimental), he could take it to Mr. Heald with the recommendation that it be transmitted to the Foundation board. From the point of view of the staff it was much easier to take a proposal to the Fund but most of the larger grants had to be taken to the Foundation because the Fund now had very limited resources.

In the Fund, Faust and Eurich had worked together essentially as equals but in the Foundation the fact that Faust was a vice-president while Eurich was not, plus the fact of a much greater emphasis on rank in the Foundation, made it difficult for them to work together as harmoniously as they had in the past. The relationship between them deteriorated to the point where communication was minimal and this caused uncertainty on the part of staff members.

Under the new arrangement, staff members were unclear as to whether they were expected to be guided by the policy of the Fund board or that of the Foundation board but — because of the permanence of the Foundation and the uncertain future of the Fund — it was obvious to those who wished to make careers of philanthropic work that their futures lay within the Foundation.

At the time he became president of the Ford Foundation, Henry Heald was quoted as saying that it was the duty of a

foundation, "to be ahead — but not too far ahead." [13] In earlier years the officers of the Fund would almost certainly have
disagreed with so cautious a statement — they would have
said that it is the duty of a foundation to be as far ahead as
possible. But after the Fund joined the Foundation the staff
became less venturesome — more willing to play it safe. It
continued to give assistance to the educational enterprise but
became less eager to shatter tradition or break down barriers.

One result was that, after 1957, the Fund received much less
criticism from the professional educators. But there was another reason for the decline in criticism. By the late Fifties the
Fund had identified a number of very able educators with
whom it could work harmoniously and whose activities it was
glad to support. Since some of these individuals were moving
into the seats of power, the Fund was no longer in serious conflict with the educational establishment.

After 1958 the officers and staff members who preferred a
more daring approach to educational reform began to look
around for other employment. Within five or six years after
the Fund joined the Foundation, all but two or three members
of the Fund's professional staff left, although only two of
them had reached retirement age. By the time the Fund entered its terminal phase, in 1967, only one man who had been a
member of the professional staff of the Fund in its independent days still was with the Foundation. The Education Division of the Foundation continued to grow and prosper but it
was in new hands.

From 1957 until 1967 the Fund continued to operate with
about two million dollars a year at its disposal. But during the
Sixties the separate identity of the Fund became increasingly
obscured as the staff came to think of itself as the Education
Division of the Foundation rather than as the staff of the
Fund. Frank Bowles, who became president upon Mr. Faust's

[13] *Time,* June 10, 1957, p. 61.

retirement, soon came to the conclusion that the Fund had lost
its effectiveness as a separate institution and ought to terminate
its existence.

The directors of the Fund were well aware of their decreasing influence but they were so deeply committed to the Fund
that they were reluctant to let it go out of existence. When
President Bundy of the Foundation appeared in a Fund board
meeting in 1966, to announce that they could no longer expect
support from the Foundation, some members of the board
were angry and indignant. They rejected an invitation from
the Foundation to continue in an advisory capacity but without any real authority. "There is just no way to wither away
gracefully," one member said.

The termination of the Fund's activities was announced in a
news release dated April 30, 1967, in which Roy E. Larsen,
chairman of the Fund board, said that the decision marked the
final stage in a transition that had been under way since 1957
when the staff of the Fund and the Foundation's Education
Division became one and the same, and added that the Fund's
efforts to advance education had now become an integral part
of the Foundation's activities and were being continued by the
Foundation. "Since the Fund and Foundation began coordinating their activities closely in 1957," said Mr. Larsen, "the
Fund has concentrated on breaking new ground with initial
support of promising experiments and developments in education, and the Foundation on amplifying, refining and more
broadly demonstrating many of these. Both have also supported activities which were not shared, but the dominant
theme has been partnership" (see Appendix, page 288).

The same release included a letter to Mr. Larsen from President McGeorge Bundy of the Foundation in which he expressed the Foundation's appreciation of the "pioneering and
highly effective work of the Fund and its many stimulating
contributions to the Foundation's own program in education."

And Bundy added, "The new massiveness and scope of Federal support to education has changed the previous relationship between the Fund and the Foundation, putting the Foundation in the Fund's special role of experimental 'pilot' much more often than in the past. In this role, we know that the Foundation will draw strength from the venturesome and inventive example set by the Fund's directors and staff since 1951."

The Foundation has indeed expanded and built upon many of the programs initiated by the Fund, notably in its contribution to educational television, in the Foundation's "breakthrough" program in teacher education, and to a lesser degree in many other activities. It has also initiated many new programs in areas in which the Fund was not involved. Although it is not yet entirely clear that a large philanthropic foundation with comprehensive goals can play the same role as a smaller fund dedicated to education alone, most observers agree that the Education Division of the Foundation is making a vigorous attack on the problems of education, that it now operates with a considerable degree of independence, and that, under the presidency of Mr. Bundy, the Foundation has become more venturesome than it was under the previous presidencies and consequently better able to play the role of innovator.

3

The Educational Milieu

AT midcentury the nation was ready for substantial changes in education. It was obvious that the kinds and quality of education that had been provided to American children during the first half of the twentieth century would not be adequate for children who would spend a part of their lives in the twenty-first. Consequently the Fifties and Sixties were years of reassessment and reform, the reforms being a natural result of the reassessment.

During the early Fifties a number of long-smoldering controversies came to the surface, forcing the schools to reexamine their policies. Parents as well as educators became involved in the debate, an involvement that reflected an increased public interest in the schools. This interest resulted in part from the fact that the number of parents had increased sharply, but it was related, too, to the migration of middle-class families from cities to suburbs. When he lived in a big city the parent often had a frustrated feeling that he could do little or nothing about the schools his children attended because the system was too big, too complex, and too remote. But when he moved to the suburbs the situation changed — in many cases the desire to find better education for his children had been the main reason for leaving the city.

In the suburbs the school district was small enough to give the parent a feeling that he had some real hope of improving the schools and the suburban parent usually was sufficiently well educated to have confidence in his opinions of what the characteristics of a good school should be. But when parents tried to change the local PTA from a friendly social gathering, with perhaps a speech followed by tea and cookies, to a forum where serious educational problems were debated, they quickly discovered that the policies of the national PTA, as well as its traditions, discouraged such a transformation. As a next step parents in many communities organized citizens' committees or ran for the school board. No longer were they content to leave education entirely to the educators.

Though some school administrators welcomed the new public interest in the schools, many of them found it troublesome. Frequently the demands of the parents were contradictory. Some wanted more vocational training in high school while others wanted better preparation for college. Some thought the schools needed stronger discipline; others were critical of the rules imposed upon their children. Administrators found that their soothing publicity releases, couched in the best educational jargon and planned in accordance with advice they had received in courses in school administration and public relations, were waved aside as mere clichés. They came to see the youthful, educated, and sometimes opinionated suburban matron and her articulate, aggressive husband as a threat to the stability of the schools. Some called for help from professional organizations, others denounced critical parents as "enemies of the schools." But the more able and imaginative administrators set out to improve the schools and it was they who were most likely to turn to philanthropic foundations for assistance because it is always easier to get money from local sources for the support of traditional programs than for innovations, even when the public is crying for changes. Taxpayers are reluctant to have their money used as "risk capital."

THE GREAT DEBATE

At the time the Fund for the Advancement of Education came onto the scene, the public schools were undergoing some of the sharpest attacks on the nationwide level in their entire history. Schools have always been subject to periodic waves of criticism in the press, from the pulpit, and over a million dinner tables where children report on the day's activities while parents express their views of the curriculum and the teacher, but the wave that hit the schools at midcentury was of a new level of violence. During the years 1949, 1950, and 1951 entire issues of popular magazines and journals of opinion were devoted to critical examinations of the schools. During the early Fifties, books highly critical of prevailing educational theories and practices were more widely read and discussed than ever before. In state legislatures, meetings of boards of education, and the citizens' committees, loud voices were raised demanding changes in the schools.

While professional educators were well aware of this criticism, they did not meet it squarely or respond to it in a way that was convincing to parents and other citizens. During the preceding decades the leaders of American education had grown both powerful and complacent; like any professional group in positions of authority they disliked having their views and decisions questioned by "laymen." Instead of answering the arguments of their critics, often they were content to question the critics' motives. And because they did not answer the criticism effectively, it continued to grow.

Before the Fund could plan a program of support for educational reform it was necessary for it to sort out the many criticisms directed against the schools and decide which were soundly based and which reflected misinformation, malice, or bad judgment. And in the emotionally charged climate of the times this was not an easy assignment.

Much of the difficulty resulted from the fact that, during the late Forties and early Fifties, the schools were subjected to two separate waves of attack which arose from different causes and were carried along by different groups of people. The first wave, which began soon after the end of World War II and continued through the McCarthy period, grew out of uncertainties of the international situation and a fear that subversion, particularly Communistic subversion, was sweeping the land. It took the form of a search for subversive teachers, a critical examination of textbooks, efforts to censor the books in school libraries, and a wide variety of attacks on academic freedom. This wave, which led in a number of states to the imposition of loyalty oaths for teachers, created an atmosphere of tension and fear which did not make for good teaching. Many teachers responded by becoming reluctant to discuss controversial issues in their classes. During this wave of controversy, classroom teachers in the public schools and professional educators had the full support of academic scholars, other intellectuals, and the liberal press. And during this period the officers and directors of the Fund were sympathetic with the plight of the schools and eager to aid teachers in their defense of academic freedom.

The second wave of criticism started a little later and continued throughout the decade of the Fifties, but, because it overlapped the first in time, it was confused with it by some educators who grouped all critics together as "enemies of the schools." In fact, the second source of criticism was almost completely *un*related to the first. It was not an attack upon the principle of free public education or the right of the child to learn the whole truth; in a sense it was a defense of these things. Rather it was an attack along a broad front upon a set of educational philosophies and practices which the critics believed had come to dominate the schools and which, they were convinced, were false and dangerous. In this debate the great majority of intellectuals, including professors of academic subjects in the universities, stood in opposition to the spokesmen for public school education, including most professors of education. This was not a debate from which any philanthropic fund, committed to the improvement of education, could easily stand aloof.

Though there were significant differences among them, most of these new critics were opposed to some of the theories and practices which in the 1920's and 1930's had been called "progressive." They felt that the emphasis on the "whole child" had resulted in a neglect of intellectual emphasis in the schools. They were critical of what they considered an excessive emphasis in teacher education on professional know-how at the expense of academic scholarship. And they were convinced that a small but powerful group of professional educators in the National Education Association, the state departments of education, and the university schools of education, had come to play too large a role in the determination of public school policy to the exclusion of both academic scholars and the general public. Indeed this was an attack on "educationists," on "education" as a subject of instruction in colleges, and upon the "educator" as distinct from the academic scholar. It was also a counterattack upon the forces deemed responsible for what many saw as the anti-intellectual drift of the times.

Among the most widely read of the new critics were Albert Lynd, Arthur Bestor, Harry J. Fuller, Bernard Iddings Bell, and Mortimer Smith. Most of these were polemicists who wrote with vigor and dash and who indulged in the deliberate hyperbole, satire, and the sweeping generalization that delights or infuriates a reader, depending on whether he agrees or disagrees. The titles of their books and articles (respectively), *Quackery in the Public Schools, Educational Wastelands, The Emperor's New Clothes, Crisis in Education,* and *And Madly Teach,* offer a clue to their approach. These critics were highly successful in calling attention to excesses and stupidities in some of the schools, in deflating the more pompous of educational spokesmen, and in probing the soft spots in the educational philosophies of the day. But because most of them had little firsthand familiarity with the problems facing schools in which children of all levels of ability must be educated, they were less successful in proposing workable alternatives. Often they attacked a specific practice without understanding its relation to other activities in the schools or to education as a total enterprise. Frequently they overgeneralized from a few local instances that were not typical of most schools.

The polemicists got most of the attention from the general public. But their criticism bore a marked similarity to that contained in the less strident statements of such men as Presidents Griswold of Yale, Dodds of Princeton, and Chalmers of Kenyon, as well as in the articles and occasional comments of a great many other scholars and scientists.

Though the adverse criticism was sometimes based on an incomplete understanding of the problems facing the schools, it could not be ignored or taken lightly because it came from thoughtful and intelligent men whose wish was not to destroy the educational system but to improve it. It was a far cry from the random and reckless pot shots of those who saw a Communist behind every teacher's desk, who had a nostalgic wish to return to the little red schoolhouse, or who would solve all problems by teaching the three R's from the first grade right up through the twelfth.

Though some educators failed to see the difference between this and the earlier criticism, the distinction was noted by Fred Hechinger who, in the *Saturday Review*, said:

. . . for the first time in a long while, serious thought is being given to the *content* of public education, not just to buildings, salaries, and tax elections. This is progress. It may signal the end of one phase and the beginning of another, and since none of the books recently published advocate less public education or less money spent for it, it would appear that the basic battle has been won. Now that we seem to agree that we want public education, and ought to pay for it, there is nothing wrong with a critical, hard-hitting discussion of what we want the schools to teach.[1]

It was not at all clear just what kind of education the general public did want. And although dissatisfaction with the schools was widespread in 1950, it was by no means universal. A Roper Survey, commissioned by *Life* magazine, the results of which were published in the issue of October 16, 1950, revealed that 67 per cent of the sample polled agreed that the things being taught in the schools at that time were more useful and worthwhile than those that had been taught twenty years earlier. But when the people were asked, "Are you satisfied with the public school system in your own community?" only 33.4 per cent were "really satisfied," while 38.2 per cent were "only fairly satisfied," and 16.8 per cent were "not satisfied at all."

When they were asked to comment on the high school curriculum, those who responded to the survey were, in *Life*'s words, "magnificently inconsistent." Though 86.6 per cent said it was the school's duty to supply vocational training, build character, and polish personality, three out of four said they wished they had had more mathematics, English, grammar and spelling when they were in school.

[1] Fred Hechinger, "Fate of Pedagoguese," *Saturday Review*, December 12, 1953, p. 18.

In commenting on other parts of the survey, *Life* concluded,

In the old days it was felt that the school's job was to teach reading, writing, arithmetic, and little else. But now, the survey shows, some 90% of the general public feel that it is also the school's business to train the whole child — even to the extent of teaching him honesty, fair play, consideration of others and a sense of right and wrong. Most of them agree that sex should be taught in the schools. And in rural farm areas and in the South a majority feels that the schools should go on to teach religion as well.[2]

These expectations reflected the wide range of responsibilities which educators had accepted for the schools. During the first half of the twentieth century the public schools, faced with the problem of educating an ever larger proportion of the population up through the secondary school level, had transformed themselves from strictly academic into general purpose institutions which accepted some measure of responsibility for the child's social and recreational life, his physical health, and his vocational training, as well as for his intellectual and moral development. During this period most academic scholars in the universities had turned their backs on the lower schools, leaving them to professional educators. After World War II, when the academic scholars discovered how greatly the schools had changed, they were appalled by the educational philosophies espoused by educators, or "educationists" as they preferred to call them, and they began to express their criticism loudly.

In the universities, particularly among scholars in the humanistic disciplines, there still were many who held to the classic or traditional view that the purpose of education is the development of the mind — a view that is more likely to be held by philosophers, historians, and professors of literature than

[2] *Life*, October 16, 1950.

by psychologists, sociologists, or biologists because it implies a radical discontinuity between the physical and spiritual realms. According to the classic view of education, rational thought and intellectual excellence, because these are the characteristics of man's best development as man, must be the chief goals of educational institutions. The classic view stresses values but holds that these must be rationally determined — a code more stable and more fundamental than the mores or the preferences of a cultural group.

A curriculum based upon the classic or traditional view of education has two goals: the development of the mind and the transmission of the cultural heritage. Subject matter is emphasized and usually is presented in a disciplined and orderly manner, based upon the internal logic of the material rather than on the interests of the student. Linguistic skills are emphasized because language is at once the medium of thought, the basis for communication, and the best means of transmitting culture from one generation to another. Mathematics is stressed because it treats of the exact relations existing among quantities, magnitudes or operations and because it represents the highest development of rational thought. Many traditional scholars also hold that the study of mathematics and grammar — particularly Latin grammar — is conducive to clear thinking.

By midcentury, the great majority of professional educators, whether or not they called themselves "progressive," had moved a long way from this view of education. Influenced by pragmatic philosophies, by research evidence from psychology, sociology and biology, and by a growing dissatisfaction with the results of the traditional curriculum in schools required by law to enroll pupils of all ability levels, they had become convinced that a new approach was necessary to meet the needs of education in the twentieth century. During the first half of the century, the public schools, particularly the secondary schools, had broadened their courses of study to include a wide variety of subjects that were rare or unknown in 1900. Vocational, homemaking and physical education courses were expanded. There was a new emphasis on social development and mental health as educational goals. And the schools came to include in their programs many activities that were essentially social and recreational rather than educational in nature.

Because the amount of time available to the individual student is limited, the inevitable result of this expansion of offerings was that less attention was given to the traditional academic subjects: languages, mathematics, literature, history, and the arts. Because a much larger proportion of the age group was in high school in 1950 than in 1900, the actual number of boys and girls studying the academic subjects during their adolescent years had risen but the proportion of students who studied these subjects had declined. This alarmed many academic people who were convinced that the essentials of education were being neglected.

Many parents, including some who had no great enthusiasm for Latin and algebra but who were convinced that students ought to work hard at academic subjects of some sort, had become convinced that the schools had grown soft — that far too little was being demanded of students by their teachers. Some protested that the schools had taken over responsibilities that more properly were those of the home. "Time was," said one irate father, "when parents took their children to the circus and the teacher taught them to read. Now the teacher takes my boy to the circus and *I* have to teach him to read."

The concern for academic rigor was most conspicuous in the affluent suburbs where parents expected the schools to prepare their sons and daughters for admission to college. It was intensified by the rising standards for college admission. After the end of World War II, prestigious colleges, faced with many more applicants than could be admitted, demanded more rigorous high school preparation in the traditional academic subjects.

This demand for academic rigor in the traditional disciplines dealt the death blow to progressive education, that nebulous set of philosophies, principles and practices that had dominated much of educational thought, if not the schools, during much of the first half of the twentieth century. But the progressive movement had already entered its twilight phase. It had reached the height of its popularity in the Twenties and Thirties and in the Forties had begun a slow decline which led to the eventual disbanding of the Progressive Education Association (for lack of members) in 1955. At midcentury the term "progressive education" rarely appeared in the professional literature, though it was frequently used by critics of the schools, some of whom found it a convenient category for everything of which they disapproved. (Max Rafferty of California was still using it as his favorite target during his unsuccessful candidacy for the U.S. Senate in 1968.)

The progressive movement in education had been in part a victim of its own success because its best features — an emphasis on understanding the nature of the child as an individual, the use in the classroom of psychological knowledge gained during the first half of the century, a freedom from repressive discipline and the employment of student interest as a motivation for learning — had, by 1950, become standard practice in many schools and hence were no longer considered "progressive." But some of the more questionable features of the various radical wings of the movement — an insistence that the schools must accept responsibility for the total growth and development of the "whole child" (as though parents did not exist), an excessive emphasis on social and recreation activities at the expense of academic learning, a scorn of factual knowledge, and a demand that the school be used as an instrument to "build a new social order" — could still be found in some schools and occasionally were espoused in the professional literature. These offered the critics suitable targets for attack.

Any philanthropic organization wishing to undertake the advancement of education in the early Fifties had to ask itself which way was forward. It had four alternatives: (1) it could support the critics; (2) it could support the upholders of the status quo; (3) it could support programs which represented compromise solutions; or (4) it could look for new approaches to education. No matter which course it chose it was certain to arouse animosity.

TEACHING JOHNNY TO READ

One of the major controversies of the decade concerned the teaching of reading. After smoldering for several years, the debate was brought to public attention in 1955 with the publication of *Why Johnny Can't Read* by Rudolph Flesch, a book which remained on the best-seller list for many weeks and sold in hundreds of thousands of copies. It was Flesch's view that most American children were not learning to read nearly as well as their ancestors and that the fault lay almost entirely with a fallacious "look-and-say" method which had become dominant in the schools. His solution was simple; "teach phonics" and if the schools would not do it the parents should take over and teach phonics to their own children.

The popularity of the book gave evidence that a great many parents were dissatisfied with their children's ability to read. Ignoring this evidence, professional educators defended the status quo, insisted that reading was being taught better than ever before, and said that critics such as Flesch did not know what they were talking about.

The debaters could not agree even on what they meant by "reading" — whether it is the art of identifying and pronouncing words or the ability to get meaning from a printed page. Nor did they agree about the basic premises that underlie any sound program of reading instruction. Some contended that the average child has a vocabulary of ten thousand words or more when he enters school and needs only to learn to recognize and pronounce them when he sees them in print. Many professional educators, however, estimated the child's vocabulary at a much lower figure — some put it as low as twenty-five hundred words — and insisted that a long period of "reading readiness," including vocabulary building, must precede reading instruction. When the experts were so far apart in their interpretation of the basic facts (both sides cited "research evidence"), it was difficult for a layman to have much confidence in either group.

It was not easy for him to choose on the basis of the professional qualifications of the protagonists because the defense of the prevailing system was led by professional educators who had devoted their lives to research on reading. On the other hand, the critics included both university professors of English and some elementary reading teachers of long experience who reported excellent success in their own classrooms with some variant of the phonics methods. Rudolph Flesch, foremost and most strident of the critics, held a doctor's degree in education from Columbia University (Teachers College) and he, too, had spent many years studying the problem of reading.

Although both groups wrote a great deal, they did not really communicate. The education professors wrote for professional journals which were not widely read even by teachers, while the critics wrote for a more general public in popular magazines as well as in books. The educators wrote scathing denunciations of these popular books and articles and found many errors in them but did not come squarely to grips with the central arguments of the critics. The critics, on the other hand, were prone to ignore the evidence offered by the educators. The arguments presented by the two sides bypassed each other and the public was left confused.

In the Sixties, calmer voices were heard. By then it seemed clear that despite all the alarm, the great majority of children who were in the elementary schools in the Fifties somehow *had* learned to read but a growing number of educators also came to accept the view that a child without a knowledge of phonics, or of some similar way of attacking unfamiliar words, was unnecessarily handicapped. By the late Sixties most of the reading textbooks used in the elementary schools included a substantially more comprehensive introduction to phonics than had been the case in the early Fifties. Many of the reading specialists began to say, "This is what we have been proposing all along."

In 1967 Professor Jeanne Chall of the Harvard Graduate School of Education published the results of a three-year research project which had been made possible by a grant from Carnegie Corporation (*Learning to Read: The Great Debate*). After analyzing sixty-seven research studies comparing different approaches to beginning reading, interviewing twenty-five proponents of various approaches, analyzing widely used basal reading programs, observing how reading is taught in over three hundred classrooms in the United States, England and Scotland, and talking with teachers and school administrators about the issues in the debate, Dr. Chall concluded:

My review of the research from the laboratory, the classroom, and the clinic points to the need for a correction in beginning reading instructional methods. Most schoolchildren in the United States are taught to read by what I have termed a meaning-emphasis method. [She added in a footnote that there were definite signs, however, that more children were learning to read by a code-emphasis method in 1965 than in the early 1960's.] Yet the research from 1912 to 1965 indicates that a code-emphasis method — i.e., one that views beginning reading as essentially different from mature reading and emphasizes learning of the printed code for the spoken language — produces better results, at least up to the point where sufficient evidence seems to be available, the end of the third grade.

The results are better, not only in terms of the mechanical aspects of literacy alone, as was once supposed, but also in terms of the ultimate goals of reading instruction — comprehension and possibly even speed of reading. The long-existing fear that an initial code emphasis produces readers who do not read for meaning or with enjoyment is unfounded. On the contrary, the evidence indicates that better results in terms of reading for meaning are achieved with the programs that emphasize code at the start than with programs that stress meaning at the beginning.[3]

Though the results of this study made it difficult for anyone to continue to defend the "look-say" approach, they did not constitute a clear-cut victory for the phonics enthusiasts because Dr. Chall added:

I cannot emphasize too strongly that the evidence *does not endorse any one code-emphasis method over another*. There is no evidence to date that ITA [Initial Teaching Alphabet] is better than a linguistic approach, that a linguistic approach is better than a systematic-phonics approach, or that a systematic-phonics is better than ITA or a linguistic approach . . . nor can I emphasize too strongly that I recommend a code emphasis only as a *beginning* reading method — a method to start a child — and that I do *not* recommend ignoring reading-for-meaning practice. Once a pupil has learned to recognize in print the words he knows (because they are part of his speaking and listening vocabulary) any additional work on decoding is a sheer waste of time. It saddens me to report that some authors and publishers of reading materials are already misinterpreting the evidence. They are developing decoding exercises for upper elementary and high school pupils, erroneously assuming that if this approach is good at the beginning, it is also good for later on.[4]

[3] Jeanne Chall, *Learning to Read: The Great Debate* (New York: McGraw-Hill, 1967), p. 307.   [4] Ibid., p. 307.

The reading controversy continued but with the publication of this report, one phase of it came to a close. The subject no longer got nearly the attention in the popular press that it did in the early Fifties.

OTHER ISSUES

In one of the most controversial of issues — the question of the proper education of teachers — the FAE was so deeply involved that a more thorough examination of it will be reserved for chapter four, in which Fund programs are discussed and evaluated. It will suffice to say here that during the Fifties there was an increased emphasis on liberal education for teachers in nearly all the colleges and universities that offered programs leading to certification. And during these years the teachers college, as a separate undergraduate institution, all but disappeared from the American scene, to be replaced by more comprehensive state colleges or universities which, though they continued to prepare many teachers, now offered programs leading to the liberal arts degree and, in many cases, other undergraduate and graduate programs. In 1950 there were 138 separate teachers colleges, most of which were supported by the various states. In 1967 only a few remained.

The controversy over teacher education gave rise to an equally bitter one concerning certification requirements for teachers. During the first half of the twentieth century each state had established procedures designed to assure that teachers in public elementary and secondary schools had some minimal qualifications for the job. The purpose was an admirable one — to protect children from incompetent teaching. But, in most cases, the requirements were established at the behest of professors of education and other professional educators whose primary concern was the strictly professional aspect of the teacher's preparation rather than the teacher's liberal education or his knowledge of academic subject matter. Consequently, by 1950, most state laws or regulations were fairly specific concerning the teacher's required preparation in child psychology, educational principles, methodology, and practice teaching but were vague in establishing standards for his knowledge of academic subjects.

Because of the nature of certification regulations, principals, particularly in the smaller high schools, often assigned courses to teachers without much regard for their qualifications. An English teacher, for example, might be required to teach a course in algebra — for which he was totally unqualified — simply because the algebra teacher was overloaded. A football coach might be asked to round out his schedule by teaching one course in English regardless of his own ability to use the language correctly.

During the Fifties a number of critics pointed out that while it was legally possible for a teacher to teach a subject in which he had little or no background, even the most scholarly mathematician or historian could not teach in the same school if he lacked certain specified college courses of a professional nature. An article in a national magazine was titled "They wouldn't let Beethoven teach music in Indiana." And it was true that they would not have allowed him to teach it in a public high school.

Educators responded that a Beethoven ought not to be allowed to teach without professional preparation for teaching because, however much he might know about music, he would not understand the special musical needs of adolescents and would not know how to teach them. This reply merely convinced the majority of educated citizens of the stupidity of "educationists."

The fact that many educators defended the certification laws reflected a philosophy of teaching that had become widespread during the first half of the century — one that placed the major emphasis on the process rather than on the content of education. But intelligent state certification officers and other educators recognized that while they might be able to defend some professional requirements for teachers they could not legitimately defend laws that permitted teachers to teach academic subjects of which they were ignorant. In one state after another, certification requirements were tightened to give assurance that teachers — particularly those employed to teach academic subjects in secondary schools — would have some minimal amount of competence in the subjects taught and that school administrators could not assign teachers to teach subjects in which they lacked such qualifications. The consolidation of small rural high schools into larger units also made it easier to avoid assigning teachers to subjects outside their range of competence.

The question of the constitutionality of religious observances in public schools was brought to the U.S. Supreme Court in several different forms during the postwar years. The Court had previously upheld the right of the state to supply textbooks to children in parochial schools (*Cochran v. Louisiana State Board of Education*, 1930) and to allow parochial school pupils to be transported in public school buses (*Everson v. Board of Education*, 1947). In 1948 it had invoked the Establishment Clause of the First Amendment in ruling against released time for religious instruction in Illinois (*McCollum v. Board of Education*) but in 1952 it upheld a released time provision in New York (*Zorach v. Clauston*). The difference, according to the majority of the Court, lay in the fact that the classes in New York City were not held on school premises.

In 1962 (*Engel v. Vitale*) the Court examined the question of religious exercises in the classroom. Here the point at issue was the use of a prayer adopted under the auspices of the New York State Board of Regents and recommended by them for use in the schools. The Court ruled that the use of this prayer was a violation of the Establishment Clause, noting that the prayer had been composed officially by an agency of the state. In 1963 the Court invalidated a state law in Pennsylvania that provided for the reading without comment of the verses from the Bible on the ground that such reading was a religious exercise. In a companion case from Baltimore it ruled that exercises involving the use of the Lord's Prayer violated the Constitution even though pupils could be excused on the basis of parental request. Nearly all these rulings were split decisions that included vigorous dissenting opinions, and though they provided legal guidelines for the schools they did not end the debate.

Some of the criticism that was heaped upon the schools in the early Fifties clearly was related to the fact that the cost of education was rapidly rising. The primary reason for this was the larger number of children of school age, but a secondary reason was that teachers' salaries — which had been too low for centuries — were rising in response to the teacher shortage, which made school boards more competitive with each other. The higher tax rates alarmed taxpayers who had previously been indifferent to the fate of the schools and caused them to scrutinize educational budgets in search of "frills." There was never much agreement as to what a frill was — to some it was art or music, to others vocational education, and to still others it was any course that had been introduced into the schools after their own graduation. Yet, at a time when schools were providing institutes for drum majorettes and cheerleaders, it could not easily be denied that the taxpayers were paying for some activities which, if not frivolous, were recreational rather than educational.

It was clear enough, however, that the growing number of children, coupled with rising building costs and the legitimate demand of teachers for higher salaries, made it necessary for school revenues to be increased dramatically just to maintain existing standards. A massive effort was made by educators, assisted by the news media, citizens' committees, and foundations including the FAE, to alert the public to the need. The legislators listened and responded: the total revenues made available to public elementary and secondary schools from federal, state, and local sources were increased from $5.4 billion in 1950 to $30 billion in 1967. The proportion of the total contributed by state governments remained at about 40 per cent throughout the period, but the contribution from local and intermediate sources (though it increased greatly in actual amount) decreased proportionately from 57 per cent of the total to 52 per cent. Meanwhile the federal contribution increased from a little less than 3 per cent of the total amount to over 8 per cent, or in dollars from $156 million to $2.2 billion.

The need for this federal aid was one of the major subjects of controversy during the period. The federal government has always been prone to leave the responsibility for education to the separate states on the grounds that the Constitution does not specify education as a federal responsibility. Most of the earlier contributions to education — the Land Grant College Act of 1861 and the Smith Hughes Act of 1917, for example — have been for specific purposes and have provided for vocational rather than for general or liberal education. The GI Bill that made it possible for several million veterans to resume their schooling was looked upon as a responsibility more to veterans than to education itself. After the Soviet Union launched Sputnik I in 1957, an alarmed Congress, prodded by citizens who blamed our backwardness in space upon the failure of the schools to prepare a sufficient number of scientists, passed the National Defense Education Act, taking care to make it plain that the purpose was not to provide liberal education for citizens but rather to increase the pool of skilled manpower. The Act had the effect of shifting the emphasis in the schools away from the humanistic disciplines and toward the sciences and technologies.

Not until the Sixties, and particularly after Lyndon Johnson became President, did the federal government make any really substantial contribution to education as distinct from vocational training. Though the amounts contributed between 1963 and 1967 were indeed substantial, the state and local governments continued to be the major sources of income for the public schools. And though federal aid brought with it some modest degree of federal influence over policy and program, the major responsibility for the public schools continued to rest with the separate states and with local government as it has throughout the nation's history.

PUPILS AND TEACHERS

In 1951, when the Fund for the Advancement of Education was established, the postwar baby boom had not yet begun to affect school enrollments. The number of pupils in elementary schools had increased only slightly between 1940 and 1950 while the enrollment in secondary schools had actually declined — from 6,625,000 to 5,752,000 — because of the low birthrate in the Thirties. But early Fund reports called attention to the fact that the number of babies already born would soon dramatically increase the number of pupils in the schools and consequently the number of teachers needed.

Between 1951 and 1967 the number of pupils enrolled in public elementary schools increased from about twenty million to thirty-two million. During the same period high school enrollments (grades eight through twelve) more than doubled, increasing from slightly under six million to more than twelve million. And since it is obvious that the rise in the birthrate which followed the war could not have had much effect on high school enrollments until 1960, it seems clear that the enrollment increase during the Fifties — from six to nine million — as well as part of the increase in the Sixties, must be accounted for not by the postwar birthrate but by the steadily rising proportion of students that chose to stay in high school until graduation. Although there was much careless talk about "the rising number of dropouts" by people who ought to have known better, the fact was that the percentage leaving high school before graduation *decreased* from a high of 41 per cent in 1950 to 25 per cent in 1967 or, to put it another way, the percentage of young people remaining in school until graduation rose from 59 per cent to 75 per cent. The number of high school graduates increased from 1.2 million in 1950 to 2.6 million in 1965. The alarm about dropouts resulted, not from a growing number of them, but from the fact that during these years automation was eliminating many unskilled jobs that dropouts usually filled. But the dimension of the problem was artificially and unnecessarily increased when many employers adopted the practice of requiring evidence of high school graduation for jobs that could easily be done by individuals with less formal education.

College enrollments increased from 2.7 million in 1950 to more than six million in 1967 (about one-third of these were part-time students), and since the postwar babies did not reach college age until about 1964, most of this increase resulted from a larger proportion of high school graduates going to college. In 1950 the number of college graduates (432,000) was inflated by the large number of veterans who had attended college under the GI Bill. The figure dropped to 290,-000 in 1954, but rose steadily after that to more than 600,000 in 1967. When this figure is compared to the total number of students in college during the preceding years, it becomes obvious that the dropout rate in *college* remained very high in the sixties. The best estimates were that not more than 40 per cent of those who entered as freshmen graduated with their own classes four years later and that no more than 50 per cent to 60 per cent were likely ever to receive degrees from any college.[5]

In spite of alarming reports of a teacher shortage running into the hundreds of thousands, very few classrooms were without teachers. The estimated shortages reported by the NEA and the U.S. Office of Education in the Fifties and Sixties were arrived at by subtracting the number of "fully certified" teachers on the job from the number of teachers that theoretically would be required to staff the classrooms if the pupil-teacher ratio were held to an ideal figure. To fill the real and existing gap many teachers were given "provisional," "temporary," or "substandard" certificates. Although these were counted as a part of the teacher "shortage," many of them were better qualified in all respects than were some of the "fully certified" teachers of earlier decades.

As for the pupil-teacher ratio, it was true that there was serious overcrowding in some classrooms, particularly in rapidly growing areas. (There were also double sessions in a number of schools, but these resulted from the shortage of classrooms rather than from the shortage of teachers.) But average class size did not grow during the period 1951–1967. At the secondary level the number of pupils per teacher on a national average actually dropped from thirty in 1955 to twenty-seven in 1966, during a period when the teacher shortage was said to be at its height.

It seems remarkable that we were able to staff the nation's classrooms during a period when it was necessary to educate

---

[5] The enrollment figures provided by the various sources differ substantially because of differing definitions of "elementary," "secondary," and "higher," of "public" and "private," and of "full-time" and "part-time" education as well as because of inaccuracies of reporting. The estimates given here are based upon figures from the U.S. Office of Education and the NEA, but even the figures provided by documents from these sources are sometimes in disagreement.

all the children born during the postwar period of very high birthrate with teachers born a decade or two earlier during a period of low birthrate, but we did, and we actually upgraded the preparation of teachers at the same time. Between 1950 and 1967 the percentage of public school teachers (elementary and secondary) holding at least a bachelor's degree rose from 60 to 93 and the percentage holding master's degrees increased from 15 to 23. By 1960 all the fifty states required at least a bachelor's degree of high school teachers and all but two or three states required it of beginning elementary teachers as well.

The demand for teachers in the Fifties and Sixties was met, in substantial part, by the growing number of college graduates who wanted to become teachers. Between 1950 and 1964, while the total number of graduates was growing, the percentage of college and university graduates who were prepared for teaching at either the elementary or the secondary level increased from 20.6 to 38.9.[6] The teacher shortage was further eased by the fact that a substantial number of older women who had left teaching after marriage returned to the profession during this period. This was made possible by relaxing rules which had previously prohibited the employment of married women, and was further encouraged by rising salaries.

The number of teachers in public elementary schools rose from slightly under 600,000 in 1950 to over a million in 1967. The number of secondary teachers increased from 324,000 to 763,000 during the same period. Meanwhile the number of college and university teachers in the nation rose from about 200,000 (or perhaps 250,000)to somewhere between 450,000 and 600,000, depending on how many of the part-time instructors and graduate students one chooses to count.

Throughout the Fifties it was anticipated that the rapid

[6] *NEA Research Report*, 1964-R, p. 13.

growth of college enrollments would soon result in a drastic shortage of college teachers with the Ph.D. degree. But those who made these predictions underestimated the capacity of the graduate schools for turning out more doctorates. The annual production of Ph.D.'s rose far more rapidly than anyone had thought possible — from 6,400 in 1950 to 18,000 in 1967. As a result the proportion of faculty members holding the degree did not change very much and the shortage of teachers at the university level was much less acute than had been anticipated.

During the Fifties and Sixties the income of teachers increased sharply in terms of dollars, substantially in terms of buying power, and slightly even in comparison with relative income of other workers, though it decreased in comparison with that of members of the fee-taking professions. During the Fifties the average annual rate of increase in teachers' salaries was 5.6 per cent.[7]

Reported salaries are confused by the fact that the various reporting agencies use different definitions of "teacher" — some including specialists and part-time supervisors while others do not — but it is essentially accurate to say that the mean salary of public school teachers in the United States increased from $3,000 in 1950 to $5,000 in 1960 and to $7,000 in 1967. Throughout the period teachers' salaries were highest in the Far West, lowest in the South, with New England falling approximately midway between the extremes.

During the Fifties, the most rapid rise was in the salaries of elementary teachers, an increase that was a reflection of three facts: the demand was greatest at the elementary level, a growing number of elementary teachers were acquiring college degrees, and many school systems which had paid higher salaries to high school teachers in 1950 adopted uniform salaries during the decade so that by 1960 they paid the same salaries to

[7] *NEA Research Report*, 1963-R9, p. 9.

elementary and secondary teachers who had similar education and experience. Since most cities had adopted uniform schedules by 1960, the increases after that date were about the same for teachers at all levels.

At the college level the increase in faculty salaries was about 6 per cent annually. The estimated mean for full-time faculty members of all ranks (on a nine-month basis) rose from $4,300 in 1950 to $7,600 in 1960 and to $10,500 in 1967. Throughout the period from 1950 to 1967 the highest salaries were paid by a few large affluent private universities, and the lowest by the hundreds of small parochial colleges that dot the American landscape, with the publicly supported colleges and universities falling between the extremes.

Although Americans have been prone to think of a teacher as "she," the fact is that women have dominated the profession only at the elementary level. The great majority of college teachers have always been men. At the secondarary level, the percentage of male teachers, after dropping to a low of 30 per cent in 1930 has been rising steadily and has been above 50 per cent since 1957. This increase, which reflects both higher salaries and the growing prestige of the profession, is probably one reason for the greater willingness of teachers to fight for higher salaries, using such weapons as the strike when they deem it necessary. At any rate the profession seems much less docile and subservient than it was a generation ago.

During the 1950's and 1960's the once popular stereotype of the teacher as a spinster became completely outmoded. The proportion of married women teachers increased steadily. The change resulted from the fact that the increased demand for teachers came at a time when more women were marrying and they were marrying at an earlier age. The number of women who never married decreased from about 11 per cent in 1910 to 5 per cent in 1960. School boards which had once refused to employ married women were forced by the statistics to change their rules. In the Sixties the typical or modal elementary teacher not only was married but had two or three children.

These years saw substantial changes in both the student bodies and the faculties of colleges and universities. The more prestigious private colleges, finding themselves faced with many more applicants than they could accept for the freshman class, steadily raised entrance standards with the result that academic talent — as measured by college entrance examinations — came to replace social class as the basis for deciding who should be admitted to the colleges that once had been considered socially exclusive.

At first this seemed to be a move toward greater equality of opportunity. It soon became apparent, however, that the scores on the entrance tests were substantially affected by social class and family background. Very few boys went from the slums to Harvard even when the move was made possible by scholarships, which, at best, were available to only a few of the most talented. For those who failed to score in the top few percentiles on the tests, the economic barriers to college remained substantial. But the availability of scholarships (with a choice of schools granted to those receiving them) had the effect of concentrating student talent in a few institutions. This was particularly true in the East — less true in western states, in many of which the publicly supported colleges and universities are more prestigious than private ones. But one result of the talent search was that a steadily growing percentage of students admitted to Ivy League and other sought-after colleges came from public high schools rather than from private preparatory schools.

Faculties also changed. The high mobility of professors, and the fact that promotions often came more easily by moving to a new institution, caused professors to feel more loyalty to their disciplines than to the institutions that employed them.

Foundations and the federal government unwittingly contributed to the trend by providing research grants to individuals
rather than to institutions — when a professor moved he took
his grant with him.

Because college professors and university professors became
interchangeable — for promotion to the upper ranks in either
institution the Ph.D. was required — the college professors,
too, became more preoccupied with research and less interested in teaching undergraduates. Whether the quality of
teaching in undergraduate colleges actually declined is debat-
able — at any rate it was debated — but there is no doubt that
professors in colleges as well as universities devoted a smaller
portion of their time and energies to teaching and more to research. The prestigious jobs came to be those in which a minimum of teaching was required. Again foundations and the
federal government contributed substantially to the shift of
emphasis away from teaching by offering rewards in the form
of research grants that seduced some of the most able teachers
away from the classrooms and made project administrators of
them. By the mid-1960's there was no great shortage of applicants for faculty positions but there was a serious shortage of
men and women who wanted to teach college students. And
the students knew it.

THE PERSISTING PROBLEM

During the Fifties and Sixties the nation became acutely
aware of its most persistent problem — that of providing
equality of opportunity, social as well as economic, to dark-
skinned American citizens. Racial discrimination is not a new
problem in the United States; it has been a blot on our history
since colonial days when Indians were being driven back along
the advancing white frontier and Negroes were being im-
ported from Africa on slave ships. But during the first half of
the twentieth century most white Americans rarely thought

about the Indians, most of whom had been relegated to reservations; and most of the white people living in the North placidly accepted the view that racism was a southern problem which northerners could safely ignore. In the South, where the problem could not be ignored, segregation had become a way of life; only a minority of the more sensitive and better educated white southerners were willing to face the fact that segregation and denial of opportunity on the basis of race could not continue on a permanent basis in a nation living under the United States Constitution in a postcolonial world that has rejected long-held notions of racial superiority and inferiority.

After World War II, a growing number of Negro Americans, supported by powerful groups within the white community, increased their demands for rights that had been guaranteed to them by the U.S. Constitution and its Fourteenth and Fifteenth amendments, but had been denied to many for nearly a century. Partly as a result of legal decisions, but even more because of changing social attitudes, the barriers that had been imposed by the white community began slowly to give way. In the late Forties the various races within the Armed Forces of the United States were integrated by Presidential decree and with much less difficulty than had been anticipated. In the late Forties and early Fifties professional baseball began to admit Negroes, some of whom quickly became popular heroes with the fans. Show business increasingly opened its doors to all races, not only to play racially stereotyped roles, but to compete with white actors on equal terms, with the result that many talented Negroes gained fame and fortune as actors, dancers, musicians, and motion picture stars. By the middle Sixties dark faces began to appear in advertisements in magazines of general circulation. And the publishers of schoolbooks, prodded by articles in *Saturday Review* and other magazines, belatedly became aware that pictures of a blond

Dick and Jane playing happily in the spacious front yard of an upper-middle-class suburban home do not accurately reflect the lives of the majority of American children.

Some progress was made in opening up public accommodations to Negroes. In 1950 it was not unusual, even in the North, for a Negro to be refused admission to a restaurant or hotel but in 1967 such refusal was very rare outside the Deep South. It was during this period that many national groups began to refuse to hold their conventions in cities where racial discrimination was practiced. But even in 1967, a Negro still was likely to face embarrassment, evasion, or actual violence when he tried to buy or rent a home in a white neighborhood, even though the law prohibited realtors from discriminating among buyers or renters on the basis of race.

Lyndon Johnson appointed the first Negroes to the President's Cabinet and to the Supreme Court. In 1966 a Negro was elected U.S. senator from Massachusetts. In the same year a Negro became mayor of Cleveland, Ohio; another, mayor of Gary, Indiana. Though these achievements were scorned by some as "tokenism," they were in fact symptoms of real progress toward racial equality. It seems highly probable that the number of Negroes holding high political office will continue to grow.

In other sectors of American life the picture was less bright. Though a number of industries began recruiting young Negroes with college degrees for training as junior executives, some of the labor unions which controlled the skilled trades continued their practice of excluding Negroes. Exceptions were made so rarely that "tokenism" was indeed a fact. Bright Negro boys commented bitterly that it was easier for them to be admitted to Harvard than to gain entrance to the New York City Plumbers' Union. And in this there was truth for, by the Sixties, Ivy League colleges were making a vigorous

effort to find Negro boys eligible for admission to the freshman class.

It was in the public schools that the nation's effort to move
toward racial equality met its most rigorous test. In 1950
nearly all the public schools in the South, and many of those in
the border states, were rigorously segregated on the basis of
race. In most cases segregation was sanctioned by state law.
Only at the college level had a few Negroes been admitted,
reluctantly and under pressure, on the grounds that equivalent
education was not available in colleges for Negroes.

On May 17, 1954, the U.S. Supreme Court, reversing the
famous "separate but equal" doctrine outlawed the practice of
compulsory racial segregation in public schools.[8] The reversal
was long overdue and should not have come as a surprise: as
early as 1950 it had become clear that the Court was no longer
prepared to accept the proposition that segregated facilities
could be equal. In a case testing the right of a Negro to attend
the law school of the University of Texas when a separate law
school was available for Negroes, the Court had ruled that the
separate school could not be equal because "the University of
Texas Law School possesses to a far greater degree those qual-
ities which are incapable of subjective measurements but
which made for greatness in a law school." [9]

The 1954 decision relied heavily on evidence of the psychological and sociological effects of segregation and said in part
"To separate [children in grade and high schools] from others
of similar age and qualifications solely because of their race
generates a feeling of inferiority as to their status in the community that may affect their hearts and minds in a way unlikely ever to be undone." [10] The decision made it apparent

[8] *Plessy v. Ferguson,* 163 U.S. 537 (1896).
[9] *Sweatt v. Painter,* 339 U.S. 629 (1950).
[10] *Brown v. Board of Education of Topeka,* 346 U.S. 483 (1954).

that Southern schools, and Southern society, was to undergo a period of vast and painful change.

Most of the border states began immediately to take steps to comply with the Court's ruling that desegregation be achieved "with all deliberate speed." Within three years all or most of the public schools in the District of Columbia, West Virginia, Maryland, and Missouri were desegregated and substantial progress had been made in Delaware, Kentucky, and parts of Texas. But in the Deep South, particularly in Alabama, Florida, Georgia, Louisiana, Mississippi, the Carolinas, and Virginia, progress was very slow and, as the years passed, the resistance stiffened. In 1956 Mark Ethridge, publisher of the Louisville *Courier-Journal* wrote:

Desegration, integration — call it what you will — hangs like a dark cloud over the South, and no editor can dare ignore it as a major editorial problem. Unfortunately, even tragically, the Supreme Court decision has set in motion some of the evil forces and evil actions which are too reminiscent of our darkest days. Councils have sprung up through the South that are, despite the feeling of their responsible sponsors, nothing more than up-town Ku Klux Klans, using instead of tar and feathers and the lash, the equally destructive economic pressure. They say they are dedicated to the idea of defeating desegregation by "means short of violence!" But already the spirit of violence has manifested itself.[11]

Desegregation would have been easier for white southerners to accept if the school had been strictly an academic institution in which boys and girls studied the academic subjects and then went home or elsewhere for their social and recreational activities. But the public schools of the Fifties, which with few exceptions were coeducational institutions, were the local centers of social life as well as seats of education. The activities of a typical high school included dances, parties, and clubs. The

11 Mark Ethridge, "A Southerner Faces the Facts," *Time*, March 5, 1956, p. 21. From an address delivered at the University of Florida.

high school was the place where the dates were made and where boys and girls began looking for future mates. Behind the angry opposition to desegreagated schools was a haunting fear that integration in the schools would lead to interracial dating and eventually to interracial marriages. To many of those reared in the southern tradition, such a prospect was abhorrent.

In the Deep South, segregation persisted as the prevailing pattern despite the efforts of courts and the federal government to enforce the law. When school integration became an established fact in the border states many white parents responded either by transferring their children to private or parochial schools or by moving to suburbs which were predominantly white. These alternatives were legally possible because the Supreme Court had ruled in 1925 that no parent could be required to send his child to a public school if he preferred to send him to a private or parochial school, and because parents are obviously free to move their families to new communities when they have the financial means for doing so. But the result was that the problem of integrating the races within the public schools was left to the poorer whites and Negroes who could not escape the central cities and who could not afford the additional expense of private schools.

In the North the flight of white families from the central cities, coupled with the persistence of segregated patterns of housing and with the tradition of sending children to the schools nearest their homes, resulted in a problem of de facto segregation which grew steadily worse during the Fifties and Sixties. Even in cities which were predominantly white, the public school population became predominantly Negro. By the early Sixties more than 90 per cent of the children attending the public schools of Washington, D.C., were classed as "nonwhite." By the school year 1965–1966 two-thirds of the children in the public elementary schools in Newark, Baltimore, and St. Louis were Negro, as were more than half of those in Philadelphia, Detroit, Cleveland, Chicago, and Oakland.

The U. S. Riot Commission Report of 1968 said:

The vast majority of inner city schools are rigidly segregated. In 75 major cities surveyed by the U.S. Commission on Civil Rights in its study "Racial Isolation in the Public Schools," 75% of all Negro students in elementary grades attended schools with enrollments that were 90% or more Negro. Almost 90% of all Negro students attended schools which had a majority of Negro students. In the same cities 83% of all white students in those grades attended schools with 90% to 100% white enrollments. Segregation in urban schools is growing. In a sample of 15 large Northern cities, the Civil Rights Commission found that the degree of segregation rose sharply from 1950 to 1965 . . . by 1975 it is estimated that if current policies and trends persist, 80% of all Negro pupils in the 20 largest cities, comprising nearly one-half of the nation's Negro population, will be attending 90% to 100% Negro schools.[12]

During the Sixties many Negroes transferred their allegiance from the moderate leaders who had promised desegregation and equality of opportunity to more militant spokesmen who promised something more, or at least something different. Instead of wanting to be assimilated into the white community the militants demanded their right to establish their separate identity. They rejected the word "Negro" and preferred to be called "Black." "Black is Beautiful" became the slogan, "Black Power" the demand.

It was understandable that men who have been humiliated, frustrated, and denied equal opportunity should, when the restrictions are removed, express their anger by asserting themselves and demanding compensation for past injustice. But to many of the more moderate Negro leaders, as well as to most liberal whites, the reversal of mood and the new demands

[12] *The U.S. Riot Commission Report* of 1968, p. 426.

were alarming because they seemed to signify the beginning of a return to a new kind of segregation and a denial of the possibility that the two races can ever live together in harmony. Liberal Americans, both white and Negro, continued to look for solutions that would bring not merely desegregation but true integration of the various races in all parts of the nation and to hope that the younger generation, when it comes to maturity, will be able to solve the problem where its elders have had only partial success.

4

The Fund as a
Grant-making Agency

THE officers and directors of the Fund were well aware
of the problems discussed in the previous chapter and
responsive to them. The problems, and the controversies over
educational goals and methods, were discussed at length in
meetings of the board of directors and in Fund staff meetings.
But, though none of the problems could be ignored — because
they were all interrelated — it was obvious that the Fund
could not undertake the support of solutions to all of them. A
choice had to be made.

In his foreword to the first annual report Frank Abrams,
chairman of the board, said, "The Fund has had to be selective. The worthy calls upon its resources have greatly exceeded its means. The Board of Directors therefore felt required to select a few of the most critical areas in education,
and decided to support those activities within this limitation
which seem to be most promising for the advancement of education." [1]

[1] *Annual Report*, 1951–52, p. 1.

In his "Report of the President" contained in the same annual report, Clarence Faust offered evidence to back up Mr. Abrams's statement, saying,

A flood of applications for assistance from educational institutions followed the announcement of the establishment of the Fund. To have met all the requests received during the first year of the Fund's existence would have required more than $300,000,000. [The Fund's initial grant from the Foundation was $7,154,000 and the total made available to the Fund by the close of the 1952 fiscal year was $16,650,580.] The problem for the Directors and staff was [therefore] not whether the Fund should be selective, but on what principles it should select.

There was obviously the danger that the Fund might spread its resources too thin. It was concerned with all levels of education and was rightly open to suggestions from all educational institutions. Yet its annual budget was only a fraction of that which a large university devotes to the work of a single institution. Moreover, most of the requests presented to the Fund, certainly far more than could be granted, were meritorious. In an effort to be useful at too many points in the whole system of education it could easily fall into what an earlier officer of the Rockefeller Foundation called "scatteration giving" and thus fail to be of any real value to education anywhere. Given limited resources, selection was inevitable. Given a desire to be of maximum usefulness, concentration was essential. And if, in concentrating its resources, the Fund was to avoid a haphazard or accidental application of them, it was necessary to formulate policies and to develop a program based upon an analysis of the major needs of education and of the role of the Fund working in this field.[2]

Soon after the establishment of the Fund, the directors decided that they would not make grants for building programs, the increase of endowments, or the general operating expenses of institutions. It was not their intention to make grants to enable schools or colleges to do things that they ought to do or could do with money available to them from the usual resources. It was their hope, instead, that grants made by the

[2] *Annual Report*, 1951–52, pp. 5–8.

Fund would support the efforts of educators to make necessary changes and improvements in the schools — particularly changes that could not be made without philanthropic assistance.

Preference was given to programs that seemed likely to result in improvements beyond the boundaries of any single institution. Mr. Faust said "the Fund cannot limit its attention to particular institutions. It exists to serve education generally. It is, therefore, driven constantly to ask, with respect to particular educational experiments, what effect they promise to have upon the course of education in general. Is a project likely to have an influence beyond the school conducting it? Will it be generally or widely applicable? Perhaps above all, does it stimulate general or widespread reconsideration of important problems in education?" [3]

As was indicated earlier (see pages 65–72) the Fund decided at the outset to limit its activities to five broad program areas: the clarification of educational philosophy; clarification of the function of the various parts of the educational system and the articulation of these parts; the improvement of the preparation of teachers; improvement of opportunities for education in the armed services; and development of financial support of educational institutions. In 1959 the program was redefined without basically changing its character or substance to include just three somewhat broader objectives: the improvement of educational personnel; the improvement of educational programs; and the improvement of the relationships between educational institutions and society. The first two of these major objectives were achieved primarily through grants while part of the effort to improve the relationships between educational institutions and society took other forms which will be discussed in chapter five which deals with the Fund as an operating agency.

[3] *Annual Report,* 1951–52, p. 7.

THE IMPROVEMENT OF TEACHING

During the first decade of its existence the Fund committed approximately half of its total resources to just one of the five purposes for which it had decided to make grants: the improvement of teaching. After careful consideration of all the possible approaches to the advancement of education, the officers and directors of the Fund had come to the conclusion that no other single approach was as likely to bring about improvement in the nation's schools and colleges. Consequently any evaluation of the Fund's achievements must rest in substantial part on judgments of its success in this area.

The Fund's approach to the improvement of teaching took two forms: (1) fellowship programs to enable experienced teachers to broaden and deepen their liberal education, and (2) sponsorship of new programs for the preparation of teachers for the elementary and secondary schools. Both approaches reflected a deep-seated conviction on the part of the officers and directors of the Fund that every teacher — regardless of the subject or age group he is to teach — should first be a liberally educated individual of broad vision and deep understanding beyond the specific subject of instruction.

The first attack on the problem took the form of a program of fellowships for college faculty members who desired to broaden and deepen their liberal education in order to improve their competence as teachers of undergraduates. This was a large and expensive program. During the first fifteen months of its operation (the period covered by the first annual report and ending June 30, 1952) the Fund made grants for all purposes totaling $9,073,275. More than half of this amount — $4,600,100 — was contained in a single grant to the Committee on Faculty Fellowships. Since the committee was established by the Fund for this one purpose it may be argued that this allocation was not actually a grant but rather an internal operation. However, it is listed in the annual report as a grant.

The Committee on Faculty Fellowships, which had the responsibility for reviewing applications and selecting candidates, was made up of presidents and deans, twelve from private colleges and universities and three from public ones. Under the policy established by the committee, the fellowship recipient received an allotment approximately equal to a year's salary, plus travel and tuition expenses where these were appropriate. He designed his own program of study with the understanding that his time was not to be used for the pursuit of additional degrees.

Though the improvement of teaching was its primary purpose, the program also had a secondary purpose. In 1951 colleges anticipated a sharp drop in enrollment when the bulge resulting from the enrollment of veterans under the GI Bill began to subside. The temporary shortage of teaching jobs threatened to drive promising younger faculty members from the teaching profession; yet these instructors would be badly needed within a few years when the postwar babies reached college age. The fellowship program helped to take care of the temporary surplus of college teachers, while enabling them to improve their competence.

The response to the fellowship program was so encouraging that in June 1953, the directors approved a plan to expand the program to include high school teachers. Another national committee was appointed, this one made up mostly of high school principals and superintendents, to administer the program. This committee agreed with the Fund officers that the greatest need of high school as well as college teachers was not for additional professional training but for more general education. It offered grants of approximately one year's salary to high school teachers who would design programs for themselves with this end in view. But the selection of applicants for fellowships under the high school program differed from that for college teachers in that the choice was made by local committees of laymen and educators appointed by the school superintendent in each community. Such use of laymen was designed to stimulate community concern for teaching and for teachers and had that effect in many communities.

In all, about twelve hundred college faculty members and one thousand high school teachers participated in the fellowship programs, which were applauded by both school and college educators. Although there is no reliable, objective way of measuring the actual improvement of teaching that resulted from the program, many of those who participated in it returned to more responsible positions of leadership in their own institutions. And although programs of this magnitude could not be continued by all the participating schools and colleges, some of them that had not previously provided sabbaticals for teachers were stimulated to do so by the success of the program.

The Fund's second major effort to improve the quality of teaching was the support of programs that gave promise of improving the quality of education received by elementary and secondary teachers prior to initial certification. This effort, which took a variety of forms and continued throughout the history of the Fund, received far more attention than the scholarship programs. It caused the Fund to become involved in bitter controversy with a great many professional educators and some of the major professional organizations.

The conflict was inevitable because the Fund's philosophy made it impossible for it to lend support to the kinds of programs for teacher education that were standard in the early Fifties. The directors of FAE were convinced that much of the criticism being leveled against these programs had a sound basis and that substantial changes were necessary. Many leaders of the teaching profession were prone to defend the programs of teacher education that were then in operation.

It is in the field of teacher education that the problems of educational philosophy are brought most sharply into focus. Any program of teacher education must be based upon assumptions, stated or implied, regarding the goals of education, the nature of the educational process, and the role of the teacher. The officers and directors of the Fund were convinced that the programs through which most of the nation's elementary and secondary teachers were being prepared in 1951 were based upon mistaken assumptions and unsound philosophies.

At that time most of the programs for the preparation of elementary teachers — in university schools of education as well as in teachers colleges — were based upon a set of assumptions that had come into prominence in the nineteenth century, had dominated the normal schools of that period, and had been transferred in somewhat revised form to the teachers colleges and schools of education of the first half of the twentieth century. These assumptions, which in varying degrees reflected the thoughts of Rousseau, Herbart, Pestalozzi, Froebel, and later James and Dewey, had led to the development of programs which stressed the teacher's responsibility for understanding the child, for motivating him, guiding his growth, and supervising his learning.

Programs for the education of secondary school teachers represented an uneasy compromise between this point of view and the older tradition that a teacher should be a competent academic scholar. If he possessed the necessary scholarship he could learn the process of teaching on the job. At midcentury, certification laws in most states required those preparing for secondary school teaching to take a number of professional courses that were similar in many respects to those required for elementary teachers. And during the first half of the twentieth century the colleges and universities had built up a large corps of professors of education whose job it was to teach the professional courses for teachers. In many colleges these professors found themselves in frequent ideological conflict with the professors who taught the academic disciplines.

At midcentury both elementary and secondary teachers were being prepared in a wide variety of institutions: universities, private and church-related liberal arts colleges, state colleges, municipal colleges, teachers colleges both public and private, and a few normal schools. The distribution of graduates completing their preparation for teaching in 1949–1950 is given in the accompanying table.

TYPES OF INSTITUTIONS IN WHICH TEACHERS WERE
PREPARED, 1949–1950

	PERCENT OF GRADUATES	
Prepared in	Elementary Teachers	Secondary Teachers
Public colleges and universities	31.1	40.2
Private colleges and universities	28.3	38.9
Teachers colleges	33.5	16.8
Other, including technical schools and junior colleges	7.1	4.1

Source: Edgar Wesley, *NEA: The First Hundred Years* (New York: Harper, 1957), p. 91. The figures are from a 1952 report by T. M. Stinnett titled "Accreditation and the Professionalization of Teaching," *Journal of Teacher Education* (March, 1952), pp. 30–38.

Contrary to widespread belief, the great majority of teachers did not, at midcentury, come from "teachers colleges." In many states such colleges, as separate institutions, had already disappeared from the scene, having been replaced by general state colleges or universities. And some of the private institutions, though they called themselves "liberal arts colleges," prepared the majority of their graduates for teaching, offering them professional courses very similar to those offered by the teachers colleges.

In 1951 a number of states still allowed beginners to become elementary teachers after only two or three years of college preparation. A few states required a fifth year for high school teachers but the most common preparatory program for both elementary and secondary teachers consisted of a four-year college course leading to either an A.B. degree or a degree in education — usually the B.S. in Ed., or the B.A. in Ed. The first two years of this program were generally academic or liberal in nature while the last two years combined a subject-matter major and a sequence of professional courses, including classroom observation and practice teaching. If the candidate were preparing for teaching in an elementary school, a third to a half of his work during the four college years might consist of either professional courses or "professionalized subject matter" such as "science for the elementary school." If he were preparing for high school teaching a smaller proportion of his time would be spent in professional courses — usually from one-fifth to one-third. The high school teacher usually spent more time on his academic major than the elementary teacher who devoted more time to learning the techniques of teaching special subjects such as reading.

While these programs had much to recommend them — they gave assurance that each teacher would have some background of liberal education, some knowledge of an academic subject or subjects, and some introduction to the professional aspects of his work — they also had serious defects. The liberal portion of the teacher's education rarely was extended beyond the requirements of two academic years and in many colleges even a part of that time was devoted to professional courses. Specialization was in many cases inadequate to give the teacher a firm grasp of the subject or subjects he was to teach. But the most frequently heard criticism of the standard program was that the professional courses had been expanded beyond reason, that there was much duplication of content among the required courses, that much of their content was trivial, and that in many cases they were badly taught.

Though such charges were often made by people who had no real knowledge either of professional courses in education or of the problems faced by an elementary or secondary school teacher, and though they were repeated on hearsay without adequate supporting evidence, similar charges were also made by some professional educators who were in a position to know what they were talking about. And many students who had taken such courses joined in the criticism which by 1951 had mounted to a point where it could no longer be ignored.

At best the standard program of teacher education, which attempted to include all the elements of teacher education within a four-year college course, led to a vicious battle for the student's time on the part of the various groups within the college faculty. The academic scholars in each department insisted that no one should be allowed to teach their subject without a much more elaborate subject-matter major than could be provided within the available time. Professors who saw a need for broadly liberal education — a smaller group on most campuses — insisted that two years was not nearly long enough time for such an education. But the professional educators saw a need for more and more professional courses and for more time for classroom observation and practice teaching. And it was the professional educators who most often had the support of the state departments of education, who in turn controlled teacher certification. In many states certification regulations were highly specific in requiring a list of professional courses in education but extremely vague about the requirements in liberal education. At about the time when the Fund was established, a number of academic professors, of whom Arthur Bestor was the best known, were loud in their denunciation of certification laws and the professional educators' responsibility for them. Some thought they saw a conspiracy on the part of professional educators to take the responsibility for teacher education away from the world of scholarship.

There was no conspiracy, of course, but it is quite true that the responsibility for teacher education had been allowed to slip out of the hands of the academic scholars. What had happened was that during the first half of the twentieth century, while academic scholars were loftily ignoring the problems of teacher education, a group of school administrators, professors of education, and educators in state departments of education had come to agreement among themselves on the necessity for professional preparation for teachers and had transmitted their convictions into law. And it was during this same period that the educators had become imbued with a new philosophy which was far removed from the traditions of the liberal arts college — one which placed much less emphasis on academic scholarship and more on understanding the child and the learning process. The new philosophy also held the schools responsible for guiding the development of the "whole child," not for his intellectual development alone.

The Fund was not opposed to professional preparation for teachers; in fact all the projects which it sponsored made provision for *both* liberal and professional education, and rested upon the assumption that both are essential to sound preparation for the task of teaching. But the Fund did hold that the liberal education should come first and that if possible it should engage the full time of the future teacher during his undergraduate years. It believed, too, that the professional preparation should be closely correlated with actual classroom practice and should include a year or at least a semester rather than only a few weeks of "practice teaching." It doubted that many of the professional courses then being taught at the undergraduate level represented either sound scholarship or a useful approach to the classroom problems that the teacher would face.

The Fund decided to attack these problems by supporting programs that might point to solutions. The various projects that received Fund support differed in the hypotheses that they sought to test and in the sources of teacher supply that they tried to tap. Some projects were designed to bring older liberal arts graduates into the classroom but most of them were intended for young men and women then in college.

THE ARKANSAS PROGRAM

The Fund's first large-scale attack on the problem of teacher education was a statewide project — the Arkansas program — which aroused more controversy and brought the Fund more criticism than any other program in its entire history. Though many individuals have been given the credit or the blame for what its critics were to call "The Arkansas Purchase" or "The Arkansas Rape," the idea for a statewide program was first proposed by Abraham Flexner who some four decades earlier had made a report on medical schools that brought dramatic reforms to medical education.

Early in 1951, Mr. Eurich asked Mr. Flexner, then an elderly man, what he thought of the idea of a "Flexner report" on teacher education. Flexner said it could not be done — that teacher education involved so many different ingredients, was carried on in so many different kinds of colleges, and reflected so many diverse philosophies that it could not be compared to medical education where goals are fairly well agreed upon and the number of preparatory institutions is much smaller. Instead Flexner suggested an action program that would involve changes in all the teacher education within a single state — preferably a small state.

The directors of the Fund found the idea attractive. Several states were considered: Connecticut was the first choice but it was found impossible to secure the necessary cooperation of the public and private colleges in the state. Arkansas was chosen primarily because Lewis Webster Jones, then president of the University of Arkansas, was enthusiastic about the idea and because Arthur Kronenberg, the dean of education at the University and once a graduate student of Eurich's at Minnesota, was a man in whom Eurich had great confidence.

In October 1951, after conversations with the officers of the Fund, President Jones submitted a formal request to the Fund for a grant of $85,000 "to be used by the University of Arkansas for the period from November 1, 1951, through August 31, 1952, in the initiation of an experiment in the education of teachers." The proposal stated: "The purpose of the project is to launch a large-scale attack on the problem by setting up and carrying forward a program of teacher education based upon a four-year program of broad liberal education to be followed by a period of combined internship and professional study as a requirement for certification."

Three distinct phases of development were anticipated:

1. A survey of basic liberal education offerings at the University and cooperating Arkansas colleges to strengthen and improve these programs and to develop a well-rounded basic program for all prospective teachers, with suitable areas of specialization.

2. The development of a system of internships so that graduates with four years of liberal education could be placed under the direc-

tion of master teachers, employed jointly by the local school district and the University. These interns would participate in teaching, and study the problems of education at the same time.

3. Revision of certification requirements so that teachers prepared in this manner would receive valid certification and appropriate salaries.

The initial planning grant was made in November 1951, and a committee of thirty-six members, selected from the various colleges and public school systems of Arkansas, was appointed to plan the program. In March 1952, the committee presented to the Fund a "basic document" which provided the groundwork for a much larger grant of $2,441,978 to get the program underway.

All the colleges in the state which prepared teachers — both state teachers colleges and private liberal arts colleges — were to participate in the program. It was expected that the teachers colleges would expand their liberal arts offerings into four-year programs and that their staffs of professional educators would assist in the professional programs in the fifth year.

In the original plan the Fund was to provide stipends of $125 a month for students during their fifth-year internships, with the hope that eventually the state of Arkansas would underwrite this cost. When it was decided that it would be impossible for the state to support the plan after the expiration of the Fund grants, an alternate program was devised which placed the responsibility for payments to interns upon the schools.

The Arkansas plan received a great deal of publicity from the first. Many lay citizens and academic scholars welcomed it as a way of restoring the liberal arts to their rightful place in teacher education while at the same time providing a full year of professional preparation, but the opposition from professional educators mounted steadily. The professional teachers' organizations resented the fact that they had not been consulted prior to the announcement of the plan. Teachers colleges saw the plan as a threat to their separate existence and resented the implication that they were not already providing liberal education for teachers. Although the planning group had included several professional educators, other educators felt that too much of the original planning had been done by people unfamiliar with the problems of the schools. Professors who had struggled for years to establish the respectability of undergraduate courses in education saw the gains of a half century about to be wiped out in one move. The plan ran directly counter to the then prevailing trend toward increased integration of professional and liberal education with an early introduction to professional studies. And, because the grant came from outside the state, there was local resentment of what was considered outside interference in Arkansas education. One bitter educator who thought he saw the shadow of Robert Maynard Hutchins hovering over the program said, "Hutchins is trying to buy what he couldn't sell."

Perhaps the amount of opposition might have been reduced by working more closely with professional organizations at the outset, but it is doubtful that anything the Fund could have done would have made the program acceptable to the majority of professional teacher educators in 1951 since the controversy reflected basic differences in educational philosophy between the Fund and many educators. It must be said that although some of the controversy arose from legitimate differences in point of view, part of the criticism of the Arkansas plan was either irrational or based on misinformation.

One widely voiced criticism was the charge that the Arkansas plan was a return to the past. The American Association of Colleges for Teacher Education condemned it as "The universal imposition of a highly unpromising pattern upon all participating institutions" and an adaptation of an eighteenth-century model. Later in the same document it called the plan "a scheme comparable to that used 500 years ago." [4] An editorial in *School and Society* suggested that the program was a revival of nineteenth century practices.[5] Still other critics saw it as a return to the Middle Ages!

Such charges were merely the polemics of angry men for at no time in the nineteenth century or in any previous era had teachers been prepared through a four-year liberal arts course on the college level supplemented by a fifth year of professional internship with correlated professional seminars. In earlier centuries most elementary teachers had no college education of any kind and prior to the development of the normal schools in the nineteenth century, most of them had no professional preparation. Secondary teachers, even when they were college graduates, had no professional preparation comparable to that proposed for the teachers of Arkansas during the fifth year. Whether or not the program proposed for Arkansas was the best possible solution — whether or not it was sound — it definitely was not a return to the past.

But however unjust the criticism of the program may have been, it was effective. The attacks upon the program from professional educators and teachers' organizations caused teachers and prospective teachers in Arkansas to lose confidence in the program and to be reluctant to go along with it. Faced with opposition from teachers as well as from those who controlled accreditation in teacher education, the plan never had much chance of a fair trial. To make matters worse, Lewis Webster Jones, the program's most vigorous and influential supporter within the state, resigned from the University of Arkansas in 1952 to accept the presidency of Rutgers University. In retrospect it seems clear that the Fund should have pulled out at that time and written the program off as a lost

[4] New York *Times,* February 24, 1952, p. 68.
[5] "An Experiment or a Revival," *School and Society,* August 2, 1952, p. 75.

cause. Instead it poured more money — a total of some three million dollars — into the state.

Whether the Arkansas project in teacher education was a disaster or a partial success is still open to debate. It failed in its primary purpose of establishing a new program of teacher education for all the tachers in the state. When the assistance from the Fund was terminated, most of the colleges in the state returned to more conventional programs and the number of teachers prepared through fifth-year internship programs was sharply reduced. The project was a disaster in the sense that it aroused a degree of hostility to the Fund among professional educators that hampered that organization in the years to follow. It was a success in the sense that it stirred widespread interest in teacher education and led to reforms in other states. It also helped to improve the liberal arts offerings at several of the participating colleges.

Whether or not the plan was basically sound, it now seems clear that the teacher-educators of the nation were not ready for it. And the Fund made a serious strategic error in underestimating the power of the professional groups that opposed so dramatic an innovation in teacher education. Although these groups were unable or unwilling to initiate reforms in teacher education themselves, except very slowly and on a small scale, their power to obstruct innovation was very great indeed, and when the Arkansas project was announced they made full use of their power. Although the Fund officers had anticipated the opposition, and obviously were not seeking to be popular with professional educators, they seem not to have anticipated that the opposition could undermine the whole project.

OTHER PROGRAMS

But the Arkansas project served one useful purpose: By drawing to itself all the criticism from professional educators who opposed programs in which professional training was postponed until the fifth year, it provided an effective smoke screen which made it possible for other fifth-year programs, operating in many parts of the country but with less visibility, to develop successfully. (Dean Francis Keppel of Harvard spoke of working "behind the Arkansas shield.")

Some of the most successful of these programs led to the Master of Arts in Teaching degree — MAT or AMT. The idea behind this degree did not originate with the Fund and was not new in the Fifties, but the Fund did more than any other organization to promote it and make it possible for substantial numbers of future teachers to pursue it.

The idea had its origins in 1936 at Harvard where President Conant, aware of the conflict of view which had arisen between academic scholars and professional educators, saw the need for a new kind of preparation for secondary teachers which would represent the best thinking of both groups. The program was first described in the *Official Register of the Graduate School of Education for 1936-7*.

During the early years the program did not attract many students because the demand for teachers was limited in the late Thirties and because salaries were too low to attract able liberal arts graduates into a difficult and expensive period of graduate training in preparation for a profession which they could enter without such preparation. After World War II the situation changed. The demand for teachers was much greater and salaries were higher. Some of the better-paying school systems preferred candidates with a substantial background of liberal education and a master's degree.

The Fund made it possible for Harvard greatly to enlarge its MAT program by establishing an arrangement with twenty-nine distinguished undergraduate colleges, all of which agreed to carry on a vigorous recruitment campaign to arouse interest in secondary teaching on the part of able liberal arts students. After completing the A.B. degree, these students went on to Harvard for a year of graduate work which combined graduate work in one of the academic disciplines taught in high school with professional courses in education. The Harvard program included a semester of supervised teaching experience, for which some of the students received a stipend of $1,500 out of the Fund grant. A number of other universities developed similar programs with Fund assistance.

Although these programs are similar in some ways to the Arkansas project, the MAT programs did not meet anything like the amount of opposition and criticism that fell upon the Arkansas plan. There were a number of reasons for this. Because the Master of Arts in Teaching degree was much older than the Fund, no one could accuse the Fund of originating the idea and forcing its acceptance upon reluctant educators. Most of the MAT programs included at least two or three professional courses with substantial intellectual content in educational psychology and the history and philosophy of education, taught by competent scholars. The original Arkansas program made inadequate provision for such content. But the most important reason for the relative lack of criticism was the fact that the MAT programs were small at first and consequently much less visible than the statewide program in Arkansas. When publicity was given to the MAT, it was usually Harvard or some other prestigious university, rather than the Fund, that got the credit or blame. The MAT, though it has not yet become the standard program for secondary teacher education, has gained widespread approval and has become a permanent part of the scene in teacher education.

Similar programs — but usually leading to a master's degree in education (M.Ed.) rather than the MAT — were supported by the Fund in a number of universities for the education of elementary school teachers. These, too, included a supervised internship with closely correlated professional seminars but they usually also included a larger component of professional courses than the MAT programs and less time for academic subjects at the graduate level.

The best evidence of the success of the Fund-supported fifth-year programs is the fact that the idea of preparing liberal arts graduates for teaching by means of a program that combines an extended internship with both professional and academic courses is no longer nearly so controversial as it was in 1951. Whether or not it is desirable to offer some of the professional work during the undergraduate period is still a matter for debate, but few educators now question the feasibility of preparing excellent teachers in programs which delay professional training until the fifth year.

Another group of fifth-year programs was designed to tap an additional possible source of teacher supply — older liberal arts graduates, particularly women, who wanted to become teachers but were reluctant to enter upon the program of studies required under the certification laws. The officers of the Fund believed that many such individuals would be willing to become teachers if programs were adapted to their special needs, and that, because of their maturity, they would be excellent teachers.

Between 1952 and 1954 the Fund received several proposals for plans to exploit this possible additional source of teacher supply. Although they differed in details, all the programs supported by the Fund were planned for mature college graduates who had had some kind of adult, nonteaching experience since leaving college. All involved cooperation between a school system or systems and a nearby college or university. All provided for specially planned professional experiences designed to eliminate duplication of professional content, and combined extended professional experience in the classroom with closely integrated professional education. Most of these programs provided for a summer's attendance at college prior to a year of internship and required evening courses or seminars in education during the school year. In most of the programs during the intern year, the teachers were paid a fraction of a teacher's salary, either out of the Fund grant or directly by the school system.

The teachers who graduated from these programs were welcomed by the school systems, and most of the reports from administrators regarding their success were highly favorable. The numbers declined, however, as the teacher shortage abated. There was evidence, too, that the number of older college graduates who were eager to teach was somewhat smaller than the Fund had anticipated.

The programs so far discussed were based on the assumption that a sound liberal education of the kind needed by teachers cannot be acquired in less than four full years of college, and that consequently professional training should be postponed until the fifth year. But the Fund also lent its support to a number of projects which were designed to test the hypothesis that better ways can be found for combining professional and liberal education within the four-year programs. Among the first of such experimental programs were those at Carleton, Swarthmore, Wilson, and Barnard, but the list eventually was a long one.

Some of these colleges, with assistance from the Fund, fostered projects for the reexamination of their programs in teacher education or for the development of such programs where none had existed. Though they differed in scope and purpose, most of these projects included the following aims:

1. To find ways of attracting more and better students into the teaching profession.

2. To resolve the conflicts between professors of education and academic scholars by finding ways of reconciling the views of the two groups.

3. To determine what professional preparation is essential for teach-

ers and to find new ways of providing such preparation without emasculating the program of liberal education.

4. To make teacher education a responsibility of the entire faculty.

5. To achieve better integration of liberal and professional courses with classroom practices.

Most of the Fund-assisted programs for teacher education in liberal arts colleges reported some success in resolving the conflicts between academic professors and professors of education. Academic professors became better aware of their responsibility for teacher education, and in several colleges teacher education became a responsibility of the entire faculty or of a committee drawn from the many departments rather than from the department of education alone.

During the first few years of the programs most of the colleges reported a substantial increase in the number of students preparing to teach in the public schools — at Carleton the number of graduates prepared to teach rose from eleven in 1953 to thirty-two in 1956. These graduates were in great demand as teachers, particularly to teach the academic subjects in high school that prepared students for entrance to similar colleges. But the total number of teachers produced by the prestigious and highly selective private liberal arts colleges remained very small compared to the number produced by less selective and less prestigious colleges, both public and private.

Beginning in 1958 the support for most of the fifth-year programs in teacher education was shifted from the Fund to the Foundation which made grants totaling $29 million to forty-two colleges and universities in support of a "breakthrough" program designed to develop further the features that had been found most successful in earlier Fund programs. These projects were characterized by the following features:

First, they were designed to prepare teachers not for the self-contained classrooms of the past, but for the schools in which teachers are most likely to be teaching in the years and decades ahead — schools with ungraded classes, teaching machines, educational television, and team teaching with its flexible use of time, space, and personnel.

Second, they were to be planned jointly by university departments of education, representatives of academic departments of the university, and public school teachers and administrators.

Third, they were expected to incorporate changes in the elementary and secondary schools as well as in the colleges.

Fourth, a considerable amount of the responsibility for teacher recruitment, teacher education, and the introduction of the teacher to his profession, was to be accepted by the public school itself.

Fifth, they were to represent an effort to place teacher education in the mainstream of higher education by bringing academic professors and professors of education together for joint planning and to create a better articulation of elementary, secondary, and higher education through the cooperative efforts of college faculty members and teachers and administrators from the public schools.

Sixth, they were to build upon earlier Fund-supported programs by providing for (a) liberal education extending well beyond the sophomore college year for all teachers, (b) scholarly academic instruction at the graduate level for all secondary teachers, (c) improved professional courses or seminars in educational psychology and educational philosophy that are firmly grounded in parent disciplines and planned so as to avoid duplication of content, and (d) an extended supervised internship during the post-baccalaureate period accompanied by closely correlated professional seminars.

The breakthrough programs had an impact that went far beyond teacher education and extended into the public school classrooms. By preparing teachers to be ready and eager for change and for the acceptance of new ideas, they made reform more possible. The teachers emerging from these programs were better prepared than conventionally trained teachers to become members of teaching teams, to make use of new technological developments in education, and to use the newer curricular materials.[6]

EDUCATIONAL TELEVISION

At the time the Fund was established in 1951, television was just beginning to make its vast impact on American life. The officers, particularly Mr. Eurich, recognized the enormous potential of the new medium as a means of instruction and as early as 1952 began exploring the possibilities of using television to bring the best teachers and the best teaching to larger numbers of students.

The obstacles were formidable. Educators have always been slow to accept innovations that alter the role of the teacher — earlier technological tools of communication such as films, radio, and recordings were introduced slowly into the classroom and had never been used as widely or as intelligently as might have been hoped. There was a very real danger that television, too, would be overlooked as an instructional medium.

Moreover, the hardware necessary for televised instruction was very expensive. Appropriate programs of instruction were yet to be developed. Very few teachers had any experience with teaching by television and many educators were reluctant to accept the possibility of using such instruction in the classroom.

A considerable part, probably the major part, of classroom instruction in conventional schools and colleges has always

[6] For a detailed description, analysis, and evaluation of the breakthrough programs, see James C. Stone, *Breakthrough in Teacher Education* (San Francisco: Jossey-Bass, 1968).

been provided by teachers who describe, explain, inform, clarify, exhort, or demonstrate while the children watch, listen, and hopefully react in more complex ways as well. Those who endorsed the use of the new medium, including the officers of the Fund, were convinced that a child is likely to learn more about counterpoint, for example, by watching and listening to a discussion and demonstration presented by Leonard Bernstein, backed up by the New York Philharmonic, than by listening to the local music teacher, backed up by a student pianist. Television obviously makes it possible for a superior teacher to bring his talents to a larger number of students.

The educators who opposed televised instruction saw it as an extension of the lecture method which they were convinced is educationally unsound. They insisted that a child learns best in an intimate environment in which the teacher and the students can exchange views. This view is widely held by educators though it does not rest upon experimental evidence. Similarly the belief that physical distance between pupil and teacher is an important variable in learning has not been scientifically demonstrated.

Despite opposition, the Fund decided to lend its support to programs using television for purposes of instruction, by working in close cooperation with the Fund for Adult Education which was providing for the establishment of educational television stations and assisting national programming of an educational nature for adult audiences. In 1953 it began with a modest grant to help teachers at Montclair State Teachers College in New Jersey to transmit fifth-grade history lessons in nearby schools by means of closed-circuit television. Over the next ten years the Fund, and later the Ford Foundation, made major investments in experiments in both closed-circuit and broadcast television. Between 1953 and 1958 the Fund made a total of seventy-six grants totaling $5.6 million for forty-eight separate educational television projects in schools, colleges, and universities.[7]

The feasibility of closed-circuit televised instruction was clearly demonstrated in a five-year project in the public schools of Washington County, Maryland, for which the telephone and electronics industry provided much of the hardware while the Fund made substantial grants to support the program. Hagerstown — the county seat of Washington County — became the showcase for closed-circuit educational television. Educators from across the nation and around the world came to observe the results and many went away convinced that the new medium had great possibilities.

Despite the initial skepticism, most of the Hagerstown teachers soon reacted favorably to the innovation. A poll of science teachers showed that after trying the use of televised programs to supplement classroom instruction, only 2 per cent preferred teaching without TV. Other polls indicated that about two-thirds of the parents endorsed the use of television while only 20 per cent were opposed, the others having no preference. When pupils were asked their opinion, 71.8 per cent said they liked science better with television and most of them responded favorably to the use of TV in teaching other subjects. The scores on standardized achievement tests rose after the introduction of televised instruction.

Hagerstown schools made important contributions toward solving the problem of how best to integrate the televised portion of the instruction with the instruction provided by the regular classroom teacher. Plans were made jointly by the television instructors and the classroom instructors. Television teachers visited the classrooms as often as possible in order that they might get the reaction of students to their teaching.

Television became so much an accepted part of the standard

[7] Ford Foundation, *Annual Report 1958*, p. 22.

procedure in the Hagerstown schools that when a visitor, in 1963, asked an eighth-grade pupil if he liked school better with or without television the boy replied: "Why, we've always had television in the school." [8]

William Brish, Hagerstown superintendent of schools, said in 1963:

Since our school system had the unique opportunity of working with television in major subject areas at all grade levels in successive years, we are often asked to point out the most significant achievement of the project. While we may seem to oversimplify the findings, we believe that the use of instructional television has stimulated teachers, supervisors, and administrators to examine more closely the teaching-learning process and to pursue curriculum development with new interest. Early in the project it became evident that the important issue was not *whether* television should be used for direct instruction but *how* it should be used and *what* it could contribute to the improvement of instruction.

And he added, "We in Washington County are convinced that television has a definite place in the program, and, if properly used, can add a new dimension to education." [9]

Not only was the Hagerstown experiment clearly successful in demonstrating the feasibility of television as an instructional medium, but the Hagerstown educators were convinced that "the television system can effect sufficient savings to pay for itself. These savings result from re-deployment of teaching equipment, changed organization within the schools, and altered scheduling of personnel. It may also be possible to develop savings through television to increase teachers' salaries." [10]

A number of colleges had experimented with televised instruction before the Fund was established, but on a small scale.

[8] *Washington County Closed-Circuit Television Report* (Hagerstown, Md.: Washington County Schools, 1964), p. ii.   [9] Ibid., p. ii.   [10] Ibid., p. 3.

The first large-scale program at the college level was at Pennsylvania State University, to which the Fund made a grant for this purpose in 1954. By 1958 some 3,700 of the University's 14,000 students were registered for one or more of the thirteen courses taught over closed-circuit television on the campus.[11]

When the results of televised instruction were compared with conventional teaching methods, no significant differences in achievement were found but a majority of the students in large classes expressed a preference for TV.

Closed-circuit systems have spread more rapidly in colleges than at the lower levels. Of the approximately one thousand closed-circuit television installations serving educational purposes in 1966 (including 275 systems of substantial size and scope) it was estimated that slightly over half were in colleges and universities, about one-fourth in elementary and secondary schools and the others in medical institutions or military installations.[12]

In the public schools the spread of closed-circuit television has been delayed by the high initial costs of the necessary hardware as well as by the continued opposition to all televised instruction from many educators and from classroom teachers who fear that the significance of their own role will be impaired.

Though the first projects supported by the Fund were for closed-circuit television, the Fund also made large grants for the development of broadcast educational television — an approach that is less expensive to individual schools and might be just as effective if suitable programs could be made available at the right times. Broadcast television also has the virtue of reaching many people who are not enrolled in the schools but who would like to broaden their knowledge.

One of the most dramatic and effective uses of open-circuit

[11] FAE, *Teaching by Television*, 1959, pp. 16–23.
[12] Judith Murphy and Ronald Gross, *Learning by Television*, 1966, p. 23.

television was a program known as *Continental Classroom*, which opened in 1958 with a course in modern physics taught by Professor Harvey White of the University of California and which was followed by courses in mathematics, and other subjects, including one in chemistry taught by Professor John Baxter of the University of Florida. Although support came from many sources the Fund and the Ford Foundation made the major contribution to the cost of *Continental Classroom* during the first three years.

The original purpose of the program was to bring high school teachers up to date in their subjects by exposing them to current developments. The instructors were distinguished scientists and scholars, selected for their effectiveness as teachers. Seven Nobel Prize winners were brought in as guest lecturers for the physics course. In spite of the fact that the courses were broadcast at the improbable hour of 6:30 A.M., the response was overwhelming. Within the first week 13,000 textbooks were sold and about 5,000 students enrolled for credit in 250 colleges and universities. The daily viewing audience was estimated at 270,000.

Efforts to use television as a means of reducing the shortage of teachers by teaching students in large classes had less satisfactory results. The National Program in the use of Television in the Public Schools, supported by the Fund and the Foundation, was designed to use television not as an adjunct but as "an integral part of the instructional program" in order to reduce the need for teachers and at the same time to improve the quality of instruction. School systems throughout the United States were included in the program and though the programs varied from one system to another, all of them offered instruction in large classes with up to 175 students in elementary schools and 200 to 500 in junior and senior high schools.

The somewhat ambiguous results were summarized by Murphy and Gross:

In general, the results showed that television could be used to teach very large classes, with corresponding savings in teacher time and classroom space, and there was at least tentative confirmation of the hypothesis that television could improve the quality of instruction with no increase in cost . . . [But] in attempting to integrate television into the instructional process, the National Program encountered serious difficulties, particularly in the secondary schools: most classroom teachers resisted the sharing of responsibility with the studio teacher. It became clear, too, that televised mass-teaching was unworkable unless the programs were of high quality. Thus the emphasis of the National Program shifted from the large-class objective to that of achieving quality, and of supplementing and enriching regular classroom instruction. Of the schools that participated in the National Program which are still using television, most use it now in classes of conventional size, and usually to supplement or "enrich" standard classroom fare.[13]

The most imaginative of all the projects designed to provide televised instruction for elementary and secondary schools was the Midwest Program of Airborne Television Instruction which was initiated by Philip Coombs of the Fund but supported in large part by the Ford Foundation. MPATI programs, which were broadcast from an airplane circling high over Purdue, Indiana, were expected to be available to some five million school children in six midwestern states.

This program encountered many unanticipated technical difficulties. In the fringe areas the quality of picture received was less than adequate for instructional purposes. Many of the schools that could have received excellent pictures failed to tune them in because of indifference, or because the time of broadcasting the various subjects did not coincide with the time these subjects were being taught, or because the schools were unwilling to change their schedules. Many of the small rural schools that could have profited most from televised in-

[13] Ibid., pp. 36–37.

struction did not own receiving sets. In spite of these difficulties MPATI programs for a time reached an estimated half million pupils in fifteen thousand schools — a not inconsiderable achievement. But when the period of Foundation support drew to a close, the schools failed to pick up the cost, as had been hoped, even though the cost per pupil would have been very low if all the schools had contributed. Consequently the program was discontinued in 1967. It is hoped that at some time in the future a similar program may be initiated, using communication satellites instead of an airplane.

In the late Fifties a number of educators, including some in the Fund, optimistically predicted that within a decade there would be a TV set in almost every classroom and that televised instruction would transform American education. For a variety of reasons it didn't happen. The decade passed and television still is used sparingly and in the majority of classrooms not at all. In the previously mentioned report published by the Fund in 1966 by Judith Murphy and Ronald Gross, the authors ask:

After more than a decade of intensive effort and the expenditure of hundreds of millions of dollars, has television made a real impact on America's schools and colleges? Has it made a worthwhile contribution to education?

The short answer to such a sweeping question would probably have to be "no." Whether measured by the numbers of students affected, or by the quality of the product, or by the advancement of learning, televised teaching is still in a rudimentary stage of development. The medium can take credit for helping understaffed schools to cope with ever increasing enrollments. But television has not transformed education, nor has it significantly improved the learning of most students. In short, TV is still far from fulfilling its obvious promise. Television is *in* education all right, but it is still not *of* education.[14]

14 Ibid., p. 9.

What went wrong? Why was the promise not fulfilled? There are many answers. The resistance of teachers to a medium that threatened to transform their role and required them to learn new skills was undoubtedly a factor. The logistical problem that put new demands on school administrators was another. But the basic problem was that the quality of programming did not keep pace with the development of the hardware. This danger was anticipated by the Fund but not enough was done about it. John Scanlon, of the Fund, had pointed out a decade earlier that television, like the book, is a neutral medium — it transmits good instruction and bad instruction with equal ease. And just as it takes both time and talent to prepare a library of great books, or of competently written textbooks, it takes time and talent to develop instructional programs for television. Even if the time had been available the talent was not — not in sufficient quantity. In the early Fifties no one had yet learned the subtleties of programming televised instruction and even in the Sixties the number who had learned to do it well was far too small to meet the demand. Though some excellent programs appeared on TV sets in the early days, the number of poor or inadequate ones was large enough to discourage many educators and to cause them to ignore the medium, for mediocre instruction of a kind that is often tolerated in the individual classroom seems appallingly bad when seen on the television screen.

In his preface to *Learning by Television* Alvin Eurich said:

> The findings reported in this study indicate that there are two prime causes for instructional television's limited acceptance: the quality of the transmitted instruction, and the way it is used in the classroom.
>
> As applied to education thus far, television has largely put current modes of teaching on the screen. The result has been widespread disenchantment as the mediocre level of much instruction has been ex-

posed to professional and public scrutiny for the first time. The need for imagination, ingenuity, and innovation in the whole process of education has been forcefully demonstrated.

The primary goal of ITV in the future must be to raise quality and improve classroom utilization. Here, as elsewhere in education today, mere expansion of present practices is not enough. The way forward is necessarily a new way. To create the new some of the old must be constructively destroyed.[15]

BETTER USE OF TEACHER TIME AND TALENTS

In the Fifties, the typical American elementary school consisted of a series of boxlike rooms assembled like an egg crate. In each room a single teacher accepted most of the responsibility for the education of approximately thirty pupils. This was the "self-contained classroom," applauded and defended by many professional educators and their professional organizations.

Fund officers were convinced that the self-contained classroom was wrong in principle because it made no provision for individual differences among teachers and required every teacher not only to teach a wide variety of subjects but to accept responsibility for conferences with parents, pupil guidance, playground and lunchroom supervision, and a wide variety of secretarial duties. Many city school systems had taken hesitant and tentative steps away from the completely self-contained classroom by making some provision for school psychologists and counselors as well as for specialists to teach music, art, and sometimes physical education, but the general principle had remained intact. Teachers still were required to do many things that could be done just as well or better by adults without professional training.

The prospective, and in some cities immediate, shortage of teachers made it imperative that the schools make better use of

[15] Ibid., p. 6.

the time and talents particularly of the most able teachers. Consequently the Fund supported a wide variety of programs designed to enable teachers to use their talents more effectively.

The first large grant for this purpose went to Central Michigan College of Education (now Central Michigan University) to provide teacher aides for the public schools of nearby Bay City. The plan provided for the employment of carefully selected and trained individuals, mostly housewives who possessed good educational backgrounds but had no professional training as teachers, to take over some of the nonprofessional or semiprofessional parts of the teacher's work — keeping records, collecting lunch money, assembling equipment, and other housekeeping chores — in order that the teachers might have more time to teach. A preliminary survey had provided evidence that teachers spent anywhere from 21 to 69 per cent of their time on such nonteaching tasks.

The teacher-aide plan spread rapidly to other Michigan cities and soon to other states. Persons trained in Bay City helped to set up similar programs, with Fund assistance, in Utah, Colorado, Minnesota, and Iowa. A slightly different program at Fairfield, Connecticut, made use of unpaid volunteers as well as paid assistants and produced a practical handbook to guide other communities in the best ways of recruiting and training volunteer assistants such as mothers and other citizens eager to help out.

One purpose of the plan was to improve the status of teaching as a profession. The hypothesis underlying this aim was that professional teachers ought to spend their time in professional activities in order to make the most of their special training. Nonprofessional tasks essential to the activities of the schools should be assigned to aides who presumably are available in larger numbers and at lower salaries because they do not require as much professional preparation.

In defense of this hypothesis the Fund cited the example of the medical profession: By letting nurses and nurse's aides take over many of the tasks of patient care, physicians can diagnose and treat larger numbers of patients without a deterioration of service and at the same time enhance their own prestige and greatly increase their incomes.

Professional educators, including spokesmen for the teachers' organizations, were reluctant to accept the analogy. Some of them insisted that the principle of the self-contained classroom was sound and that no one, except a fully certified teacher, should be allowed to work with school children in any capacity — some even opposed letting aides supervise playgrounds and lunchrooms. Professors of education who were not at all reluctant to employ secretaries to do their own paper work and graduate students to grade their papers were strongly opposed to permitting elementary and secondary teachers the same kinds of assistance.

Classroom teachers, however, were much more willing to accept aides than were those who professed to speak for them, and as the years passed their numbers increased. A poll conducted by the NEA, the results of which were published in the *NEA Journal* for November 1967, revealed that while only one out of five public school teachers had an aide in 1967, 84 per cent said they would like to have such assistance with their clerical duties and 51 per cent would be willing to turn the grading of papers over to a nonprofessional aide. Of the teachers having aides, nine out of ten said they found them helpful. The teachers did not believe, however, that the availability of aides would enable them to teach more students or that hiring aides should take precedence over improving teachers' salaries.

Today it seems safe to predict that the number of schools employing teacher aides will continue to grow. Teachers want them and professional opposition to them is subsiding. For this development the Fund deserves a large measure of credit. Without a boost from an outside agency, it seems clear that no school system would have the initiative to start such a program or the courage to push it in the face of the known opposition from professional educators and teachers' organizations.

The use of aides has undoubtedly made the teaching profession more attractive because it relieves teachers of dull chores and gives them more time to do the things for which they are professionally qualified. Consequently it has probably improved the quality of teaching. But, in retrospect, it seems that the Fund may have made a mistake in encouraging the belief that the employment of aides would make it possible for a school system to operate with fewer teachers. It has not had that effect and the fear that it might was the source of much of the professional opposition to the plan. Though it probably is possible for a teacher with an aide to teach more children, elementary teachers work hard enough even with an aide and thirty children. There is no need to increase their load, particularly since the teacher shortage is no longer acute in most parts of the country. It has proved more acceptable to everyone to keep the same number of teachers while employing aides in order that the teaching may be of higher quality.

The team-teaching plan is a logical extension of the effort to make better use of teacher time and talent that was begun with the teacher-aide programs, but it goes much further. Under the plan, which has many variations, a group of professional and subprofessional individuals takes responsibility for the education of a group of children, each individual accepting the tasks for which he is best qualified by virtue of his education, professional training, and personality. A team may consist of only two or three individuals but often it includes a larger group with a team leader, master teachers, specialists, aides, and apprentices. Whether it is found in an elementary or a secondary school, the team offers an opportunity to improve instruction by making the best possible use of individual talent.

Team teaching met with a considerable amount of opposition because it was working against several well-developed trends in American education. Like the teacher-aide plan, it was a challenge to the principle of the self-contained classroom. And in the Fifties the teaching profession was just emerging from a long and hard-won struggle for higher salaries, tenure, and equal pay regardless of the sex of the teacher or the grade taught. Strict equality among teachers was stressed, and teachers prized their individual autonomy — they saw team teaching as a threat to both equality and the autonomy because the members of a team are not entirely equal in responsibility and they must work together.

In spite of opposition, team teaching caught on rapidly. Judson T. Shaplin, who has been a leader of the movement, first at Harvard and now at Washington University, says:

Team teaching, a new pattern for school organization which has emerged in American education since 1954, has rapidly assumed the dimensions of a major educational movement. Starting with a few pilot projects in 1956 and 1957, the movement has now spread to several hundred communities distributed widely throughout the country, and plans under development suggest increasingly rapid growth. A number of major universities are participating actively in the development of team teaching, and there is a high level of professional interest, both pro and con, expressed in meetings organized for the description and analysis of team teaching at local, state, and national conferences of teachers, supervisors, administrators, and school board members. In some communities programs have progressed far beyond the pilot stage and include the reorganization of entire schools, the spread of teams throughout the school system, and even the construction of school buildings designed to meet the requirements for the new program. Substantial sums of money have been allocated for these developments by local school boards and by one major foundation, the Fund for the Advancement of Education.[16]

At the secondary level, departmentalized instruction has been the rule and class size has tended to be standardized regardless of the talents of the teacher or the subject of instruction. The Fund supported programs to investigate the possibilities of reallocating the variables of the teaching-learning situation — pupils, teachers, time, space, and equipment. Most of these experiments also made use of some form of team teaching.

In 1956 the Fund gave support to a Commission on the Experimental Study of the Utilization of the Staff in the Secondary School, a group whose members had been appointed by the National Association of Secondary-School Principals. The commission undertook a nationwide search for ideas and research on such critical problems as curriculum development, teaching methods, space arrangements, and staff utilization. It explored and promoted the use of teaching teams in more than a hundred high schools throughout the country. The activities of the commission were reported by Lloyd Trump, the director, in a number of documents which were widely read by secondary school educators and which stimulated widespread experimentation with the variables of instruction.[17] The result was a much more open attitude on the part of educators toward this kind of experimentation.

The Dual Progress Plan, a variant of team teaching devised by George Stoddard, a psychologist who was dean of the School of Education of New York University, received support from the Fund during a period of experimentation in

[16] Judson T. Shaplin and Henry F. Olds, Jr., eds., *Team Teaching*, 1964, p. 1.
[17] Lloyd Trump, *Images of the Future*, National Association of Secondary-School Principals, 1958. (See also other books by Trump listed in chapter five.)

three school systems adjacent to New York City. Under this plan the child spent half of the school day in a classroom with children of his own age while he studied what Stoddard calls "the cultural imperatives" — English and the social studies — and the other half of the day with individuals of his own achievement level while he studied mathematics, science, music, and other subjects. He might be in an advanced class in mathematics, for example, but in a slow class in music. Subjects other than the cultural imperatives are taught by specialists rather than by the regular classroom teacher.[18]

The results were exhaustively investigated by Glen Heathers who found that although students, teachers, and parents generally endorsed the plan, no major improvement in instruction could be found. (He notes that organizational changes rarely result in measurable improvements in learning.) The ability grouping for part of the day seemed to have some harmful effects on low-ability pupils. Mr. Heathers concludes:

In assessing the dual progress plan, it is probably best to view it as a vehicle for introducing a number of themes into the instructional program at the elementary and middle-school levels. These themes are specialist teaching; differential, non-graded advancement on an individual basis in the elective subjects; mastery of the essential common learnings; and an emotional-social home base to provide security and to foster personal-social growth. Assuming the validity of these themes, it remains to be determined whether the dual progress plan or some other organizational plan, can most effectively incorporate them.[19]

EARLY ADMISSION AND ADVANCED STANDING

At midcentury the educational program in the United States required a standard number of years of schooling for all,

[18] For a detailed description of the plan and the psychological principles underlying it, see George Stoddard, *The Dual Progress Plan* (New York: Harper, 1961).
[19] Glen Heathers, *The Dual Progress Plan* (Danville, Ill.: The Interstate Printers and Publishers, 1967), p. 197.

regardless of rate of maturity or level of intelligence. Except for the rare child who was allowed to skip a grade or two, elementary and secondary education took exactly twelve years. The result was that few had an opportunity to enter college before their eighteenth year. Some of the most able students found themselves marking time during their last years in high school, facing assignments too easy for them, losing interest in learning, and developing poor work habits.

The Fund officers were convinced that some way should be found of making better provision for individual differences in learning capacity and level of maturity in order that boys and girls more mature and more academically talented than their classmates might enter college at an earlier age, with or without a high school diploma. The University of Chicago had admitted such students during the years when Mr. Faust was dean but other colleges had not followed the example.

Early in its history the Fund made the first of a series of grants to enable colleges and universities to experiment with early admissions on a substantial scale and to provide scholarship assistance for such students. Between 1951 and 1954 1,350 carefully selected students with less than a full high school education were admitted to college and provided scholarships, under this program, with grant assistance totaling $3,429,045.

The announcement of the program set off a violent reaction in public school circles. Paul Elicker, executive secretary of the National Association of Secondary-School Principals, called it an A-bomb dropped on secondary education.[20]

A considerable number of educators joined Elicker in opposing any acceleration of education even for the brightest and most mature students. Some high school principals even refused to inform their pupils of the opportunity to earn

[20] C. Winfield Scott and Clyde M. Hill, *Public Education under Criticism* (New York: Prentice Hall, 1954), p. 74.

scholarships from the Fund. But in spite of this opposition the cooperating colleges had no great difficulty in locating a sufficient number of well-qualified students.

The evaluation of the program was turned over to the Educational Testing Service of Princeton and the results of the evaluation were reported in a Fund publication, *They Went to College Early*, published and distributed by the Fund in April 1957.

Though the evidence was somewhat conflicting, on the whole the results were highly encouraging. All the participating colleges considered the program successful. The rate of failure of the students admitted early was slightly higher than that of a control group of older students of similar academic talent, but it was lower than that among classmates as a whole. The academic averages of the experimental group were higher than those of the control group, and while those admitted early encountered more initial difficulties in adjusting to campus life than their older classmates, most of the difficulties were minor and soon overcome.

There was evidence that in many cases early admission to college freed students of the boredom and frustration of an unchallenging high school environment, gave them new intellectual momentum, and enhanced their social and emotional maturation.

After the period of Fund support ended, eleven of the twelve colleges incorporated the early admission idea into their regular admissions policy, and in 1956 the College Entrance Examination Board reported that 29 of its 169 member colleges had established early admissions programs. Only six of these were participants in the Fund-supported experiment.[21]

But after the termination of Fund support, the early admissions programs languished. The number of participating students declined in the colleges that had participated in the ex-

21 FAE, *They Went to College Early*, 1957, p. 89.

periment and in other colleges the number never rose to a substantial figure. There was insufficient interest on the part of college and high school administrators to keep the program going. One reason was that many high school principals, while agreeing that many students could successfully enter college after the sophomore or junior high school year, were reluctant to lose the potential leaders of their high school classes. And the growing number of high school graduates who sought admission to the more selective colleges in the Fifties made these colleges less interested in attracting candidates without the high school diploma. The program died away, not because it was unsound, but because no one was willing to support it vigorously after the termination of Fund support.

Opponents of early admission, some of whom seem to confuse a "peer group" with an "age group," have emphasized the danger of placing a student with others older than he. But a student whose intellectual ability is far beyond that of his own age group often can find no true peer group among his high school classmates, who resemble him only in chronological age. The dilemma was well stated by one of the scholars who wrote in his senior essay: "There is some danger a young student's talents will be harmed by being thrust among older students who do not accept him. But the greater danger is that he will be allowed to stagnate in secondary school and will arrive in college lacking imagination and ambition, these having been 'educated' out of him. The harm to him and society is great." [22]

The advanced placement or advanced standing programs supported by the Fund were designed to serve a purpose similar to that of the early admissions programs — to break the academic lockstep and make it possible for bright students to graduate from college at an earlier age. Though these programs were much less costly than the early admissions pro-

[22] Ibid., p. 90.

grams — because they did not require scholarship assistance — they met with much less opposition and have had a greater long-range influence on higher education.

Under this program the colleges agreed to give advanced standing to unusually capable students who had taken special college-level courses in high school and had demonstrated their competence by passing special subject-matter examinations devised by the College Entrance Examination Board. By 1960, 567 colleges, mostly in the East, had agreed to accept students on this basis and advanced placement programs have since spread across the country.[23]

Many high schools found that the advanced placement courses exerted a subtle beneficial effect on the entire curriculum and proved a stimulus to the entire student body.[24] Today the principle of college credit for college-level work done in high school — when achievement is demonstrated by examination — is widely accepted among the colleges. Most individual students, however, receive such credit for only one or two subjects, consequently it is rare for the entire period of college attendance to be shortened by more than one quarter or one semester as a result of advanced standing. But these programs and the planning involved in them have helped to provide better articulation of school and college courses.

EQUALIZING EDUCATIONAL OPPORTUNITY

Throughout much of the period of the Fund's operations the nation was increasingly turning its attention to the problem of eliminating the social and economic barriers that have prevented equal access to educational opportunities for culturally disadvantaged, particularly Negro, children. The Fund's first approach to this problem was to provide better information concerning the effects of racial segregation in the schools. Projects with this aim will be described in chapter five. But, in

[23] FAE, *Decade of Experiment*, p. 88.   [24] Ibid., p. 89.

addition to its own operations, the Fund made a considerable number of grants to other institutions that were trying to solve the problem.

In all the major programs which it supported, including teacher education, improved curricula, better use of resources, and efforts to locate and foster talent, the Fund sought to include educational institutions serving Negroes as well as institutions admitting students without regard to race.

Between 1951 and 1967 the Fund made grants totaling approximately $4 million that can be classified under the general heading "Educational Opportunity for the Culturally Disadvantaged"; of this sum approximately $2.5 million was specifically in support of Negro education. Nearly $300,000 went to twenty-four Negro colleges and universities in fourteen states which took part in the Fund's efforts to make teaching a more attractive profession for Negroes and to increase the opportunities of teachers for further intellectual growth. Qualified college teachers were awarded fellowships which allowed them a year of self-planned study and work at a college or university other than their own.

Harvard University and Morgan State College received Fund assistance for experiments in the better utilization of teachers. Fisk University and Morehouse College, both Negro institutions, participated in the Fund's early admission program, under which able students were admitted to college before finishing high school and, between them, received some $450,000 in support of this program.

To provide better teachers for educationally depressed areas and to improve the preparation of Negro teachers in schools and colleges, the Fund supported experiments at Hampton Institute and Dillard University. The program at Hampton — one of the nation's outstanding training centers for Negro teachers — included in-service training for teachers in the Virgin Islands and the preparation of new teachers at

Hampton for island assignments. Dillard (in cooperation with Harvard and Cornell) carried out a program to prepare superior Negro teachers for the New Orleans public schools.

During the school year 1953–54 the National Scholarship Service and Fund for Negro Students, aided by a grant of $175,000 from the Fund, began a talent search among the seniors of eighty-one segregated Negro high schools in forty-five southern cities. During that year and the year that followed, 2,178 seniors who represented the upper 10 per cent of the classes of these schools were examined through a modified version of the Scholastic Aptitude Test of the College Entrance Examination Board. More than half of these students made at least the minimum qualifying score set by the Fund as the lowest possible indicator of probable success in college.

In the late Fifties and Sixties the Fund enlarged its contribution in this area by making grants for remedial and supplementary work designed to make up for past educational deficencies of Negro institutions and Negro students. A grant was made to the Human Relations Center of the Department of Education of St. Louis University for experimenting with principles and practices that might help teachers working with culturally deprived children to meet the special problems resulting from such deprivation. In 1959 the Fund made a grant of $30,000 for a cooperative effort to devise ways of educating culturally handicapped children in large cities. In 1966 it initiated a program to distribute paperback books as part of an effort to encourage disadvantaged children and adults to improve their cultural background through owning and reading books. Grants totaling nearly a half million dollars were made to fourteen institutions, including the Southern Association of Schools and Colleges which administered the grant for 108 Negro colleges and Project Opportunity Schools.

The causes of educational inequality are so deeply ingrained in the nation's social and economic structure that the efforts of a private foundation cannot be expected to produce change rapidly. Nevertheless the Fund made a substantial contribution to the examination of the problem. The portion of its grants that went for the improvement of education in Negro slums of large northern cities was small considering the fact that this is one of the major problems of our day, but fortunately some of the programs initiated by the Fund have been greatly expanded by the Ford Foundation.

OTHER GRANTS

A complete description of all the grants made by the Fund for the Advancement of Education would require far more space than is available in this volume. In addition to those already described, the Fund made many grants which can be mentioned only briefly even though some of them have had, or may ultimately have, a profound effect on American education. (See the annual reports for lists of all grants.)

As a part of its effort to contribute to better public understanding of education and to encourage better public support for the schools, the Fund made grants totaling nearly $2 million to the National Citizens Commission for the Public Schools (later renamed the National Citizens Council for the Public Schools) which had been established in 1949 by a distinguished group of concerned citizens who were convinced that the public schools faced a crisis. The NCCPS encouraged the development of local citizens' committees and published a series of pamphlets to guide them. It also published a periodical, *Better Schools*, to keep school board members and other interested citizens informed about their schools. Throughout its history the organization sought desperately to find ways of reconciling educational conflicts and looked for compromises that might gain general acceptance. It played a notable part in alerting the general public to educational problems and school needs.

The majority of the grants made by the Fund for the improvement of public school education went to urban or suburban systems, but a few notable ones were designed specifically to meet the special problems of rural schools. It was during these years that James B. Conant, in his influential series of reports on American secondary education, emphasized his conviction that most American high schools were too small to be effective and insisted that consolidation of rural schools should continue until each high school was at least large enough to have an annual graduation class of one hundred. The Fund favored consolidation where distance made it favorable but it did not agree with Conant that a small school must inevitably be a poor school. It pointed out that many excellent private schools were smaller than the size suggested by Conant as minimal. The difference in opinion reflected the fact that Conant wanted every high school to offer not only an academic program but also a wide variety of vocational courses in order that each student might have a marketable skill at the time of graduation. The Fund took the position that the high school curriculum should be mostly academic and liberal in content and that most vocational training should be postponed until the post-high school years. To offer a variety of vocational courses requires a large staff of specialists but a sound academic program can be provided by a smaller staff.

The Fund was aware that a substantial number of small schools were located in areas so isolated that consolidation would require students to spend many tedious and wasteful hours each day in school buses. Some schools were located on offshore islands or in mountain valleys isolated in winter — circumstances which made consolidation all but impossible.

To provide better instruction in schools that must remain small, the Fund supported projects in twenty-three high schools in the Rocky Mountain area of Colorado, twenty-five schools in the Catskill area of New York, and about one hundred rural schools in Vermont and Maine. These projects included the use of teacher aides, correspondence courses, and extensive use of tapes, films, and recordings. Where specialists were needed for subjects taught to only a few students in each school, it was found much less expensive and more practical to transport the teachers than to transport all the students.

To develop educational leadership in rural schools, particularly those in remote, outlying areas, the Fund appropriated $1.5 million in 1966 to provide fellowships for teachers from such areas who had displayed leadership potential, but who had inadequate opportunity for advanced study because of a lack of nearby institutions of higher education. This Leadership Fellows Program was continued by the Ford Foundation after the Fund ceased operations.

A number of Fund-assisted projects were designed to bring improvements in the content of the curriculum, particularly at the secondary school level. Many of the early programs involved curricular changes of one kind or another, and after 1957 the improvement of the curriculum became a major goal, though it proved to be one not easily achieved. The difficulties faced by those who would reform the curriculum were pointed up in *Decade of Experiment:*

Of the Fund's five major areas of interest, curriculum reform is probably the most difficult to accomplish. We are not a homogeneous nation with a well-defined set of goals, but a diversity of peoples and cultures. Our very variety, which we have always cherished, keeps us from general agreement about what should be taught to our children. Many a curriculum has been achieved, not through rational consideration of the goals of education, but by compromise among several factions in the community; the result is not a school with the most beneficial curriculum but with a hodgepodge of curriculums. Complicating the situation further is the national desire to educate every

American child. The curriculums of our schools have increasingly been designed for quantity output, to the serious neglect of quality. Only recently have world events reversed this trend and aroused interest in the reshaping of curriculums so as to emphasize quality.[25]

The most notable of the world events referred to was the launching by the Russians of Sputnik I in 1957. An alarmed American public, looking for a scapegoat, blamed the schools for our failure to launch rockets into orbit ahead of other nations. This attribution of blame was not entirely logical. Our nation could have launched the first satellite earlier if we had been willing to spend the necessary funds and to give the project top priority. In any case both the Soviets and ourselves relied heavily on scientists who had been educated in Germany rather than in our own schools. But our failure to be the first to launch a satellite had the fortunate result of making the American people more willing to accept educational reforms.

In response to a widespread demand for better courses in science, the Fund gave support to a group of outstanding scientists who worked with high school teachers to bring the curriculum in chemistry, physics, and biology up to date. By means of films and other technological innovations, these improved courses were made available to a large number of high school students. It was obvious that if a revised and updated curriculum was to be offered in subjects which were rapidly changing, teachers already on the job would need additional instruction in preparation for teaching them. The television program, *Continental Classroom*, discussed in a previous section, was the most dramatic of the Fund's efforts to provide such instruction for large numbers of teachers.

The Fund also assisted programs in mathematics, foreign languages and a number of other courses including a fourth-year high school course to replace the conventional survey

[25] P. 83.

course, "Problems of American Democracy." It supported a program in which the public schools of Portland, Oregon, collaborated with nine Oregon colleges and universities in a comprehensive reevaluation of high school courses. A series of early grants to Educational Services, Inc. (now Educational Development Center, Inc.), for the outline of a new social studies sequence based on case studies and original sources, led to support from the Ford Foundation for actual unit design and development of course materials.

In a series of grants totaling $832,000 made between 1951 and 1961, the Fund assisted in a variety of experiments and demonstrations designed to enable bright pupils to move more rapidly through the schools. These included the early introduction of intensive foreign language and science, multiple tracking according to ability, special classes for the able, summer enrichment programs, and college-level courses in a variety of subjects.

Although a number of earlier Fund-assisted programs in elementary education extended into preschool experiences, the first grants directly intended for the support of preschool programs were made in 1965, after experience in the national Head Start program suggested a need for further basic research and program development, especially for deprived children. Under a $400,000 appropriation, seven institutions explored such facets of early childhood education as the relevance of parent orientation, the role of the mother in preschool programs, adaptability of existing programs for gifted children to the needs of disadvantaged children, and a systems approach — with continual feedback and analysis — to curriculum development.

Although the Fund's primary emphasis in teacher education was the preparation of teachers for the public schools, the officers were also concerned with improving the preparation of college teachers. They were aware that the improvement of college teaching requires an approach substantially different from that they had followed in their efforts to improve public school teaching. The Fund Report for 1952–54 says:

in one respect the situation as regards preparation for college teaching is the reverse of that for public school teaching. If the latter has tended to overdo methods at the expense of subject matter, the former has tended to concentrate on subject matter specialization to the neglect of teaching competence. It oversimplifies the matter to some extent, yet perhaps not too much, to say that the ideal of the scholar-teacher has suffered in our graduate schools, on the one hand from a too narrow view of scholarship and, on the other, from an almost complete disregard for preparation for teaching.[26]

Teaching quality was not the only problem. In the Fifties it appeared that there was soon to be a serious shortage of faculty members. Statistical projections made for the Fund early in its history had indicated that in the Sixties the demand for college teachers would far exceed the supply and that the percentage of college teachers holding the doctorate might drop from forty to about twenty. To alleviate the anticipated shortage and at the same time encourage the development of better programs for the education of college teachers, the Fund assisted fourteen universities in the development of a new rigorous three-year master's degree program. Undergraduates began taking graduate-level courses during their junior and senior years and then proceeded with a fifth year that combined additional graduate work with a supervised internship in college teaching. Though this plan was proposed and developed by the Fund staff, it was supported by a grant from the Ford Foundation, which committed $2.4 million to the program in 1960. Oliver Carmichael, while a consultant to

[26] *Annual Report*, 1952–54, p. 32.

the Fund, played a large role in the development of the three-year master's program.

In an effort to enable colleges to make better use of their resources, the Fund assisted a nationwide program of experiments in new patterns of college teaching, including independent study programs, better use of graduate and undergraduate teaching assistants, and greater use of tape, film, and other media as well as curriculum reform under the Committee on Utilization of College Teaching Resources. It also made grants to forty-one colleges and universities for self-studies to redefine their role in American life. The Fund also supported efforts to make long-range financial and development planning a standard procedure in colleges and universities, and helped to establish the financing of higher education as a distinct area of study within the field of economics.

Between 1953 and 1958 the Fund granted a total of $970,-000 to eighteen colleges and universities to enable them to provide internships to young college instructors who had plunged into their teaching careers after intense academic specialization which permitted little opportunity to acquire practical experience in the art of teaching. Some three hundred interns worked under the guidance of experienced teachers, observed effective teaching, and engaged in discussions of curriculum development, course planning, and instructional techniques. In another approach to improved college teaching, the Fund granted $1.4 million to ten colleges and universities to experiment with cooperative programs of graduate study, focused on the establishment of a "common core" of work, leading to the doctorate and dealing with fundamental problems in the humanities and social sciences.

To lend more realism to the training of school administrators, the Fund granted $1.7 million for experiments which emphasized the clinical aspects of administration through internships and workshops. The programs encouraged closer cooperation between institutions training administrators and the schools which employ them. They also exposed administrators in service to a wider range of practical problems and solutions by enabling them to visit selected institutions notable for their effective administrations.

In 1952 the Fund made a grant of $565,000 to Mortimer Adler for the establishment of an institute for philosophical research. The stated purpose of the grant was "support for three years of studies concerned with the clarification of Western thought and educational philosophy." [27]

Adler's comprehensive familiarity with the history of Western thought had already been demonstrated by his part in the preparation of the fifty-four-volume *Great Books of the Western World*. It was he who had conceived and constructed the *Synopticon* which classifies 163,000 references under 2,987 topics and 102 "great ideas," selected from the 443 basic works included in the fifty-four volumes of *Great Books*. His interest in *educational* philosophy, however, seems to have been secondary to another purpose. It was his lifelong ambition to prepare a summary and synthesis of the entire body of Western thought since the time of ancient Greece. This was to be the *Summa Dialectica*, which Adler hoped would compare with the *Summa Theologica* of *Thomas Aquinas*. There was, as Adler himself admitted, "a touch of megalomania in it." [28]

Adler set up the institute in a thirty-room mansion in San Francisco, assembled a fourteen-man staff, and called a number of famous philosophers as consultants. But progress was slow, the hoped-for meeting of minds did not occur, and the plans had to be revised downward. The several volumes

[27] *Annual Report*, 1951–52, p. 37. [28] New York *Times*, June 7, 1952, p. 21.

that emerged from the work of the institute fell short of the original goals.

Insofar as the purpose of the grant was to find a basis for a consensus among educational philosophers or to harmonize the conflicting views of educators as to what the schools ought to accomplish, Adler was an unfortunate choice to head the institute because his Neo-scholastic views are far distant from the pragmatic views held by most of the educators responsible for policy making in American educational institutions and because Adler's convictions do not permit of compromise. It is doubtful that the work of the institute has had much influence on the activities of the schools, or on the thinking of educators.

In 1965 the Fund made a series of grants to colleges, junior colleges, and technical institutes in support of cooperative work-study programs. Such programs are not new, but the older ones, notably the one at Antioch College, were designed for academically talented students and did not substantially lower the cost of education to the student.

The new programs were available to a much wider range of academic talent and in many cases made it possible for the student to pay a substantial part of his education by alternating periods of on-campus study with periods of paid off-campus work related to his field of study. These programs reflected a conviction that academic studies and career goals should be related directly and realistically — that the intervening periods of work would give meaning to the periods of study. The Ford Foundation, which has had a more sustained interest than the Fund in vocational education, has given further aid to these programs. They are continuing to expand.

Many of the innovative programs initiated by the Fund later received a part of their support from other foundations.

Conversely the Fund gave assistance to projects that had been started with help from other foundations. One of these that seems likely to have great impact on American education is the National Assessment Program which was initiated in 1964 by Carnegie Corporation in cooperation with the U.S. Office of Education.

In 1965 an "Exploratory Committee on Assessing the Progress of Education" with Dr. Ralph Tyler, director of the Center for Advanced Study in the Behaviorial Sciences in Palo Alto, as chairman, held conferences in various parts of the country with teachers, school superintendents, and school boards. The committee came to the conclusion that the assessment of the progress of American education was both feasible and desirable provided it was done wisely and covered the whole range of educational objectives. Plans were made and testing instruments developed in several fields: reading and language, arts, science, mathematics, social studies, citizenship, fine arts, and vocational education. (This list has since been expanded.)

In February 1966, the Fund for the Advancement of Education made a grant of $496,000 to assist in the support of this program. Later grants brought the amount committed by the Fund to this program up to a total of $1,336,000.

To many people in and out of education the need for such an assessment has seemed obvious for a long time. For lack of it, no one has been able to say with confidence just what or how much American children are learning or have learned. The widely used standard achievement tests, including college entrance examinations, offer some clues but the sampling has not been adequately controlled and the results have not been reported in such a way as to provide a basis for educational planning. When critics have charged that "Johnny can't read," that "Swiss schools are better than ours," that "children are learning less than their parents did at the same age," or that "today's children are not learning what they need to know about history, grammar, or mathematics," endless and futile debate has resulted because no one had persuasive evidence based on a nationwide sampling of children and adults, in school and out. It seemed entirely possible that the facts, if known, might astound the critics and provide educators with a sound defense of their schools. But whatever the facts might be, it was reasonable to expect that educators would welcome the prospect of having reliable data regarding the results of their endeavors.

This, however, proved to be an unwarranted assumption. When the plans for a national assessment were announced, educational organizations and many individual educators expressed their angry opposition. One, writing in the *Educational Forum*, called it a "recipe for the control of the many by the few." The American Association of School Administrators condemned the plan as "coercive" and said it would produce unfair comparisons of school systems, force teachers to teach for the test, and reveal little not already known. Spokesmen for the Council of State School Officers and the Association of Supervision and Curriculum Development expressed fears that national assessment would lead to a national curriculum and federal control of education. William Carr, executive secretary of the NEA, saw no need for an assessment based upon nationwide tests. At the White House Conference on Education of 1965, when asked "Should there be periodic assessments of American education?" Carr had replied, "Yes, and this is being done every day by those who should continue to do it, the teachers in the classroom. We should not substitute a national assessment for this."

Many of the fears expressed by the educators were caused by a reluctance to have the achievements of children in their own schools compared with those of children in other schools; others indicated a failure to grasp the distinction between probability sampling and every-pupil testing. In response to the critics, Dr. Tyler made it clear that no comparison of schools was intended:

This is not a national testing program, it is an effort to develop an inventory of educational progress roughly comparable to the Gross National Product, a concept which economists have developed to assess the growth of the American economy. Furthermore, it is not an effort to impose national standards on American education because we are not engaged in giving marks to individual students, teachers or school systems. Unlike achievement tests, the instruments we are trying to develop are designed to tell us what proportion of a given age group has mastered certain knowledge or skills that thoughtful educators and lay citizens believe are important for children to learn. Because of the absence of dependable data, public opinion about the schools is based largely on personal views and popular impressions. This situation will be corrected only by a careful, consistent effort to obtain valid data aboumt the progress of American education.[29]

To obtain such data, Dr. Tyler's Exploratory Committee made plans for assessing the educational achievements of a sample of four age levels — nine-, thirteen-, and seventeen-year-olds, and adults — in four geographic regions, Northeast, South, Midwest, and Far West. In each region the individuals were to be drawn from urban, suburban, and rural areas, and from the various socioeconomic levels in each community.

Though some of the assessment, particularly that of adults and of adolescent school dropouts had to be done outside of school, the work of the committee could have progressed much more easily and economically if school facilities could have been used. But a number of school administrators, following the advice of their national organization, refused to cooperate and refused to allow their staffs to do so.

[29] Ralph Tyler, "Assessing the Progress of Education," *Phi Delta Kappan,* XLVII (September, 1965), p. 13. See also Ralph Tyler's *Challenge of National Assessment* (Columbus, O.: Merrill, 1968).

But a substantial number of professional educators endorsed the assessment program. Shortly after the American Association of School Administrators vigorously condemned the program, a group of eight faculty members of the Harvard Graduate School of Education replied with equal vigor that the AASA seriously misconstrued the problems and the possibilities of national assessment and expressed the view that "teachers and administrators will be freer than they are now from undesirable pressures once they possess greater knowledge about what different sorts of Americans know at various ages."

As time passed, the opposition to the program subsided, and support for it grew. It now seems all but certain that assessment on a national basis is destined to become a permanent part of the nation's educational system. The need for the kinds of information that will be provided by the program seems obvious; the danger that it will lead to a national curriculum or to federal control of education seems remote.

The history of this program provides an excellent illustration of the value of philanthropic support for innovative projects. Although the need for a national assessment had existed for many years, the nature and extent of the opposition to it makes it apparent that it could not have been started without the support and encouragement of philanthropic funds.

5

The Fund as an Operating Agency

Although making grants for educational purposes was the primary activity of the Fund, that was not, and was never intended to be, its only responsibility. The Fund's Certificate of Incorporation, dated March 29, 1951, states clearly that in addition to making grants to "worthy students, teachers and organizations duly organized to carry on educational functions," the Fund's responsibility would also include "conducting educational research [and] publishing or otherwise making available the results thereof. . . ." If grant making had been its only goal the Fund might never have been established. But Hoffman and Hutchins were convinced that in addition to being able to give closer attention to applications for grants within the field of education, a separate fund could assemble a staff well qualified to carry on operations of its own when no existing agency could be found to undertake them.

As an operating agency, the Fund disseminated information in the form of reports, statistics, and projections; sponsored the writing of books dealing with educational problems; promoted new approaches to educational journalism; and conducted conferences on a wide variety of educational problems. It also sponsored various kinds of activities that might be called research.

"Research" is a word that does not lend itself to sharp definition because it means different things in different disciplines. Webster says it may mean: "1: careful or diligent search" or "2: studious inquiry or examination; *esp:* investigation or experimentation aimed at the discovery and interpretation of facts, revision of accepted theories or laws in the light of newly discovered facts, or practical application of such new or revised theories or laws."

In physics, chemistry, biology, and some aspects of psychology, "research" usually refers to a carefully controlled experiment conducted under laboratory conditions. But in other disciplines, such as astronomy, anthropology, and archaeology, which do not lend themselves to such treatment because some of the data cannot be brought into the laboratory, research means careful observation of phenomena, a meticulous collection of empirical evidence, and the deduction of laws or principles from the measurable data. In the humanities, and some of the social sciences, research often is an activity carried on in a library rather than a laboratory. It consists of scanning the literature for pertinent information which may throw light on a principle to be investigated or a theory to be proved or disproved.

Professional educators have not been able to agree among themselves on the kinds of research most appropriate to their discipline. Some, in their efforts to make education a science and as much as possible like the "hard" sciences, have restricted their efforts to the investigation of those aspects of the educational process which can be subjected to laboratory controls. But the Fund officers and directors — including Mr.

Eurich who, as an educational psychologist, was thoroughly familiar with educational research — doubted that more research of this kind was what was most needed in education in the 1950's. They noted that a large proportion of the studies of the relative merits of various educational methods led to the finding of "no statistically significant differences," and that even when significant differences were found the report of them rarely led to changes in teaching. One of the most controversial issues in elementary education was the methodology for teaching reading. Since 1920, more than four thousand "research" studies had been reported on this subject in the English language alone, and yet there was no agreement whatever as to how reading should be taught. The officers doubted that more research was likely to lead to agreement.

Although research ought to lead to some conclusions regarding the relative merits of various methodologies, it is doubtful that research of the laboratory variety can ever result in firm conclusions regarding the things that matter most in education. No laboratory experiments can tell us what the goals of education ought to be. But the offices of the Fund agreed on the need for accurate information regarding the schools and educational problems and on the necessity for the dissemination of such information to all those concerned.

THE ASHMORE REPORT AND SERS

If the collection, analysis, and dissemination of accurate information regarding an important problem can be called research, the largest and most rewarding research effort sponsored directly by the Fund was that which led to a report by Harry S. Ashmore, titled *The Negro and the Schools*. By fortuitous circumstance this was published on May 16, 1954 — the day before the U.S. Supreme Court ruled that racial segregation in the public schools is a violation of the United

States Constitution. The study had been undertaken to fill the need for fuller, more up-to-date information on a problem which the directors agreed was among the most urgent in the field of education — that of equalizing educational opportunity for children of all races.

Early in 1953 the Fund held a series of conferences with leading educators, white and Negro, to discuss the problem. Among other things it was suggested that the Fund support an objective, scholarly study of racial segregation in the public schools. The need for such an investigation, which had been long apparent, was then pressing in view of the five segregation cases then pending before the Supreme Court. Whatever the outcome of these cases might be, information regarding the extent of segregation and its effects would be useful to school board members and administrators in reaching wise decisions in an area supercharged with emotion. It was primarily with the needs of these practical decision makers in view that the Fund chose to support the proposed study.

It was decided at the outset that the Fund would avoid direct or indirect involvement in the litigation before the Court and that it would not attempt to argue the case for or against segregated schools. The study was to gather the facts and to present them as objectively as possible. These policies were fully accepted by all participants in the investigation.

The Fund was fortunate in securing the services of Harry S. Ashmore, executive editor of the *Arkansas Gazette*, a widely known and respected editor deeply interested in the problems of race relations. Mr. Ashmore was given complete freedom to assemble the staff, to plan and carry out the research, and to write the report. Upon his recommendation the Fund appointed Mr. Philip Hammer of Atlanta as research director. The research was carried on by forty-five scholars, most of them from southern colleges and universities, recruited from a wide variety of fields including sociology, law, political science, economics, population analysis, and public education.

These researchers analyzed the legal background of segregation in the public schools, studied the experience of communities outside the South which had recently shifted from segregated to nonsegregated systems, reviewed the experience of public and private colleges and universities in the South which had recently begun to admit Negro students, and collected information concerning the dual system of thirteen of the seventeen southern states and the District of Columbia. They benefited from the cooperation of many individuals, institutions, and agencies of the state departments of education in the southern states.

The direct sponsorship of research on such a scale was a departure form the Fund's usual procedure but a wise one because it had the great advantage of making it possible to draw quickly upon the experience and talents of many men and women in a variety of institutions who had spent many years in the study of a wide range of aspects of the problem. In no other way could so comprehensive a study have been completed in so short a time.

In his foreword to *The Negro and the Schools*, Justice Owen J. Roberts, who was then chairman of the Fund's board of directors, said:

This volume and those that follow it are intended to bring into focus the dimensions and the nature of a complex educational problem that in many ways provides a significant test of American democracy. The ultimate solution of that problem will rest with the men and women who execute public school policy in thousands of local school districts, and their action will be conditioned by the degree of understanding of the general public which supports their efforts with its tax dollars. If this project serves to assist them in their task, the Fund for the Advancement of Education will feel that it has wisely invested a portion of the "risk" capital of American education with which it is entrusted.[1]

The project served well the purpose for which it was undertaken. Newspapers throughout the country, and especially in the South, gave *The Negro and the Schools* prominent coverage in their news columns and book review sections, and a number of papers carried editorials about it or quoted from it in editorials on the Supreme Court decision. It was discussed extensively on radio and television and was made the subject of a special broadcast of the *Voice of America*. It was widely used as a source book in conferences, workshops and study groups devoted to the discussion of the Supreme Court decision, as a reference book in college classrooms, and in several southern states as a reference by committees established by the governors to chart future school policy. It became the major source book for two pamphlets which received wide circulation, one published by the Southern Regional Council and the other by the Public Affairs Committee. Teachers, parents, legislators, and leaders of civic, religious and educational organizations also found the report valuable as a timely, objective statement of the problem and the facts concerning it.

In the summer of 1954 the directors and officers of the Fund gave considerable thought to further steps that might be taken to assist state and local school administrators in meeting the many complex problems raised by the Supreme Court's decision. It became apparent that one of the most pressing needs throughout the South was for accurate and unbiased information about developments resulting from the decision in the many educationally autonomous communities affected by it. Although the problem of adjusting to the decision

[1] Harry S. Ashmore, *The Negro and the Schools* (Chapel Hill: University of North Carolina Press, 1954), p. VII.

would vary from state to state and community to community, and would have to be met by each community in its own way, it was reasonable to expect that school officials and community leaders would be better able to meet this challenge wisely and effectively if they had easy access to the experiences of other communities with similar problems.

The Fund agreed to support a nonprofit agency, the Southern Education Reporting Service (SERS) an impartial, fact-gathering enterprise intended to supplement rather than to compete with regular newspaper coverage of educational developments. Virginius Dabney, editor of the *Richmond Times Dispatch*, became chairman of the SERS board, which was made up of distinguished southern editors and educators.

C. A. McKnight, editor of the *Charlotte News*, who took a year's leave of absence to serve as executive editor of the Reporting Service, also became editor of the *Southern School News* which SERS published to provide a medium of objective information about school desegregation in the seventeen states affected by the Supreme Court decision. *Southern School News* was staffed by an experienced team of southern newspaper reporters. After 1957 the support for this enterprise came directly from the Ford Foundation.

THE EDUCATION SUPPLEMENT

Some of the programs sponsored by the Fund fell into decline or disappeared altogether after Fund assistance was terminated. One that has continued to flourish long after the period of Fund assistance is *Saturday Review*'s Education Supplement, titled "Education in America." The support for the supplement was a part of the Fund's effort to improve the relationships between educational institutions and the society that supports them by keeping the public informed about educational problems.

Throughout the Fifties, the officers of the Fund had been

aware of the need to keep the public informed of new developments in education, of alerting them to problems faced by the schools, and of analyzing and interpreting educational trends and issues. They were convinced that an informed public was essential if the schools in a free nation were to survive and flourish and that necessary reforms in education would be resisted if the public did not see the need for them. They had observed that resistance based upon a lack of understanding of the problems can thwart even the most soundly based programs of reform.

During the Fifties the magazine, as well as the newspapers and other information media, had given a great deal of attention to educational problems, but while there was no dearth of information much of it had been presented on a selective basis by individuals who had an ax to grind or a point of view to defend. Many of the critical attacks on the educational system, or some aspect of it, had been made on a hit-and-run basis without adequate follow-up of analysis and interpretation. On the other hand, many of the articles published in defense of the schools had used a public relations approach which glossed over the defects in our educational system and did not squarely meet the legitimate criticisms which had been directed against it.

Very few magazines employed full-time education editors who had a thorough understanding of the complexities of American education: public, private and parochial; elementary, secondary, and higher. Often the responsibility for covering education was turned over to a junior staff member who had a much less sophisticated knowledge of his subject than was possessed by the editors responsible for the coverage of politics, business, military operations, or sports. To cite just one example, many of the articles and editorials published during the Fifties which blamed John Dewey for the defects in American education were written by people who seemingly had never read what Dewey had to say. And though hundreds of professional journals of education were published, none of them was of much interest to the general public, and only a few reached any large segment of the teaching profession.

After pondering these circumstances, the officers of the Fund talked with a number of magazine editors and urged them to employ knowledgeable education editors and to give them more responsibility and more space in order that they might give their readers more continuing coverage-in-depth of all aspects of education. The editors were sympathetic but most of them doubted that a popular magazine that gave any large portion of its space to education could hold either its readers or its advertisers. The implication was that education was a dull subject and little could be done to make it interesting to most readers.

As a next step the officers and directors considered the possibility of sponsoring a new magazine of national circulation that would deal exclusively with education but would be edited for the general public. After investigating the idea, they came to the conclusion that such a magazine could not gain a large enough circulation and attract enough advertising to make it self-supporting after the period of Fund assistance expired. Consequently they next directed their attention to the possibility of persuading the editors and publishers of an already established magazine to offer a regular supplement on education with an agreement that the Fund would cover losses during the pilot period.

Mr. Eurich, who was the strongest supporter of the plan, carried on the negotiations. Several editors and publishers were approached and a number of them expressed an interest, though some had doubts that a supplement on education could be so written and edited as to hold the attention of their readers. But both Norman Cousins, editor, and Jack Cominsky, publisher, of *Saturday Review* were convinced that if the

Fund would help with editorial and publishing costs during the experimental period, the supplement might eventually become a self-supporting part of the magazine. Moreover, *Saturday Review* had a well-distributed nationwide circulation and offered an appropriate readership that included many of the opinion leaders in their respective communities.

It was agreed that the Education Supplement would consist of twenty-five pages, published once a month. Though *Saturday Review* is a weekly, this presented no problem because the magazine had already established the practice of offering readers supplements on various subjects on different weeks of the month. An arrangement was made for providing the necessary financial assistance and included an agreement that during the exploratory period the Fund would pay the salaries of the editorial and secretarial staff, the cost of manuscripts, and a part of publication costs.

It was also agreed that the editors would be selected by the Fund with the approval of Mr. Cousins, who would have the final editorial responsibility for the supplement as he had for the other parts of *Saturday Review*. I was asked to be the editor of the supplement and accepted the assignment with the understanding that I would be free to return to my professorship at Western Washington State College as soon as the supplement had been in operation long enough to prove its feasibility. John Scanlon was given a leave from his position on the Fund and Foundation staff to become associate editor of the supplement. Two secretaries, Thelma Coles and Eleanor Slaybaugh, also took leaves from the Fund to work on the supplement. In addition to their secretarial duties they read manuscripts and helped to select letters for publication.

The third member of the editorial team was James Cass, who had been director of research for the National Citizens Council for the Public Schools. (In 1966 Mr. Cass became editor of the supplement.) The team was rounded out by Frank

Jennings, an editor-at-large of *Saturday Review*, who had long experience in education. Though none of the editors had had very much magazine experience, as a group they had a broad and comprehensive knowledge of many aspects of American education: elementary, secondary, and higher.

The four editors worked as a team, sharing responsibility for policy and editorial content. All contributed editorials from time to time as well as their own signed columns and an occasional article. Until the load became too great it was customary for at least three of the editors to read each incoming manuscript and to share the responsibility for deciding what was to be published. During the early months of publication the secretaries as well as the editors worked excessively long hours to meet the deadlines, but the morale of the staff and their enthusiasm for the supplement was such that no one protested.

The editorial policy of the Education Supplement was announced in an editorial written by me and printed in the first issue, dated September 17, 1960, which said in part:

It will be our purpose, each month in these pages, to try to bring the problems of education into focus by providing a forum for the most literate, the best informed, and the most penetrating thinkers and writers on educational matters. Intelligent controversy will be welcomed and a diversity of views on unresolved issues will be presented; our pages will be open to those who have something important to say about education and can say it with clarity and force. Good schools and good teachers will be vigorously defended; questionable practices and viewpoints will be analyzed by qualified critics.

Attention will be given to all levels of education from kindergarten through college, and particular attention will be given to the problems of achieving better articulation of the various units of our educational structure. We shall try to avoid those biases resulting from regional viewpoints and preoccupation with a single level of education, a single kind of school, or a single academic subject. The American educational establishment is so complex, diverse, and enormous that it is difficult for anyone to see it clearly and in perspective, but we shall strive to present in these pages the wisest and most thoughtful discussions of American Education that we can discover. The Supplement will also provide continuing, critical examination of educational policies, trends, and developments, and professional evaluation and interpretation of important and influential books on education. Readers will be alerted to promising proposals for meeting the problems that confront us, including technological advances that offer promise of bringing better education to more children, but the emphasis will always be upon the goals of education and the improvement of educational quality.

In our attention to educational institutions we shall try not to forget that it is the individual human being who is being educated; his welfare including his freedom to make the most of himself as an individual, must remain our primary concern.[2]

Though the response to the supplement was predominantly favorable, a number of educators who had previously engaged in controversy with the editors or the Fund viewed the new publication with alarm. Several professors of education wrote angry letters to Mr. Cousins protesting the choice of myself (whose views they considered too controversial) as education editor. Others expressed fears that the supplement would become a house organ for the Fund, presenting only points of view with which the Fund was in agreement, or devoting its pages exclusively to Fund projects.

Such fears proved to be groundless. The officers and directors of the Fund took great care not to exert any influence whatever over editorial policy — indeed they offered neither suggestions nor advice, except for an occasional note of commendation for the overall quality of the publication. Mr. Cousins and Mr. Cominsky of *Saturday Reveiw* allowed the

[2] Paul Woodring, editorial, *Saturday Review*, September 17, 1960, pp. 65–66.

editors of the supplement a degree of freedom that is rare in magazine journalism. Whatever mistakes were made were those of the education staff.

The editorials in the supplement naturally expressed the views of the editors who wrote them but the articles selected for publication included many that expressed points of view contrary to those of the Fund officers as well as the editorial staff. It proved difficult, however, to maintain the promised balance of emphasis about the various levels of education. Excellent articles on higher education were so abundant that many had to be rejected for lack of space, but good articles on secondary and particularly on elementary education were much harder to come by. The editors had hoped to publish many articles by elementary and secondary teachers but not enough were received and many of those that came in unsolicited lacked the desired nationwide perspective or the necessary literary quality. There were some outstanding exceptions, however; among the most notable was a short piece titled "From a Teacher's Wastebasket" by the teacher named Bel Kaufman who later expanded her piece into a best-selling book, *Up the Down Staircase*, probably better known than the supplement itself.

Because of my personal association with the supplement (as editor of the supplement for six years and now as an editor-at-large for *Saturday Review*) I am not in a good position to offer an unbiased judgment of its success. It seems fair to say, however, that the experiment achieved one of its goals by demonstrating that a quality magazine of general circulation can substantially expand its coverage of education and give sustained attention to educational problems without losing readers or driving away advertisers. Within five or six years after the appearance of the Education Supplement, *Saturday Review* doubled its circulation, and this was at a time when many magazines were losing circulation. Of course the supplement cannot claim full credit for this increase (from a quarter to a half a million subscribers) because the circulation of *Saturday Review* had been rising steadily ever since Mr. Cousins became editor, but it seems reasonable to conclude that the addition of the supplement was no handicap to the magazine. The fact that the supplement was continued after the termination of Fund support may be taken as another evidence of success.

Whether the publication of the supplement has contributed to the improvement of education would be impossible to prove, but there is no doubt that the pages are read. To test reader interest the editors have occasionally offered free reprints of an article or editorial. In response to one of these offers (an editorial on the teaching of reading) the editors received requests for fifty thousand reprints.

The supplement has received a great many awards for excellence in educational journalism, including the School Bell Award "for distinguished service in the interpretation of education" (received each year since 1960), the Educational Press Association Award for editorial excellence, and the Education Writers Association Award. Norman Cousins, editor of *Saturday Review*, who must have spent some sleepless hours worrying about the supplement during the early days when it was in the hands of inexperienced editors whose talents were unknown to him, says, "The Education Supplement more than lived up to our expectations. It was able to achieve that rare combination of good writing and authority that editors strive for so valiantly but don't always achieve." [3]

STATISTICS AND PROJECTIONS

The officers of the Fund saw that the large number of children born during the years following the end of World War

[3] Norman Cousins, *Present Tense: An American Editor's Odyssey* (New York: McGraw-Hill, 1967), p. 43.

II would soon present problems for which the schools were unprepared. It was essential that the American people be alerted to the anticipated increase in school enrollments and the teacher shortage likely to result from it. Consequently the Fund sponsored the publication of a number of documents which in addition to setting forth the basic statistical facts regarding American education offered predictions about the future. Two of the most influential of these documents were *Teachers for Tomorrow* and *Teaching Salaries Then and Now*, both published in the fall of 1955.

Though *Teachers for Tomorrow* was unsigned, most of the work was done by Philip Coombs and John Scanlon. In his introduction to the document, President Faust said: "Steeply rising enrollments present a number of serious problems to schools and colleges. More buildings will be needed. Substantially larger appropriations of money will be required. Overshadowing these, however, is the problem of securing enough really able teachers. More than anything else — far more than anything else — the quality of teachers and of teaching will determine the quality of education in the years ahead. It is with teachers for tomorrow, therefore, that this study is concerned." [4]

The projected need for teachers was based, of course, on anticipated enrollments and enough time has now elapsed to enable us to evaluate the predictions in the light of subsequent events. So far as the elementary schools were concerned the enrollment predictions were remarkably accurate; accuracy was possible because the children who would be in school for at least the period up to 1960 already were born in 1954 when the statistics were assembled and because immigration was not large enough to alter the numbers substantially. Predictions for high school enrollments turned out to be a bit low. The prediction for 1967 was 11,932,000; the actual number in high

[4] FAE, *Teachers for Tomorrow*, p. 4.

school in the fall of 1967 was 13,700,000. Since the number of boys and girls who were to be of high school age in 1967 was known in 1954, it seems clear that the error resulted from an underestimation of the proportion of those who would remain in school up through the twelfth grade.

A still larger error is found at the college level. Two predictions, based on different projections, were offered. The first, based on U.S. Office of Education figures, predicted 4,710,-000 college students for 1967. The other, which made allowance for a larger percentage of the age group going to college, predicted 5,418,000. In 1967 the actual number of students in college (full and part time) was 6,500,000, a figure which substantially exceeds either of the projected figures. The combination of continued prosperity and rising desire for a college education had brought more students into college than anyone predicted in 1954.

But in spite of this larger number of students, the shortage of college teachers has turned out to be less acute than was predicted. The Fund bulletin predicted that the need for new college teachers would far outstrip the supply of new Ph.D. degrees and that, as a result, the percentage of college teachers holding that degree would decline far below the 1955 figure of 40 per cent — probably to 20 per cent. This decline has not occurred, because the number of academic doctorates granted annually by American graduate schools has risen much more rapidly than was predicted — from 9,000 in 1954 to about 16,000 in 1967 against a maximum predicted figure of 10,350.

At the elementary and secondary levels, also, the shortage of teachers has proved to be less acute than was predicted in 1955, primarily because the number of college students has increased and a larger number of those students than was anticipated have prepared themselves for teaching. It may very well be, however, that the evidence presented in *Teachers for Tomorrow* played a substantial part in causing the larger number of young people to prepare themselves for the teaching profession at all levels.

The willingness of a larger number of young people to become teachers undoubtedly reflects the rise in teachers' salaries and this rise was influenced in part by the publication in 1955 of another bulletin, *Teaching Salaries Then and Now*, written by Beardsley Ruml and Sidney Tickton. More than 120,000 copies were distributed by the Fund. To call attention to the financial plight of teachers and school and college administrators the Fund, in 1954, had commissioned Ruml and Tickton to make a fifty-year study of salaries in the teaching profession, comparing them with salaries and wages paid in other vocations.

The bulletin presented the salaries for all major classifications of the teaching profession in colleges and public schools, both for the fifty-year period, 1904–1953 and for the twenty-five-year period, 1929–1953. Estimates were made of changes in purchasing power over the years and of the salaries that would be necessary in 1953 to bring wages up to the purchasing power of the salaries paid at the earlier dates. The investigators also compared the pay of teachers with that of other professions and industries. They paid particular attention to the pay of railroad employees, the railroad industry being one of the few that has reported wages throughout the fifty-year period.

Although the facts presented in the bulletin were not entirely new to educators, they were shocking to those who had not thought much about teachers' salaries and they provided valuable ammunition to those who were fighting for higher salaries for teachers and school administrators. Throughout the fifty-year period the salaries of elementary teachers in small towns had been lower than those of railroad clerks, some of whom lived in the same towns. Salaries of full professors in colleges and universities had been no higher than those of railroad engineers and those of associate and assistant professors had been much lower. In 1904 the salaries of high school teachers in cities of 30,000 to 100,000 population had been somewhat higher than those of railroad switchtenders, but by 1953 had fallen below them.

The most serious decline in purchasing power during the first half of the twentieth century had been suffered by school and college administrators. In 1904 at least four university presidents drew salaries of $10,000. Ruml and Tickton estimated that it would require a salary of $50,000 before taxes to have the same purchasing power in 1953 and found that the salary paid to presidents in that year was far below that figure. School superintendents and high school principals in the larger cities had also suffered a loss of purchasing power.

It was useful to have these comparative statistics brought to public attention but some of the facts presented required more interpretation than was offered in the document. It might have been mentioned that in 1904 the salaries of high school teachers were nearly double those of elementary teachers; that by 1953 this gap had almost been closed for teachers of comparable preparation; and that consequently the rise in elementary teacher salaries was much greater than that of high school teachers. And in 1904 the salaries of big-city teachers were much higher than those of teachers who did similar work and carried similar responsibilities in smaller communities. During the half century this discrepancy was substantially reduced, partly as a result of more state aid. In 1904, when some university presidents drew salaries of $10,000, the average salary of full professors in large state universities was only $2,000. Part of the drop in the purchasing power of the men at the top may be accounted for by the fact that these excessive differentials were being reduced. The greatest gains in purchasing power during the period were those of elementary school teachers in small towns, whose salaries rose from $446 to $3,190 and whose "real" income doubled. And it was they, rather than the university presidents, who needed it most. But it was fair enough to emphasize the fact that the salaries of educators compared badly with those of industrial employees with much less education and were far less than those of members of other professions with similar education. It should be mentioned, of course, that the professional qualifications of teachers rose rapidly during the period, consequently it would have been reasonable for salaries to rise more rapidly than they did.

In May 1961, Sidney Tickton made a second report for the Fund titled *Teaching Salaries Then and Now — A Second Look* which updated the statistics in the earlier report to include figures through 1959. In some categories he found substantial increases. Between 1953 and 1959 the mean salaries of professors in large state universities had risen from $7,000 to $10,000, those of high school teachers in large cities from $5,526 to $6,650, and those of elementary teachers in medium-sized school districts from $3,682 to $4,900. But industrial wages had risen at about the same rate and the incomes of dentists, for instance, had increased from $8,500 to $15,000. In comparison with other groups within our affluent society, teachers were at best barely holding their own.

FUND PUBLICATIONS

In addition to the annual reports and the statistical projections discussed in the preceding section, the Fund published more than thirty volumes dealing with many aspects of American education: elementary, secondary, and higher. Some of these were written by members of the regular Fund staff but the majority were the work of consultants to whom the Fund had assigned the task of exploring some educational problem and recommending solutions, or of evaluating a group of

Fund-supported programs. Only a few of these publications can be discussed here; a complete list appears in the bibliography.

Most of the staff-written publications were reports on Fund programs. *Bridging the Gap between School and College* (1953) was an early report on four related projects supported by the Fund. *They Went to College Early* (1957) is a more complete report on one of these, the early admission program. *Better Utilization of College Teaching Resources* (1956) is a report by the Committee on Utilization of College Teaching Resources. *New Directions in Teacher Education* (1957) is a comprehensive report on the programs in teacher education which received Fund assistance between 1951 and early 1957.

Some of the publications that were not staff-written were also reports on Fund programs. John S. Dieckhoff's *Tomorrow's Professor* (1959) is a report on the College Faculty Internship Program. Robert S. Donaldson's *Fortifying Higher Education* (1959) is the story of college self-studies. Sidney G. Tickton, who collaborated with Beardsley Ruml on *Teaching Salaries Then and Now* (1955) and wrote a sequel, *Teaching Salaries Then and Now: A Second Look* (1961), was also the author of three other Fund publications: *Needed: A Ten-Year College Budget* (1961); *Letter to a College President* (1963), which is a statistical report on the need for long-term planning; and *The Year-Round Campus Catches On* (1963). Elizabeth Paschal, a staff member and later an officer of the Fund, was the author of *Encouraging the Excellent* (1960), a report on special programs for gifted and talented children which encouraged the development of such programs in many other schools. F. W. Strothmann's *The Graduate School Today and Tomorrow* (1955) is a report written on behalf of the Committee of Fifteen, which had been appointed to look into the problem of graduate education. *Learning by Television* (1966) by Judith Murphy and

Ronald Gross, is a follow-up report on a staff-written earlier report titled *Teaching by Television* (1959).

John I. Goodlad was the author of two very influential Fund publications: *School Curriculum Reform in the U.S.* (1964), a compilation of illustrative projects with an analysis of problems and issues, as well as conclusions and recommendations; and *The Changing School Curriculum* (1966), on which Goodlad shared the authorship with Renata von Stoephasius and Frances M. Klein.

Fund publications were distributed initially to a selected list of educators but additional copies were available upon request. One of the most freqently requested was *Schools for Tomorrow, an Educator's Blueprint* by Alexander J. Stoddard (1957). In January 1956 the officers had asked Stoddard, who had recently retired from the school superintendency in Los Angeles, to look at the educational programs and educational problems of the big-city school systems around the United States and submit suggestions on ways of meeting the critical shortages of teachers and buildings. Stoddard, an administrator of long experience, was eminently qualified for the task. Before going to Los Angeles he had been superintendent of schools in Bronxville, Schenectady, Providence, Denver, and Philadelphia, and had served for ten years as chairman of the Educational Policies Commission. The fact that he was already on a first-name basis with most of the big-city school superintendents made it easy for him to acquire the information that he needed for his study. Stoddard visited seventy-two communities from coast to coast, from Canada to the Gulf of Mexico, and talked with more than one thousand people deeply interested in education.

Stoddard cited statistics on the rapid growth of the educational system, called attention to the large number of classrooms on double sessions, and found evidence that the pupil-teacher ratio was growing larger. He estimated that to meet the growing need for classroom space it would be necessary for the nation to "build and open 100 new classrooms every school day before recess in the morning, 100 more before lunch, 100 more before afternoon recess, 100 more before the pupils go home at night, and 100 more while they are home at night!" He also predicted that the teacher shortage would continue to grow and said, "By 1965 there will be needed nearly 350,000 more teachers than there are now. There are no signs anywhere that such a needed increase in teacher supply will be met by the total of all present or planned training programs throughout the nation. It is likely that the shortage of fully qualified teachers will approximate a quarter of a million by 1965, if present conditions continue." [5]

As it turned out, the teacher shortage did not increase as rapidly as Stoddard had predicted because he — like almost everyone else at the time — underestimated the number of young people who would prepare themselves for teaching positions in the years just ahead.

In pointing to possible solutions Stoddard placed great emphasis on the value of educational television and urged educators to install coaxial cables in all new school buildings. He also stressed the value of teacher aides and of new approaches to scheduling in order that new educational techniques might be properly employed. Some 114,000 copies of Stoddard's report were distributed to educators. It was widely read and discussed and seems to have played a substantial role in educational planning in many cities.

In 1961 the Fund published a ten-year report of its activities, titled *Decade of Experiment*. Written by Renata von Stoephasius and Judith Murphy, the volume summarized Fund programs during the first ten years of its existence under five major categories: (1) more and better teachers, (2) efficient use of teachers' time and talent, (3) education for all,

[5] Alexander J. Stoddard, *Schools for Tomorrow*, 1957, pp. 24 and 17.

(4) improved and updated courses, and (5) modern business methods. In his preface, President Faust looked back over the previous decade:

. . . the Fifties have been exciting years in American education. There have been grave problems, many still unsolved; there has been sharp controversy, much of it still unresolved, on many questions ranging from the purposes and performance of the schools to the methods of preparing teachers. The past decade, especially since Sputnik, has been a period of extensive experimentation.

The Board and the staff of the Fund feel privileged to have been able to work on the problems of American education during these days, which have been filled at the same time with so much that is menacing and so much that is promising. The Fund has been encouraged by the mounting interest in education, by the increasing willingness of schools and colleges to engage in fruitful experimentation, and by the strong evidence that under the direction of imaginative and energetic educators certain lines of experimentation contribute constructively to the advancement of education. We have experienced many more satisfactions than frustrations during our first ten years.

We are especially pleased with the success of the experiments and new developments designed to improve the preparation of teachers, and to increase their effectiveness through the provision of teacher aides, the formation of teaching teams, and the use of modern means of communications. We are pleased, too, with the success of the new programs for meeting the needs of superior students and for challenging all students to exert themselves to the limit of their capacities. We have been heartened by signs that, in spite of pressures to meet the nation's critical needs for specialized and skilled manpower in many fields, there is a new appreciation of the central importance of general and liberal education as preparation for the wise execution of the responsibilities of citizens in a democratic society and for the full development of each individual as a person.[6]

Decade of Experiment includes a full listing of the members and former members of the board of directors of the Fund as

[6] Renata von Stoephasius and Judith Murphy, *Decade of Experiment*, pp. 8–9.

well as a list of officers and staff members, past and present, and a selected list of Fund and Fund-supported publications. In a concluding statement titled "The Next Decade," the authors look into the future, asking questions that reflect the Fund's philosophy:

The past decade [the 1950's] has been deeply concerned with a series of critical problems in education. All of them pertain to the central issue of how schools and colleges can maintain or improve quality in the fact of exploding student enrollments. Some notable gains have been made, but as we enter the Sixties, a number of urgent questions remain unanswered.

Can the function of the schools be clarified? Only to the extent that we are clear about the goals of education can we devise satisfying school and college programs. And it is plain that we can determine educational goals only after we have answered the larger question of what it is that we as a nation value most and wish above all else to accomplish in the years ahead.

Can the curriculum be designed anew to reflect all we know and still have to find out about the learning process? Schools and colleges must provide common learning that is broad and rigorous and at the same time they must meet the specialized demands of a complex society.

Will the teacher shortage be solved? Will we have to depend on traditional approaches or will we find new and better ways of utilizing teaching talent? Can we raise the status and economic level of the teaching profession and thereby attract a larger number of able people?

Will it be possible to develop schools that challenge and capture the interests of youth in the depressed neighborhoods of large cities?

Can we work out a better basis of financial support for our schools so that children in Mississippi will have the same educational opportunities as children in New York or California?

Building on the experience gained in the Fifties, will we find ways to bring all sound new ideas and techniques together to achieve not just a patchwork of improvement, but a coherent design of advancement? Such a unified effort would include curriculum reform, expansion of the team-teaching concept, provision for flexibility of student grouping as well as of time schedules, and the imaginative use of modern means of communication in the classroom; it would mean a more and more effective partnership between school systems and institutions of higher learning in the training of teachers and in educational research and development.

And above all else, can we improve our educational programs to make the most of human talent? In the pursuit of excellence we cannot afford to sacrifice the variety our educational establishment must maintain if it is to provide equality of opportunity to all.

New ideas and experiments will be needed in the decade ahead. For education is a creative process in which "principles that have served their day expire and new principles are born."

The Fund for the Advancement of Education is proud to continue to play its part in meeting one of the most serious challenges that face our nation in this revolutionary age.[7]

SPONSORED PUBLICATIONS

In addition to the books published under its own imprint, the Fund sponsored the writing of many other volumes which were published and distributed by university presses, schools, professional associations, or commercial publishers. One of the most influential of these, Harry Ashmore's *The Negro and the Schools*, has already been discussed. Another book dealing with a related problem, *The Louisville Story* by Omer Carmichael and Weldon James, was published in 1957 by Simon and Schuster; another, titled *Desegregation in the Baltimore Schools*, was published by the Maryland Commission on Interracial Problems, in 1955; and still another, *With All Deliberate Speed: Segregation-Desegregation in Southern Schools*, was edited by Don Shoemaker and published in 1957. These and other Fund-sponsored books, in combination with the publications of the Southern Education Reporting Service, contributed notably to the public's understanding of the prob-

[7] Ibid., pp. 104–105.

lems involved in desegregating schools that had long been racially segregated.

As a first step in its effort to preserve and improve liberal education, the Fund, in 1951, made a grant to support the work of faculty members in three colleges: Harvard, Yale, and Princeton, and three preparatory schools: Andover, Exeter, and Lawrenceville, who had undertaken a study of the interrelationships of the academic programs in school and college. The project, which took the name "The School and College Study of General Education," resulted in a publication titled *General Education in School and College* which was published by the Harvard University Press in 1952. This report, which includes a definitive statement of the meaning and purpose of liberal education that has since been widely quoted, concludes with a proposal for an experiment in articulating liberal education at the secondary and higher levels which led to the advanced placement program supported by the Fund.

During the Fifties, the private liberal arts colleges faced serious financial difficulties as a result of continuing inflation and the need for higher faculty salaries. There was no shortage of students, but because the tuition charges paid for only a fraction of the actual cost of instruction, more students meant a bigger deficit. In a search for solutions, the Fund, in 1958, asked Beardsley Ruml to examine the financial and structural aspects of private colleges and recommend solutions.

Recognizing that the rising birthrate would make it necessary for colleges to continue to expand, even though many of them preferred to remain small, Ruml set out to answer the question "How can our colleges organize their faculties, their teaching programs, their facilities, and their finances to provide liberal education for twice as many students as today while continuing to improve educational quality?" His report, *Memo to a College Trustee*, which includes a chapter by Donald Morrison, was published in 1959 by McGraw-Hill in paperback form. Ruml decided to address his recommendations to trustees because the trustees of colleges have final responsibility and authority for the performance of their institutions. Accordingly, they must understand the issues that the liberal colleges face and find solutions within the specific structure of the college for which they are responsible.

Because the liberal colleges were being squeezed between limited financial resources and the necessity for substantial increases in faculty salaries, Ruml urged that they give up the low student-teacher ratio in which many of them took great pride. Ruml recommended a ratio of twenty to one and offered a number of models to demonstrate that such a ratio would make it possible to raise salaries substantially without giving up all classes and tutorial relationships. This proposal was widely discussed, and though it was roundly condemned in some quarters, it stimulated many colleges to reexamine their policies in a renewed effort to provide sound instruction within the available financial resources.

Oliver C. Carmichael, after a long and distinguished career as foundation executive and university president, came to the Fund in 1960 as a consultant to undertake a comprehensive study of graduate education. He came to the conclusion that while the graduate school is the most strategic segment of higher education it is also the most inefficient and in some ways the most ineffective division of the university. He summarized his findings and presented his conclusions in a book titled *Graduate Education Today*, published in 1961 by Harper, which won the American Council Book Award for the best book of the year on higher education.

In 1960 the Fund made a grant to the Harvard Graduate School of Education to underwrite the preparation of a book on team teaching. The volume, which was published in 1964 by Harper and Row, under the editorship of Judson T. Shaplin and Henry F. Olds, Jr. — titled *Team Teaching* — became the definitive book on the subject and contributed to the further development of team-teaching programs.

Early in 1960 Mr. Eurich asked a group of men and women who had been actively involved in teacher education projects supported by the Fund to assemble for an eight-week period to make a critical appraisal of the professional aspects of teacher education. The group, which met at the Center for Advanced Study in the Behavioral Sciences at Palo Alto, included Robert Bush, Alvin Eurich, John Goodlad, Lester Nelson, Robert Pace, Elizabeth Paschal, Harris Purks, Paul Rehmus, Judson Shaplin, John Walton, Paul Woodring, Elmer Smith, and Ralph Tyler. The results of the conference were reported in a book by Elmer Smith, titled *Teacher Education: A Reappraisal*, which was published in 1962 by Harper and Row.

These are but a few examples of the many volumes published by commercial publishers which resulted from Fund conferences, the work of Fund committees, or the work of individuals whose investigations received financial support from the Fund. A more complete list will be found in the appendix.

CONFERENCES AND COMMITTEES

Before undertaking an attack upon an educational problem, the Fund officers usually appointed a committee of educators to advise them and to recommend possible solutions to which the Fund might contribute. Many of the grants described in chapter four resulted from the recommendations of such committees. The Fund also sponsored many conferences for the discussion of educational problems. The roster of men and women who served on these committees and attended these conferences — several hundred names in all — reads like a Who's Who of American education. It includes schools and college administrators, professors of education, NEA executives and U.S. Office of Education officials, members of boards of education and college trustees, education editors and reporters, and a number of individuals who fall into none of these categories. A number of college professors took part but classroom teachers from elementary and secondary schools were poorly represented.

The Fund sponsored more than seventy-five of these conferences, most of them between 1953 and 1959. They dealt with a large variety of educational problems: teacher education, utilization of teachers, graduate study, educational television, clarification of the functions of educational institutions, educational reporting, higher education, the role of education in American history, educational management and financing, merit pay, education in the armed services, equalization of educational opportunity, problems of Negro education, college self-studies, improvement of small high schools, guidance and counseling, school and college curricula, programs of testing, the teaching of various subjects, and many other topics.

These conferences, which were held in many parts of the country, ranged in length from a day or two to as long as three weeks. Some of the longer ones on teacher education were held at the Center for Advanced Study of the Behavioral Sciences at Palo Alto, others at places having special facilities for conferences such as Aspen, Colorado, and Williamsburg, Virginia, and still others at universities or in hotels. It was customary for the Fund to underwrite all costs including travel costs and in some cases wives were invited to accompany their husbands at the Fund's expense.

The formal discussions, based on an agenda sent to participants in advance with recommended reading, took place both morning and afternoon and sometimes again in the evening. Frequently these were led by either Mr. Eurich or Mr. Faust, both of whom were highly skilled as conference leaders. Informal discussion continued through the cocktail and dinner hours and far into the night. The more extended conferences inevitably took on something of a house-party aspect but the discussions were of a high level.

Most of those who attended Fund-supported conferences seemed to have been convinced that the conferences were useful and that their support constituted a sound investment of the Fund's risk capital. They enabled influential educators of diverse views to become personally acquainted and to exchange opinions. Sometimes they led to a reconciliation of differences. Unquestionably they stimulated thought. The participants went away better prepared for leadership in educational innovation and encouraged in their belief that innovation was both necessary and possible. And the conferences gave Fund officers an opportunity to become acquainted with individuals who were potential leaders of experimental projects. Though the conferences were expensive, it is doubtful that the same amount of money could have been better used in any other way.

Harold Howe II, who participated in several of the more extended conferences when he was a high school principal, and who later became U.S. commissioner of education, says, "The summer seminars at Palo Alto turned out to be real change agents. They affected the thinking and behavior of the people engaged in them and those people affected American education. I guess the generalization is that if you get the right people to a conference, it's worth having." [8]

[8] Letter to the author dated September 20, 1968; quoted by permission.

6

Judging the Results

THE difficulty of appraising the accomplishments of a philanthropic foundation was anticipated by the authors of the Ford Foundation's "Study Report" in 1949:

Probably the most difficult problem of a foundation is to determine which grants have been successful, and which have not. Foundations have experimented with different techniques for appraising their own work, including the preparation of rather elaborate analyses and reports. Such documents are useful in various ways. In addition to their primary purpose of providing a formal basis for appraising a foundation's program, they may be useful for historical purposes and for the training of new staff members — they have certainly been invaluable in informing the staff of this study. Nevertheless they should be supplemented by less formalized types of review. Any written review is likely to be a rather mechanical device to record in a watered-down form the critical self-appraisal in which foundation officers ought always to be engaged. For the officers of a foundation must be guided in their new decisions by the most candid judgment regarding old successes and failures. The most important judgments are not those that they would be willing to put into writing. Like most other policy decisions crucial to an organization's success, such judgments are most effective if they are made informally, privately, and confidentially.[1]

In the course of my work on this volume I have gone to some length to get judgments of the kind that have been expressed to me "informally, privately, and confidentially." These will substantially influence the judgments I shall express as my own in the latter part of this chapter. But before offering my own comments I shall discuss the Fund's educational philosophy, analyze the expenditures, examine the many criticisms directed against the Fund and the controversies which they engendered, present a distillation of professional opinions of the value of the Fund's contribution, and comment on missed opportunities and lost causes.

The Fund was established for the purpose of advancing education. Consequently, any appraisal of its work must be a search for evidence that education has advanced since 1951 and that the Fund contributed to that advancement.

We know that education has changed in the past eighteen years, though in most of the schools the changes have been too gradual to be called dramatic. There has been a gradual shift away from the self-contained classroom and toward some form of team teaching but the change is apparent in only a minority of school systems. The content of the curriculum, particularly in mathematics and the sciences, has been altered in most secondary schools. The methods used in teaching foreign languages have been changed in many schools. A substantial number of children now receive some of their instruction via television though the majority still know television only as a form of entertainment in the home. Beginning teachers have a background of more years of college education, and presumably better education, than those of 1951. Most of the thou-

---

[1] "Report of the Study for the Ford Foundation on Policy and Program," 1949, p. 136.

sands of school buildings that have been constructed during the Fifties and Sixties are lighter, more airy, and more attractive than those built earlier.

The most easily measured changes have been in numbers. The figures given in chapter one indicate that between 1951 and 1967 the enrollment in American elementary schools increased by 62 per cent, high school enrollments by 100 per cent and college enrollments by 117 per cent. At the elementary level the increase accurately reflects the high birthrate of the late Forties and Fifties, at the secondary and higher levels it also reflects the prosperity of the nation, the greater availability of schooling, and greater desire for it on the part of young people and their parents. Obviously the Fund can claim no credit for the higher birthrate or for the increased prosperity and only a modest amount of credit for the availability of schooling and the desire for it.

The Fund can claim credit for encouraging and assisting curricular change, the development of team teaching and other efforts to make better use of time, space, and personnel in the schools. It has also pressed for the use of television, and for changes in teacher education. But while there is no doubt that these changes occurred, and little room for doubt that the Fund contributed to them, the problem of appraisal goes well beyond the simpler task of describing change. In evaluating the changes we must ask which of them can be accepted as evidence of *advancement* or *improvement* in educational quality — which of them can be cited as evidence that the children in school today are getting a *better* education than was available to those enrolled in 1951. The answers to these questions must be based upon an answer to the question, "What are schools for?" This question in turn involves philosophical judgments analyzing the nature of the good society and the place of the individual human being within that society.

If society, or the state, is considered all important, it may be legitimate to say that a good school is one that strengthens the society or even one that satisfies the demands of the state for suitably trained manpower. But if the individual is of primary importance it would seem to follow that a good school is one that enables each individual to develop to the utmost his potentialities as a human being. But the two points of view need not be mutually exclusive. The individual who is trained to meet manpower demands can also develop his full capacities as an individual if the state or the society gives him the freedom and opportunity to do so. A sound educational philosophy can make suitable provisions for interaction between the individual and the society of which he is a part.

WHAT DID THE FUND HOPE TO ACHIEVE?

One possible approach to the problem of evaluation is to judge the success of the Fund in achieving its own goals. These are not set forth concisely in any one document but may be gleaned from a number of papers and reports.

Although there was naturally some difference of opinion among the officers and directors of the Fund, it seems to have been the consensus that the primary responsibility of the schools is to produce liberally educated citizens capable of making wise, independent decisions. The development of each individual to the full extent of his capacity was placed above the manpower needs of the society or the needs of the state. The Fund also held that the philosophy of education should be consistent with the public philosophy and in the public interest, which, in the words of Walter Lippmann, "may be presumed to be what men would choose if they saw clearly, thought rationally, acted disinterestedly and benevolently." [2]

Though the policy of the Fund evolved in response to changes in the nation and the world that occurred during the

[2] Walter Lippmann, *The Public Philosophy* (Boston: Atlantic–Little, Brown, 1954), p. 42.

Fifties and Sixties, it did not always follow the directions of public opinion or of the nation's leadership. Indeed the officers and directors of the Fund often resisted public pressures and responded to trends that they considered unfortunate or dangerous by taking steps to counteract them. After the Russians launched Sputnik I in 1957 the nation demanded that the schools take steps to restore the leadership of the United States in fields of science and technology. The Congress answered the challenge by passing the National Defense Education Act for the clearly stated purpose, not of improving education, but of creating a larger pool of skilled manpower as a contribution to the defense of the nation. Some foundations went along with the new direction but the Fund for the Advancement of Education did not alter its view that the training of skilled manpower is not properly the primary goal of education and should not be allowed to overrule the liberal goals.

In the Fund annual report for 1957–59, Clarence Faust, in an introductory section titled "The Age of Education," contrasted Russia's educational aims with those appropriate to a free nation such as the United States. Because of its significance as a reflection of the Fund's philosophy, I shall quote from the statement at some length:

Future historians looking back upon our time may be torn between the inclination to call it "The Atomic Age" and the inclination to describe it as "The Age of Education." The twentieth century has certainly seen a tremendous expansion of education and a tremendous growth of concern about it. Indeed, the burgeoning of science and technology, including the unlocking of the secrets of atomic energy, may be traced to education. Certainly, the historian will be impressed by the mounting interest in it at the middle of this century. Education has become news, often front page news. Magazines carry an increasing number of articles critical of our educational practices, urgent for reform, or ardent in defense of our educational system. Numerous books undertake to clarify our educational problems, make comparisons with other educational systems, view with alarm, or point with pride to our educational arrangements and procedures. Radio and television abound in interviews and panels dealing with the "crises" in education. Voluntary citizens' organizations have been formed to deal in one way or another with the problems of education.

The topics for discussion among laymen and educators alike cover a wide range. Should all young people go to college, or should higher education be limited to the more able and more highly motivated of our youth? Should educational opportunity at the elementary and secondary school be equal for all, or limited by considerations of race? Are our schools too "soft"? Are we neglecting an important human resource by failing to give adequate attention to the education of "the gifted"? Are the salaries and status of teachers unconscionably low? How can the amount and quality of education needed by children and young people in the modern world be financed? Should tuition in institutions of higher education be sharply raised to equal or come much nearer actual per student cost? How much and what kind of Federal financial support should education receive? How far should young people be led or pressed into educational preparation to meet the needs of our society for scientists, doctors, the foreign service, and other professions and occupations? What are the functions of the schools, and what priorities should be established for them? What should be the relationship between public and private and parochial schools?

The widespread and earnest discussion of these topics has not produced consensus. It has, indeed, often produced more heat than light. But it is possible to make out in the smoke and dust of debate an emerging central concern. The consideration of education, the analysis of its problems and proposals for their solution, has increasingly revolved around what might be called the interest in "manpower." It is pointed out, or more frequently taken for granted, that national strength depends mainly on human resources and that education is the most important means of making the most of a nation's human resources. The National Defense Education Act clearly reflects this preoccupation with manpower, not only in its title, but in its preamble and its provisions. "The Congress hereby finds and declares," the Act begins, "that the security of the nation requires the fullest development of the mental resources and technical skills of its young men and women. We must increase our efforts," declares the Act, "to identify and educate more of the talent of our nation." The Act thus represents both a development in the public attitude toward the role of Federal government with respect to education and a development in the public conception of the role of education in society.

The public conception of the role or function of education has been modified throughout our history, reflecting in successive periods of our national life our conceptions of the nature of our major interests as a people. In the earliest period of our national existence, we were primarily concerned with providing through education the opportunities for individual advancement. As expressed by Benjamin Franklin and later by Horace Mann, our schools were to provide young people with the means to get on and up in the world. As Horace Mann put it, education could solve the problems of poverty and class in America. During the late nineteenth and early twentieth centuries, when the prospect of opportunity in America had brought floods of immigrants to our shores, schools were conceived of as having an important role in the process of the American "melting pot." This role of assimilating new Americans into our national society is still very important in many of our large metropolitan school systems, but by and large the school's function of bringing about the adjustment of young people to American society merged with or shifted toward the problems of the internal adjustments of students. The conception of education of "the whole man" and an education for the development of "well-rounded individuals" bulked larger and larger in the planning of school curricula and in the arrangements and methods of education during the first half of this century.

The new concern about education as the means to increase our manpower resources, which has its major roots in an increasing awareness of the possibilities and dangers of our new relationships to other nations and especially our menacing conflict with Russia, does not fuse automatically or even easily with our earlier preoccupations with education for individual "adjustment." One may expect that as the pressure increases to use education as a means of building our national strength by developing our manpower resources, tension will develop between this view of education and the conception of it as primarily providing individuals with a means of economic and social advancement in our fluid society or as primarily developing normal, healthy, well-adjusted people. There are already signs that many parents are disinclined to bring up their children as manpower resources. The emergent debates in education are less likely to focus on such old issues as that of "progressive" versus "traditional" education than around the question of the reciprocal responsibilities of the individual and society. Preoccupation with the manpower aspects of education, however statesmanlike, runs into the fundamental question whether the individual exists for society or society for the individual. On this question, the American commitment would seem to be clear, that the individual is not primarily to be regarded as a resource of the state but the state as a means for assuring the full flowering of the individual.

A closely related question has to do with specialization in education. In the view of education expressed by Mr. Khrushchev for Russia and by the central authorities of other countries behind the Iron Curtain, education has two functions: the indoctrination of youth in Communist principles and the development of each individual's capacities for specialization in the service of the state. As Mr. Khrushchev put it in 1958 in a memorandum approved by the Communist Party Central Committee, "The most important thing here is to issue a slogan and make this slogan sacred for all children entering schools — that all children must prepare for useful work, for participation in the building of a Communist society." To achieve this purpose, he said, the schools must do two things: first, they must inculcate Communist ideas and make sure of indoctrination in Communism; second, they must develop the specialized competence of every person in that society by means of which each individual may contribute to its productivity and strength.

At first sight, and from a superficial point of view, it might seem that in these respects Russian education has aims not very different from our own, for we are concerned that students acquire the values of a democratic society and that they develop their special abilities to make important contributions to our national welfare and security. But it does not require any very profound examination of the Russian position as expressed by Mr. Khrushchev to reveal that the two chief aims of Russian education — indoctrination and specialized training — are not identical with the aims of the American educational system.

The American educational system aims not at indoctrination and absolute acceptance of a set of ideas, but at the development of each individual's capacity to think for himself. Our interest is not in conformity and the social solidarity that conformity produces, but in the development of the powers of independent thought and the independent flowering of the individual's capacity. Similarly, in the matter of specialization, our concern is not with mere training, that is, with fixing a standard way of doing things, but in the development of originality and creativity by means of which better ways of doing things may be found.

These differences in the aims of Russian and American education have very deep roots in the fundamental principles of the two societies. The Russians assume that truth has been discovered and needs only to be impressed upon the rising generation. We are convinced that every individual is entitled to discover or rediscover the truth for himself and that only as he makes the effort to do so can he really grasp it, truly understand it, and make it a part of himself. We are convinced, too, that even the things that we do well might be done better and that consequently the practitioners of any vocation or trade or art must be encouraged to do more than merely repeat the practices of their predecessors. They must be encouraged to experiment, to try new methods, and for this purpose must be given a grasp of basic principles, in light of which any originality or creative capacity they have may become soundly effective.

This picture of the difference between Russian and American educational aims may be charged, and truly, with a certain idealism when considered in contrast with actual practice of American education. The debates, therefore, which may take place with regard to specialization and more fundamentally with regard to the relation of the individual in society as it affects education may, if carried on intelligently and deeply enough, have great value in clarifying our views of the functions of education and, consequently, assist in the establishment of educational priorities and in increasing the effectiveness of our educational practices.

Perhaps we may even come to see that education should not be conceived of primarily as a means to an end, but as an end in itself, that the acquisition of wisdom is infinitely more important than the acquisition of "know-how," and that the role of education, therefore, is to provide the opportunity for the development of man's peculiarly human capacity for thought and reflection along the full range of its possibilities.[3]

Throughout its history, the activities of the Fund were consistent with these stated objectives. The goal was to assist educational institutions in making the most of man, as man.

WHERE DID THE MONEY GO?

In appraising the work of a philanthropic organization two questions seem appropriate: How was the money used? Was it wisely spent? The second question is by far the more difficult of the two.

The first question is easier to answer because the Fund kept accurate records and made public reports of all grants and other major categories of expenditure. About the only item concealed from the general public was the salaries of officials. These were roughly comparable to those paid by academic institutions to individuals of comparable background and responsibility. Because this was a period of progressive inflation in which academic salaries were rising rapidly, the salaries paid to Fund officers and staff rose by about 50 per cent between 1951 and 1966. After the staff became the Education Division of the Ford Foundation, the salaries were brought into line with those of other Foundation officials but this did not require any very substantial readjustment.

Between April 3, 1953, and September 30, 1966, the Fund spent a total of just under $71 million in the following ways:

GRANTS	$60,778,145
PROJECTS	4,355,279
GENERAL ADMINISTRATIVE EXPENSES	5,851,550
TOTAL	$70,984,974

[3] *Annual Report*, 1957–59, pp. 3–7.

Administrative expenses include the cost of travel (which inevitably is high), office rental, the purchase of furniture and equipment, and a wide variety of incidentals as well as the salaries of officers and directors, staff, consultants, research assistants, secretaries, clerks, and receptionists. Administrative costs are lowest in a large foundation that makes only large grants on a wholesale basis; higher in a foundation that makes a large number of small grants. Consequently there can be no firm answer to the question: "What portion of a foundation's resources may properly be allocated to administrative expenses?" It depends upon what kind of a foundation it is and how it operates. Warren Weaver, a foundation executive of long experience, says:

> I have seen it suggested that foundations should not enjoy tax-free privileges unless they are efficiently managed, and that one criterion of efficiency is low cost for "administrative overhead." It would in fact be not only inefficient but also scandalous for a foundation to pay excessive salaries to its officers. In general these salaries should be competitive with the salaries of distinguished professorships, deanships, and presidencies of academic institutions of comparable rank — for the simple and practical reason that persons of similar qualifications are required.
>
> It does not at all follow that the ratio of "administrative overhead" to the total of grants should be automatically accepted as an indication of efficiency. A responsible officer of a foundation may exert the critically important judgments which lead to the decisions as to how hundreds of thousands, or even millions, of dollars are to be used. If an additional $10,000 of salary will obtain an officer who increases by a few percent the wisdom, and hence the practical efficiency, of the grants, this $10,000 is clearly the best investment the foundation can make.
>
> The main variation in administrative overhead from one foundation to another is not, however, the result of salary differentials. It results from the size of the staff, and this in turn results from the nature of the foundation's activities. If the foundation is completely non-operative,

distributing all of its money as grants to other agencies (universities, research institutes, etc.) then the staff can be relatively small and the administrative costs relatively low.

If some of the grants go for development purposes to strengthen and improve inexperienced agencies (say, some of the smaller predominantly Negro colleges, as an example) then a good deal more staff work is necessary, both in working up the basis for the grants and in furnishing helpful supervision after the grants have been made. This necessarily increases the foundation's administrative costs; but it is incorrect to label this with the pejorative word "overhead." This is a vitally necessary cost of efficient operation.

This point applies even more strongly if the foundation in question carries on semi-operating or operating activities. In the former case it is again true that the foundation must maintain, and pay salaries to, a sufficient staff to supervise and carry out the semi-operating actvity in question. This might, for example, be a scholarship or fellowship program which requires a great deal of detailed attention to each individual case. And when a foundation carries on an operating program . . . then the foundation should no more be criticized for the total of the relevant staff salaries than should a university for the total amount it pays its professors.

Percentages for administration can understandably run higher for small foundations unless they can depend partly on contributed services, or unless they utilize part-time advisors. Some foundations manage in this way to keep administrative costs down to a few percent. Thus the Lilly Endowment reports administrative costs of 3.3% while the figure for the John A. Hartford Foundation is only 1.4%. Kellogg, Carnegie, and Rockefeller have administrative costs in the 5 to 7% range, while Duke is only slightly higher. Sloan is now operating with administrative costs slightly over 4%, and the administrative budget of Ford, although larger on an absolute scale ($7.2 million), is less than 3% of its high total of grants. Comparisons among the figures just stated are meaningless unless the individual situations are analyzed in detail.[4]

[4] Warren Weaver, *U.S. Philanthropic Foundations* (New York: Harper & Row, 1967), pp. 108–109.

During the years when it was independent of the Ford Foundation (1951–1957) and had an annual total budget of about $8 million, the Fund for the Advancement of Education spent an average of about $400,000 a year, or 5 per cent, on administrative costs. In the later years, when the total expenditures dropped to an average of $2 million, administrative costs averaged about $200,000 or 10 per cent. These latter figures, however, are difficult to interpret because the Fund staff was also the education staff of the Foundation, and though the Foundation paid half the salaries it is likely that the major portion of the staff's time was devoted to Ford Foundation work.

During its entire history the Fund's expenditures totaled $70,984,983, of which the "General Administrative Expenses" came to $5,851,550 for a percentage of 8.2.

Considering that the Fund was both an operating and a grant-making agency, that it was relatively small, and that it made a considerable number of small grants, the amount spent on administrative costs does not appear to be excessive.

The portion of the available money spent on "projects" — about 4 per cent of the total — was modest for a philanthropy that was an operating as well as a grant-making agency. And the results were impressive.

The $4.3 million included under this heading covered the costs of all the documents, pamphlets, and books published by the Fund, some of which were distributed to tens of thousands of educators. It also covers research and the sponsorship of many books published by commercial publishers. Some of these — *The Negro and the Schools, Memo to a College Trustee, Images of the Future, With All Deliberate Speed,* for example — may well have had greater impact on the schools and the nation than equal amounts invested in grants.

This portion of the expenditures also covered the costs of a large number of conferences which brought educators together, stimulated them to give careful thought to possible innovations, and set the wheels in motion for projects that were to follow.

Since by far the greater part of the money available to the Fund went into grants, their allocation and relative size for different purposes offers a clue to the pursuits that the Fund considered most important. The major categories were as follows:

PROGRAMS FOR THE IMPROVEMENT OF SCHOOL
AND COLLEGE PERSONNEL

including teacher education and fellowships to
enable teachers to supplement their liberal educa-
tion $26,622,523

PROGRAMS FOR THE IMPROVEMENT OF
EDUCATION

including new curricula, staffing arrangements
such as team teaching, teacher aides, and new
technologies such as television   22,392,944

PROGRAMS FOR THE IMPROVEMENT OF INSTI-
TUTIONAL RELATIONS

(this catch-all category includes college self-
studies, management studies, programs for the
equalization of educational opportunities, and
programs designed to disseminate information
about the schools)   11,487,560

(The total is slightly smaller than the amount listed for grants on page 211 because a few programs were not included in any of these major categories.)

More revealing, perhaps, is a list of some of the larger grants or series of grants made for a specific purpose:

TEACHER EDUCATION PROGRAMS

including the Arkansas project and many programs leading to the Master of Arts in Teaching as well as other fifth-year and four-year programs $9,634,450

COMMITTEE ON FACULTY FELLOWSHIPS

to enable 1,205 faculty members in 386 colleges to improve their educational background   6,674,649

HIGH SCHOOL TEACHER FELLOWSHIPS

to enable about 1,000 teachers to increase their education   4,836,517

EARLY ADMISSION AND
ADVANCED STANDING PROGRAMS   4,939,483

EDUCATIONAL TELEVISION   4,992,821

FELLOWSHIPS AND OTHER PROGRAMS DESIGNED
PRIMARILY FOR THE PURPOSE OF IMPROVING
THE EDUCATIONAL OPPORTUNITIES OF NEGROES   4,549,800

PROGRAMS TO IMPROVE THE CURRICULUM   3,256,000

NATIONAL CITIZENS COMMISSION (LATER, NATIONAL
CITIZENS COUNCIL) FOR THE PUBLIC SCHOOLS   1,890,560

PROGRAMS TO IMPROVE THE PREPARATION OF
EDUCATIONAL ADMINISTRATORS   1,708,800

PROGRAMS IN SCHOOLS AND COLLEGES FOR THE
EDUCATION OF ABLER STUDENTS   832,373

The Fund was chartered to work for the advancement of education at all levels but in the early years (between 1951 and 1956) most of the grants went to institutions of higher learning. Even when the purpose of the grant was to improve elementary or secondary education the Fund preferred to let a university school of education make the plans and redistribute the money to public school systems as it saw fit. Of the first three hundred grants (made between 1951 and 1956) about 84 per cent went to colleges or universities while only 4 per cent went directly to public schools. The other 12 per cent of the grants were made to national associations or agencies of various kinds.

In later years the distribution changed; the Fund seems to have become more willing to make grants directly to the public schools. Of the 360 grants made between 1959 and 1964, 58 per cent went to colleges or universities while 21 per cent went to public schools and 21 per cent to other agencies. Some of the grants to the schools were for advanced placement programs which probably did as much for higher education as for the secondary schools. Many of the grants to colleges were designed to improve the education of teachers for the elementary and secondary schools. Consequently it is impossible to say just what proportion of the Fund's resources were committed to the improvement of education at each level.

At the level of higher education the great majority of grants went to private and church-related colleges and universities. Only about 22 per cent of all the grants went to publicly supported institutions although well over half of all college students were enrolled in such institutions. This imbalance reflects a widespread conviction throughout the philanthropic world that private foundations, because they are the products of the free enterprise system, have a special obligation to nonpublic colleges and no similar obligation to schools and colleges supported by taxation.

CONTROVERSY AND CRITICISM: AN ANALYSIS

Any philanthropic organization that makes grants on a selective basis must expect criticism. For each grant proposal
that is accepted, many must be rejected, and the psychology
of an individual whose application is turned down is similar to
that of a rejected suitor — he is likely to be bitter and certain
to question the wisdom of the individual or organization that
has rejected him. In spite of this hazard the Fund maintained
generally good relations with the great majority of academic
men in universities and liberal arts colleges.

The Fund's relations with professional educators or "educationists" — professors of education, officials in state departments of education, and the professional teachers' organizations — was less uniformly cordial. Particularly during the
early years, when the Arkansas controversy was at its height,
the Fund was a favorite target of attack from such groups. In
addition to the occasional criticism that appeared in professional journals, there was a great deal of verbalized but un-
printed (and in some cases unprintable) criticism of the Fund
at professional meetings and wherever a group of educators
got together.

The major reason for this was that the philosophy of education implied in the Fund's grant making and operations ran
directly counter to the philosophy that prevailed among professional educators in the early Fifties. At a time when educators were stressing the importance of educating the "whole
child," the Fund stressed the priority of the intellect; at a time
when educators were urging more professional training for
teachers, the Fund supported programs that provided more
liberal education for teachers and postponed professional
training until the fifth college year; and at a time when professors of education were engaged in bitter conflict with academic professors in the universities, the Fund was lending its

support to programs that made it more difficult for them to win their battle.

The tension was heightened by the fact that this was a time when professional educators, and the things they believed in and stood for, were under heavy attack from outside as well as within the colleges and universities. At Yale, President Griswold was taking steps to liquidate what had once been one of the nation's best graduate schools of education. In many other universities, professors of education felt threatened. Consequently they had become defensive, some of them even a bit paranoid in their belief that anyone who rejected their leadership, or who tried to move education in directions different from their own, was an "enemy of the schools."

In this atmosphere it is unlikely that any organization that saw a need for substantial changes in education could have escaped vigorous criticism both from individual educators and from professional organizations. But some educators who wanted changes, and were sympathetic with what the Fund was trying to do, still believe that the Fund made itself more vulnerable to criticism than it need have by its brusque treatment of those who opposed its programs.

Though some of the attacks on the Fund hit vulnerable targets, many of them fell wide of the mark. One of the more absurd charges was that the Fund hoped to use such devices as television and teaching machines "to replace the teacher." Mr. Eurich replied to such charges in *Reforming American Education:*

I want it clearly understood that I am not advocating that television or any other device replace the teacher. Nothing could be further from my intention. A basic principle is involved, which is simply this: any device or arrangement that improves communication with the student should be used. *Used* — not merely tacked onto the existing system — in order to exploit the unique capacities of the new medium. As Marshall McLuhan delights in pointing out, the usual way of dealing with new media is to consider them mere additions to the old way of doing things. But any new medium of instruction, to be effective, means structural changes in the system and new and different ways of using individual talents.[5]

While the Fund officers had no intention of replacing the teacher, they did hope that the new approaches to education would enable the schools to make better use of the teachers available, and they at times expressed a hope that with the new technology the total number of teachers might be reduced somewhat. They supported programs that challenged the axiom that small classes are essential to good teaching. The use of televised instruction was urged as a means of bringing the best teachers to more students. The teacher-aide programs were designed originally to make it possible for schools to operate effectively with fewer teachers.

Teachers' organizations, particularly the American Federation of Teachers, consistently opposed all efforts either to increase class size or to delegate any part of the teacher's work to individuals not holding teachers' certificates. They held that not only must there be a "fully qualified" teacher in every classroom at all times but that this teacher should be responsible for at most thirty children and preferably a smaller number. Many educators insisted that the class size must be held to thirty regardless of the subject taught or the method of instruction.

The Fund took the position that even if it eventually became possible to provide a "fully certified" teacher for every classroom there was not the slightest possibility of finding enough really competent teachers for all the schools of the nation. Fund officers said it was better for a student to sit in a class fifty feet from an excellent teacher than to sit at the elbow of one less competent. They were fond of quoting the

[5] Alvin C. Eurich, *Reforming American Education* (New York: Harper & Row, 1968), p. 10.

comment of President Johnson of Fisk University, who said that "keeping classes small by staffing them with mediocre teachers merely enables the teachers to transmit their mediocrity in an intimate environment." And they called attention to the fact that such research evidence as was available seemed to indicate that pupils learn no more in small classes than in larger ones.

In *Teachers for Tomorrow* the Fund asked, "Is our conviction that small class size is always the best guarantee of quality a valid one? Is there danger that this conviction, followed blindly, may lead toward quality erosion instead of the reverse?" [6] The Fund was convinced that there was such a danger. The Fund, and Mr. Eurich in particular, believed that small classes were no guarantee whatever of quality. Eurich held that class size should be varied with the subject of instruction and the teaching techniques used; that team teaching would make it possible to offer effective instruction to groups ranging in size from eight or ten to as many as one hundred or more. He was convinced that the proper use of television could bring the best teachers to thousands of students at a time and that with teacher aides fewer certified teachers would be needed in the schools.

The Fund called attention to the fact that other professions have raised the status and income of their members by making better use of various kinds of assistants. Between 1900 and 1949 the number of people in the nation per physician rose from 645 to 826 and it has continued to rise since that time, but the quality of medical service has improved because physicians now make more use of laboratory technicians and nurses, while nurses, in turn, now delegate many of their duties to nurse's aides. But between 1900 and 1950 the number of students per teacher in public elementary and secondary schools *dropped* from 36.7 to 27.5.[7] The Fund held that there

[6] FAE, *Teachers for Tomorrow*, p. 46.   [7] Ibid., p. 70.

was little chance of improving either the status or the salaries of teachers as long as each teacher was able to work with only a small number of students and so long as the teacher accepted the responsibility for many such nonprofessional duties as collecting milk money, keeping records, administering first aid, supervising the lunch hour, and listing library books.

Eventually both teachers and the organizations that represent teachers came to accept teacher aides with the proviso that the number of teachers would not be reduced. The Fund's arguments that schools making use of teacher aides, and of televised instruction, could reduce the number of teachers fell on deaf ears. Only at the college level did large classes become common, particularly in the multiversities where, in the Sixties, freshmen and sophomore lecture classes of five hundred to one thousand students were no longer rare. But such class size is defended, not on the ground that it makes for superior instruction, but because it reduces the cost of lower division instruction and makes more money available for the instruction of upper classmen and graduate students. Students in a number of universities have protested vigorously against such large classes, and few professors really like them.

At the secondary level the feasibility of variable class size has been demonstrated in many experimental schools and the practice is spreading, particularly in schools using a team approach. It is difficult for anyone to deny that a class of thirty is the wrong size for any kind of instruction — it is much too large for an effective discussion in which all students are to participate, but if the teacher is to lecture or demonstrate, while the students watch and listen, the class can just as well be considerably larger. In the great majority of high schools, however, the class of thirty has remained the rule despite the fact that research has failed to demonstrate that students learn more in small classes.

At the elementary level the effort to persuade teachers to

accept larger classes was a lost cause from the start because the opposition to it has little to do with the quality of learning. Teachers oppose larger classes because it has been their experience that such classes impose a much heavier burden on the teacher, even when there is an aide to do the routine work. In the great majority of elementary schools (and in some secondary schools as well) a large part of the time and energy of the average teacher is devoted just to keeping order. When there are twenty-five or thirty children in the room most teachers can keep things orderly and quiet enough to make some kind of instruction possible, but when the class size is increased to fifty or sixty it reaches a critical mass which makes the maintenance of order much more difficult. Often the noise level increases to a point where instruction is impossible.

The fact that some exceptionally skillful teachers can handle large classes effectively is not persuasive to the great majority of teachers who are unable to do so. It does no good to argue that children *ought* to be quiet and orderly, that order and quiet are not necessary when sound instructional methods are used, or that a teacher *ought* to be able to keep order in large classes. The fact is that in most elementary and many secondary classrooms keeping order is still a problem. And every teacher knows it.

It seems probable that the officers and directors of the Fund, most of whom had never taught in a public school, were unaware of this problem. Their own experience as pupils was far in the past. They had visited schools, of course, but a visitor rarely sees a classroom in its normal state — his presence completely alters the situation, as every experienced teacher knows. When a visitor comes in, accompanied by a principal or superintendent, even the most disorderly class comes to attention.

In some exceptional schools, where morale is high, the children are highly motivated, and the teachers are exceptionally skilled, it may be possible, with new instructional techniques and a new curriculum, to make use of large-group instruction even for small children for a part of the day. Many experiments today are focused on "discovery learning" as a means of both reducing the teacher-pupil ratio and improving the quality of the learning experience. The use of a "prepared environment" and special educational materials, and encouraging children to teach each other are techniques designed to enable teachers to give more of their attention to helping children to learn and less to the unproductive chore of establishing and maintaining discipline for its own sake. But children will always be restless and energetic, and when they are small their attention span is short. Teachers will continue to prefer to teach them in small groups — and to hope for groups much smaller than thirty.

A commonly heard criticism of the Fund during its early years was that its officers were too eager to replace formal professional courses for teachers with seminars, held in conjunction with the internship, in which classroom problems were discussed with the supervisor. Mr. Faust denies that this was the intent. In a letter to me dated April 7, 1969, he says, "We did not propose that seminars be taught by the supervisors of interns but by scholars in the relevant disciplines (history, philosophy, psychology, etc.)."

Nevertheless, some of the programs which received Fund assistance in 1951, 1952, and 1953 do seem vulnerable to the charge that those responsible for them wished to eliminate most professional courses for teachers. These programs reflected an erroneous belief, widely held by academic scholars, that professional courses in education consist entirely of methodology. The effort to deemphasize professional courses was also an overreaction to the fact that, in the early Fifties, such courses had proliferated beyond all reason. They needed to be severely pruned, revised, and upgraded, but this is not to say that they should have been replaced entirely by seminars of a practical nature, held in conjunction with the internship, even when the candidate for teaching held an A.B. degree. A student may graduate from a good liberal arts college without having given much thought to problems of educational philosophy, without having gained much awareness of the historical development of educational institutions, and without knowing much about the psychological processes through which a child learns.

Mr. Eurich, who had been an educational psychologist, was of course aware of these facts. Writing in 1964 he said, "There was never much point . . . to irresponsible attacks that lumped together as 'method' or 'methodology' everything in teacher education that was outside the mainstream of the liberal arts. Certainly teacher education by the 1920's and 1930's had grown overfond of the methodological, but it always included professional courses or substance and, if taught well, of real value." [8]

Through the efforts of Messrs. Eurich and Faust, and partly as a result of the work of others brought into the Fund after 1954, the defects of early programs were corrected in later ones. Nearly all the projects for teacher education that received fund support after 1955 included provision for substantial courses in educational philosophy, educational psychology, and the history of education.

The inclusion of such courses in later programs reduced the amount of criticism of the Fund but did not eliminate it because, in some colleges, the professional courses were taught by psychologists, historians, or philosophers who had no professional degrees in education. Understandably, the professional educators saw this as a threat to their professional status

[8] Ronald Gross and Judith Murphy, eds., "Preparing Better Teachers" in *The Revolution in the Schools* (New York: Harcourt, Brace and World, 1964), p. 67.

as well as to their careers, even though the tradition of recruiting professors of education from these academic disciplines has a long history that includes some of the great names in American education.

Another criticism that had some basis in fact was that most of the Fund support for programs in teacher education went to private colleges and universities at a time when the majority of teachers were being produced by publicly supported institutions. (The large grant to the University of Arkansas was an outstanding exception to the rule, but a part of this money was dispersed by the University to the private colleges within the state.) During the entire period of the Fund's operations more than two-thirds of all public school teachers came from state colleges and universities, and the Fund's efforts did not alter the ratio. Of the college graduates who completed their preparation for teaching in 1964, only 10.3 per cent came from private universities and 20.1 per cent from private and parochial colleges. Public universities were responsible for the preparation of 28.6 per cent while the largest percentage, 35 per cent, came from public general colleges — mostly state colleges that had once been teachers colleges. Only about 6 per cent came from institutions still called "teachers colleges." [9]

Critics charged that most of the teacher education programs supported by the Fund (after Arkansas) seemed to reflect an assumption that the proper way to prepare a teacher for the public schools was to send him first to a highly selective, highly prestigious, and very expensive private liberal arts college and then give him a Fund scholarship for a year of graduate work in an equally prestigious private university — preferably one associated with the Ivy League. They said that such an assumption was implied in the fact that most of the large grants for MAT programs went to such universities —

---

[9] NEA news release, October 29, 1967. See also NEA's "A Manual on Certification Requirements for School Personnel in the U.S.," 1967 ed.

$535,600 to Harvard, $450,000 to Yale, $275,000 to Brown, $275,000 to Johns Hopkins, and $250,000 to Cornell. Some grants went to universities ranking lower on the totem pole: $500,000 to Yeshiva, $350,000 to Temple, and $350,000 to a joint Vanderbilt-Peabody program, but it is true that state universities with the exception of Arkansas were conspicuous by their absence during the early years.

The critics were willing to admit that these MAT programs turned out some excellent teachers but said they were excellent primarily because they had been very carefully selected to begin with. They pointed to the fact that many of these MAT programs drew their candidates from colleges attended largely by students from upper income levels. Harvard, for example, drew all its MAT candidates from twenty-nine private colleges which are highly selective as well as expensive. The critics said that such programs could not hope to become models for other universities because the number of candidates for teaching that could be drawn from such sources was much too small to provide enough teachers for the American public schools.

Such criticisms cannot be dismissed lightly. Any assumption that a large proportion of the teachers needed by our schools can be or ought to be drawn from colleges catering to the upper socioeconomic level is indeed dubious. The numbers of teachers required would preclude it even if all the graduates of such colleges chose teaching as a career. And the fact is that comparatively few women and still fewer men who attend the prestigious private colleges want to become teachers in the public schools. The father who has achieved some degree of distinction as a business executive, lawyer, physician, engineer, or architect is likely to consider it a step down for his child to become a teacher in the elementary schools or even in the high school and the son or daughter is likely to share his conviction. Perhaps this bias against teaching is changing, but not rapidly.

The great majority of public school teachers have always been recruited from the lower-middle class. They are the sons and daughters of clerks, farmers, storekeepers, postmen, skilled laborers, and small businessmen. In many cases they are somewhat brighter and more academically talented than their classmates, but they rarely have the money, the background, or the inclination to go to the highly selective private colleges. Most of them go to state colleges or universities, tuition-free city colleges such as those in New York City, or to parochial colleges near their homes. Any effort to increase the number of teachers for the public schools must make the most of these sources of supply.

Moreover, it is these teachers from modest homes who are in greatest need of financial assistance during their college years and yet are least likely to get assistance from foundations. MAT programs, such as the one at Harvard, provided financial assistance during the fifth year for students from more prosperous homes who had been able to attend expensive private schools. It did little or nothing for the much larger number of prospective teachers who needed assistance most.

Anyone examining the list of universities to which the Fund provided assistance for MAT programs might assume that the Fund preferred to give its money to universities that already were prestigious and well endowed, or that it was particularly eager to have the name of the Fund associated with Ivy League institutions. There is some basis for these assumptions. But in selecting the universities in which to support fifth-year programs in teacher education other factors were at work. Private colleges and universities made many more proposals to the Fund than did public ones and — perhaps because they were more dependent on philanthropic money and have had more experience in working with foundations — their plans usually were more imaginative and more carefully drawn. The private universities were willing, and in some cases eager, to establish or expand programs leading to the MAT degree at a time when most state institutions were reluctant to do so, preferring to offer undergraduate programs leading to the B.S. in Ed. degree followed by the master's degree in education. Moreover, the private universities were able to select candidates rigorously at a time when many state colleges and universities thought they should admit almost any college student to the teacher education program to alleviate the teacher shortage.

The Fund officers saw less need to give assistance to state institutions which they were convinced would continue to turn out many teachers even without such help. Private institutions were producing fewer than their share and needed encouragement to produce more. They justified the selection of prestigious universities for the MAT programs by observing that their purpose was to establish models which lesser institutions might strive to emulate.

After 1962 about half the grants made under the Ford Foundation breakthrough program went to public institutions: the Oregon State Department of Education received $3,500,000; the University of Wisconsin, $500,000; Puerto Rico Department of Education, $325,000; University of California at Berkeley, $235,000; and Colorado State College, $192,000. The charge that the assistance was going exclusively to private universities no longer was valid. Still, it seems probable that if an earlier effort had been made — even after the difficulties encountered in Arkansas — to launch a more direct and continued attack on the problems of improving education in the state colleges that produce most of the teachers, the results might have improved the education of a larger number of teachers with less delay.

Individuals whose applications for grants were rejected sometimes charged that personal friendships played too large a part in the grant making. They noted that some of the larger grants went to men who had been longtime friends of the officers of the Fund and came to the conclusion that individuals unknown to the officers were seriously handicapped when they applied for assistance. Probably such charges are leveled against all foundations from time to time, and perhaps it is inevitable that there will be some basis for them. Nevertheless the facts deserve examination.

It is true that some of the larger grants went to institutions headed by men who were well known to one or another of the Fund officers. Mortimer Adler, who received a half-million-dollar grant to establish the Institute for Philosophical Research, had been an associate of Faust (and more particularly of Hutchins) since their days at the University of Chicago. Arkansas was selected for the massive, statewide reform program in teacher education primarily because the dean of the School of Education at the Univeristy of Arkansas was a former graduate student of Eurich's and the president of the University was a personal friend. The Portland, Oregon, school district, which received substantial grants, was headed, in the early Fifties, by Paul Rehmus, whom Eurich had known since high school days and in whom he had great confidence. The experiment with teacher aides was located at Bay City, the town in which Eurich had gone to school, and Central Michigan College, which assisted with the program, was headed by a longtime friend.

It cannot be assumed, however, that there is anything reprehensible about these facts. Both Faust and Eurich had such wide acquaintance among the nation's leading educational administrators that they could not easily have avoided making some of their grants to men whom they had known for years. Moreover, both were convinced, and rightly so, that the success of an innovative project depends more on the imagination and vigor of its leader, and on the willingness of the top administrator to support the project vigorously, than on any other factor. They made grants to institutions where such leadership was known to exist, and turned down requests when the leadership appeared to be weak.

It is undoubtedly true that an educator who was personally and favorably known to one of the officers got a more cordial reception when he came to the Fund with a request than someone totally unknown to them. He might be given more time or taken to lunch. But unless the proposal was a sound one personal friendship did not greatly increase his chances of getting a grant. Against the list of grants made to old friends, a much longer list could be compiled of grants made to institutions headed by men who were totally unknown to Fund officers until the application was received. No grant request was turned down merely because of the obscurity of the applicant; the officers were on the lookout for original and imaginative proposals from obscure individuals in remote places. It is worth noting that although Faust and Eurich had attended the same undergraduate college, the Fund made no grants to their alma mater.

Another criticism offered by individuals whose applications for grants had been rejected was that instead of giving an equal hearing to all proposals the Fund officers decided in advance what kinds of programs they wished to support and consequently often turned down excellent proposals on the ground that they were "outside the scope of our present program." It is true that most of the grants were made within preestablished program areas which had been approved in advance by the board of directors. The question is whether such a policy is sound.

The decision to concentrate on a limited number of program areas was made after careful consideration of the dangers of "scatteration giving." It was concluded that small, isolated programs, however sound, were unlikely to survive and unlikely to have widespread influence if they did survive. The officers and directors were convinced that to break through the resistance met by any new approach to education it is necessary to establish a critical mass of experimental approaches involving many individuals in a number of institutions. Those familiar with the problems of innovation probably will agree with this judgment.

A criticism often voiced, though rarely seen in print, was that in selecting its advisory groups and committees, and when inviting people to conferences, the Fund relied too exclusively on administrators and too little on teachers. This was particularly true of the representatives selected to plan programs in elementary and secondary education. At the college level, professors were often invited to participate, but when public school education was the topic for discussion well over 90 per cent of the participants were supervisors, principals, or superintendents. On one occasion the Fund did hold a conference on the teaching of reading in which all the participants were primary school teachers but this was one of the rare exceptions.

There were a number of reasons for this neglect, which was not unique to the Fund but characteristic of other foundations as well. If a conference is held during the school year an administrator usually finds it easier to get away for a few days, even though he may pride himself on being a very busy man. If it is held during the summer months the administrator, who is paid on a twelve-month basis, suffers no loss in salary, while the teacher, who in most cases is not paid during the summer, either has other employment or is a student at a university. Consequently teachers find it difficult and expensive to attend such a conference. But the most important reason for the preponderance of administrators on committees and at conferences was their higher visibility. The officers of the Fund were personally acquainted with many school and college administrators; their acquaintance with public school teachers was much more limited.

Foundation officers and directors are familiar with the worlds of business, industry, and government, where everyone who holds a position of any real importance is in some sense an executive or at least a "junior executive." Only in teaching and a few other learned professions can an individual hold a position of great responsibility — one in which wisdom, judgment, and decision making are required — without acquiring an administrative title. But, in education, the assumption that the "best" people — those who are most intelligent, most perceptive, best informed, most intellectually sophisticated, and most deeply concerned about the improvement of education — inevitably move into administrative positions cannot be justified. Some teachers who far surpass their principals and superintendents in ability prefer not to become involved in administrative detail and choose to remain in the classroom even though it means a lower salary. The Fund could have made a real breakthrough by seeking out more such individuals, however difficult the search might have been, and by making the most of their ability to guide the course of educational innovation. A few, indeed, were brought in, but the number might well have been much larger. It is true that most of the administrators had at one time or another been classroom teachers, but the man or woman who spends a few years in the classroom and then twenty years in the front office comes to a view of education that is substantially different from that of the one who remains a teacher. The absence of teachers from the advisory groups — or the low proportion of them — gave undue emphasis to the administrative point of view in the discussions and resulted in some blind spots so far as classroom problems are concerned.

Much of the criticism received by the Fund reflected the

view that philanthropic organizations ought to *support* education instead of trying to change it. Some critics even went so
far as to contend that the officers of a foundation have no
right to promote change in education — that their purpose
should be to distribute the available money to educators holding administrative positions and let them decide how it should
be used.

The officers and directors of the Fund sharply rejected this
view. They pointed out that the Fund's name as well as its
charter committed it, not to the support of existing practices
but to the *advancement* of education. On one occasion Mr.
Eurich said, "Mere expansion of present practices is not
enough. The way forward is necessarily a new way. To create
the new some of the old must be constructively destroyed." [10]
Most of those who have had experience in philanthropic giving will agree that support of the status quo is not enough —
that philanthropic funds should indeed promote change. If
Carnegie had been interested only in supporting medical
schools as they existed in 1910, medical education in the
United States might still be in the sorry state that Abraham
Flexner found it in 1910. By sponsoring the Flexner report on
medical education — highly critical of the situation — Carnegie brought about substantial change when change was
clearly necessary and the profession itself was not prepared to
effect it.

The relationship of a foundation to a recipient of a grant,
both before and after the grant is made, is a delicate one.
Foundation officers ought to offer advice and assistance but
they should not exert so much control as to stifle the initiative
of the grant recipient. Establishing just the right balance requires tact and judgment. Some grant recipients were critical
of the Fund for offering too much advice, or for exerting too

[10] Judith Murphy and Ronald Gross, *Learning by Television*, 1966, p. 6.

much control, others for giving too little assistance after the grant was made.

Professor Robert Bush of Stanford says:

Although [the Fund] was accused of "monitoring" funds after they were granted, the exact opposite was my experience. They did scrutinize carefully, almost annoyingly, before they granted money, and at times may have tried too much to get their own views accepted by the potential grantee. He is after all in a tender state. Once they made the grant, however, they got out of the way and let me proceed with complete freedom, being even perhaps too relaxed in the kinds of reports which they exacted from the projects." [11]

The charge that foundations limit the freedom of grant recipients is also denied by Professor Robert Anderson of Harvard who worked closely with the Fund on a number of projects:

The foundations have probably made their share of mistakes, but on the whole it seems their influence has been of magnificent dimensions. Further, the writers of this volume, admittedly the beneficiaries of substantial grants, have never felt that their own freedom of thought or action was even minutely limited by the behavior and expectations of the foundation personnel with whom they have dealt. In other words, the integrity of the foundations in their relationship to educators has not seemed questionable.

What may be the real problem is the integrity of some educators. Many a school man has probably found himself hungering after the same dollars and fame to which certain of his friends have fallen heir, and cynically he may have been tempted to announce his conversion to the same religion. If team teaching (or television teaching, or foreign language laboratories, or what have you) seems to be attracting the foundation fish these days, he cheerfully baits his hook with it. Quite likely such behavior, reprehensible though it may be, is among the chief reasons for the feeling that the foundations cause educators to sell their souls. Sometimes it appears that there is a seller's market.[12]

[11] Letter to the author dated January 6, 1969; quoted by permission.
[12] Judson T. Shaplin and Henry F. Olds, Jr., eds., *Team Teaching* (New York: Harper & Row, 1964), p. 267.

The Fund was criticized, at different times and by different people, on the one hand for spending too much money on research and on the other for giving too little attention to research. It is difficult to evaluate such criticism because there is no easy way of determining just how much research is "enough" or of evaluating the long-range effectiveness of research.

While some educators continue to stress the need for more research as the solution to a wide variety of problems, others are convinced that foundations have gone too far in their willingness to ignore problems which must be dealt with immediately. This is the view of Dwight MacDonald who says, "A philanthropoid would deal with the problem of a man trapped in a burning house by subsidizing a study of combustion." [13] And indeed he might, but he would reply that the problem of rescuing the man in the burning building is one for the fire department, not for a foundation, and that the philanthropoid would only get in the way if he rushed in with a grant while the fire still was blazing. Still there are problems of immediate import, including some of broad social significance, that will not wait for further research. Sometimes a foundation, because it can move rapidly, without legislative action or the support of public opinion, is in a better position than any other agency to attack such problems immediately and directly. Perhaps there are times when it is appropriate for a foundation to put out a fire.

The Fund preferred whenever possible to give its support to action programs that would change the course of American education; it was less prone than most foundations to solve problems by sponsoring research. And for this it was often criticized by educators. It was criticized for attempting to move the entire state of Arkansas to a new approach to

[13] Dwight MacDonald, *The Ford Foundation: The Men and the Millions* (New York: Reynal, 1956), p. 105.

teacher education before the new program had been proved superior to traditional programs. It was criticized for supporting large-scale programs of televised instruction before the usefulness of the new medium had been proved to the satisfaction of the critics. In both cases, however, the kind of research demanded would have taken many years and would probably have led to inconclusive results because of the vast number of variables that influence what children learn and because educators cannot agree on what they ought to learn. For these and for many other reasons (including the difficulty for measuring accurately some of the most important but indirect consequences of education including changes in character and personality) research does not lead to the kind of conclusive results in education that it does in medicine or aeronautical engineering or other sciences.

Despite these difficulties, most of the educators who held prominent positions in the early Fifties were convinced that research is the proper approach to most educational problems and were prone to answer questions about methodology and sometimes even questions about the goals of education with statements beginning, "Research says . . ." The directors of the Fund, in contrast, had much less confidence in research as a solution to educational problems. It seems probable that most of them had only a modest degree of familiarity with such research. Mr. Eurich, who was familiar with and had conducted research on a number of educational problems, had become disillusioned about its value as a guide to action. Consequently, although the Fund supported many programs that were "experimental" in the sense of trying something new, it did not often support programs in which the scientific method of rigorously controlled experimentation was applied to educational problems.

Much of the criticism of the Fund cannot be documented because it did not appear in print. In assembling the preceding pages I have relied heavily on the recollections of men and women who worked for, with, or against the Fund and who still remember something of these events. But one painful controversy that can be specifically documented was that which came to be known as the "Briggs Affair."

When the Fund was only a month old the officers invited a small group of distinguished educators to meet with them to discuss educational problems and to advise on Fund policy. Thomas Briggs, a senior professor of education at Columbia University Teachers College was one of the group. In 1954 Briggs resigned from this advisory committee with a blast at the Fund that was printed as a lead article in *School and Society* and consequently was widely read by educators.

In his letter of resignation (addressed to President Faust) Briggs charged the Fund with taking actions that had brought discredit upon professional educators. He said, in part, ". . . as the Officers of the Fund for the Advancement of Education have not used its Advisory Committee in any effective way and as there is no indication that they are likely to do so in the future, and also as I am not in sympathy with important parts of the program that is being promoted, I tender my resignation. . . ." After offering a bill of particulars he added:

I have been disturbed by your complacent expression of opinion that the Fund has excellent public relations. On the contrary, at least among educators, I have yet to hear one word of approval of the record so far made. The fact of deterioration of public relations is concealed from you because you hear only from those who, uninformed about the real needs of education, approve, as everyone must do, the generalities expressed in your addresses and publications, and who have no basis for sound critical judgment of the particular projects that you are promoting.

Briggs charged the officers of the Fund with having a hostile attitude toward professional education and said that ". . . able and responsible people think that their proposals have not received hospitable, or even fair, consideration. Several such people . . . have reported that they have been rebuffed by a subordinate employee with no assurance that their proposals have ever been seen by policy-making officers of the Fund or by the Board of Directors." Briggs also charged Fund officers with arrogance and an "assumption of omniscience" and said that "on the policy-making staff there is not a single person who knows our schools from firsthand experience.[14]

There was much more. Briggs's letter of resignation contains in capsule form just about every accusation that was ever leveled against the Fund.

But all the other members of the Advisory Committee — Courtney C. Brown, William H. Cornog, Paul A. Rehmus, Prudence Cutright, Ed McCuistion, Lester Nelson, Willard Olson, and Ralph Tyler — sharply disagreed with Thomas Briggs. In a letter titled "We Choose to Stay," also printed in *School and Society*, they expressed confidence in the ability and integrity of Fund officers, listed some of the Fund's achievements, and disagreed with Briggs's conception of the proper role of philanthropic foundations. They said:

It is no discredit to professional education if the Fund uses its resources to test or refine existing practice, or initiates proposals which may not be according to conventional or accepted patterns. In doing this, the Fund will sometimes have to pay the price of temporary unpopularity. We believe that the vast majority of informed educators have no fear, but will welcome new ideas in the educational market place. . . . All fair men will recognize that in making selections of projects Fund officers cannot always act with invariable wisdom. Mistakes will be made. "Risk capital" cannot always be expected to bring in an oil well. . . . We do not share Dr. Briggs's views. We choose to stay.[15]

[14] Thomas H. Briggs, "I Must Resign," *School and Society*, April 17, 1954, pp. 113–116.
[15] Courtney C. Brown et al., "We Choose to Stay," *School and Society*, July 24, 1954, pp. 27–29.

Although he was outvoted eight to one by his own committee, Briggs was not willing to let the matter rest. He came back with a "Surrebuttal," also printed in *School and Society*, in which he restated his charges and added some new ones.[16]

As a result of his attack on the Fund, Professor Briggs became a star witness before the congressional "Reese Committee" which was investigating the activities of philanthropic foundations. Here he made the most of the opportunity to give greater publicity to his criticisms. He testified that all the officers of the Fund had been appointed, directly or indirectly, by one influential executive of the parent foundation (presumably Hutchins), and that these officers presented to the board of their own organization "a program so general as to get approval and yet so indefinite as to permit activities which in the judgment of competent critics are either wasteful or harmful to the education program which has been approved by the public." He added that the Fund was improperly manned with an inexperienced staff, "out of sympathy with the democratic idea of giving appropriate education to all the children of all the people," and said, "not a single member of the staff, from the president down to the lowliest employee, has had any experience, certainly none in recent years, that would give understanding of the problems that are met daily by the teachers and administrators of our public schools." [17]

The Reese Committee was not much interested in a quarrel among educators and failed to find what it was looking for — evidence of subversion in the Fund or the Foundation. But the board of the Ford Foundation was disturbed by the threatened loss of its tax-exempt status and became more cautious as a result of the investigation. It may be that this caution

16 Thomas H. Briggs, "Surrebuttal," *School and Society*, September 18, 1954, pp. 87–89.
17 Quoted in René A. Wormser, *Foundations: Their Power and Influence* (New York: Devin-Adair, 1958), pp. 253–257. (Wormser was general counsel to the Reese Committee.)

was a factor in the Foundation's decision to give less independence to the separate Funds but this could not have been a logical consequence. The most damaging testimony to come before the Reese Committee was the evidence of jury tapping as a part of a sociological investigation which had been done with grants made, not by the Fund but by the Behavioral Science Division of the Ford Foundation. The committee found no evidence that the separate funds were any less responsible or wise than the Foundation itself.

Among professional educators, particularly professors of education, the widespread publicity given to the Briggs Affair did more damage to the Fund's reputation than the officers were, or are today, willing to concede. It confirmed the conviction that the Fund was hostile to those whom it looked upon as "educationists."

This conviction was not entirely without basis. It is true that the officers and directors of the Fund had serious doubts about the ability and wisdom of many of those who held responsible positions as professional educators in the early Fifties and were so thoroughly convinced of the need for dramatic changes in education, particularly in teacher education, that they took actions that could easily be interpreted as highhanded. Though they sought professional advice, they were not easily persuaded to accept that which went counter to their own convictions. But the other eight members of the Advisory Committee, who remained after Briggs resigned, had a considerable amount of influence on Fund policy.

It is true that prior to 1954 the Fund staff was lacking in members who had a firsthand familiarity with the problems of elementary and secondary education. Whether such familiarity is absolutely essential might be debated (at any rate it was debated by the directors), but it is worth noting that after 1954 the Fund did add staff members who had been closely associated with the public schools. It seems probable that these additions may have come as a result of the criticisms that came from Briggs and other educators.

To a large extent the Briggs Affair seems to have been a clash of personalities between a strong-willed educator and an organization whose officers held educational views in direct opposition to his. In the early Fifties, Briggs's educational philosophy was closer to that of the educational establishment than was the philosophy of the Fund but it was a philosophy that reflected a period in American education that was drawing to a close. His view that education is best left to professional educators was no longer acceptable to the American people, who had become convinced that education is too important to be left to any one professional group, however well qualified. The Fund officers were better aware of the need for dramatic changes in education and more willing to challenge the traditional wisdom which many educators of the day were still defending.

THE JUDGMENT OF EDUCATORS

The long-range influence of a philanthropic foundation does not easily lend itself to objective measurement. Consequently, in undertaking an appraisal of the work of the Fund for the Advancement of Education it has been necessary to rely heavily on professional opinion, particularly the opinion of men who have been in a position to observe the work of the Fund and its influence on American education.

In 1968 I wrote to a number of educators in many parts of the nation to ask for their overall judgments of the work of the Fund, both its contributions and its most notable mistakes or failures. I tried to make it clear that I was asking not for eulogies but for critical comments regarding errors or oversights which might reflect biases, blind spots, or mistaken judgments on the part of staff members, officers, or directors of the Fund. My request went to a number of individuals who had been critical of the Fund as well as to some who had expressed admiration for its work and to still others whose views were unknown to me.

The summary of their responses, which are quoted by permission, is a revealing distillation of professional judgments full of insights on the merits and demerits of the Fund's programs. I shall present first the favorable comments and then the criticisms, though in many cases both were included in the same letters.

John H. Fischer, president of Columbia's Teachers College, says:

In my view the Fund for the Advancement of Education played a very useful role during its time on the American educational scene. When it began the American educational system badly needed to be shaken up and as I reflect upon the Fund's work, this was its principal contribution. To use a friend's words — it comforted the afflicted and afflicted the comfortable. It deserves a large share of the credit for generating in both the establishment and its critics a spirit of innovation that long was lacking. Much of the best of subsequent Federal activity is traceable directly or indirectly to the beginnings the Fund made possible.

Within the educational system, the Fund encouraged the more adventurous people whose initiative might otherwise never have had a chance to emerge, much less flourish. Outside of the establishment, the Fund persuaded many individuals and groups that they could and should play a part in educational affairs, and the consequences of the broadened involvement are still spreading. Among them is a decline in the foolish conflicts between the proponents of content and method in teacher education. While some, of course, thought that the professional emphasis was too heavily downgraded, as in some cases it may have been, the total effect, on balance, has been all to the good.

Lindley J. Stiles, professor of education for interdisciplinary studies at Northwestern University, says:

The most valuable contribution of the Fund, in my opinion, was its thrust to begin what some of us call the reform of teacher education.

To be sure the task is yet to be completed, but without the help of the Fund it would never have been begun — at least not as soon as it was. I consider the pioneering of a Master of Arts in Teaching program to be significant. Many of these [MAT programs], of course, carry the name only. They represent nothing more than the master's degree programs in education with some kind of student teaching or internship added. The original conception of the M.A.T. programs, however, has already had a significant influence upon the thinking of those who are involved in teacher education. These programs have attracted the participation of liberal arts scholars in developing programs to prepare teachers, they have recruited for teaching outstanding liberal arts graduates, and they have shifted the focus in professional preparation to the internship which in itself has been improved in a variety of ways, one of the most important of which is the intern in team plan that the University of Wisconsin developed. Looking back over the past twenty years I think nothing has stimulated more intensive innovation in teacher education than the M.A.T. program supported by the Fund for the Advancement of Education.

Henry Hill, president emeritus of George Peabody College for Teachers, agrees with Stiles on the significance of the Fund's contribution, saying:

I think the Fund gave an emphasis to teacher education and a respect for it at a time when many influential leaders in education could find no kind words for it . . . in my judgment, the Fund with its money provided for some thousands of students a better program for teaching than would have been available otherwise . . . [it] located some good leaders in the new movement in teacher education, and in some instances these leaders continue to be successful with some of the Ford ideas.

Robert Havighurst says, "From the vantage point of 1969, I would say that the most influential work of the Fund was one in Teacher Education, with the High School Curriculum second. Relatively neglected were the problems of the Big-City Education though this may have been partly due to an agreement between the Fund and the developing program of the Ford Foundation to leave that area to the latter."

Other commentators, particularly the presidents of liberal arts colleges, rate the contribution to the improvement of college teaching through the faculty fellowship program as the Fund's most significant achievement. Laurence Gould, who had an opportunity to observe the work of the Fund, both as president of Carleton College and as a trustee of the Ford Foundation, says, "I remember the great impact the Faculty Fellowships made throughout the academic world . . . if the Fund had done nothing but this, I would still have a very high opinion of it." And he adds, "I have always had some reservations about the experiment in the state of Arkansas . . . even so, I would not judge a fund of this sort on the basis of its failures. It was designed to experiment in areas where others feared to tread. Obviously it took gambles but it took them on the basis of careful study. I think Clarence Faust was extremely effective in this whole area."

Several of the respondents commented on the success of the Fund in challenging the educational axioms and stimulating innovation. Harold Howe II, who was a high school principal at Newton, Massachusetts, and then superintendent of schools at Scarsdale, New York, before becoming U.S. commissioner of education, says,

. . . the most valuable contribution of the Fund was the stirring of the complacency of the world of secondary education. The activities of the Fund called into question all of the variables in a secondary school — teachers, curriculum, organization, staffing patterns, etc. Even today some of the major directions being pursued with much larger funds by the federal government are the same directions which were instituted early in the activities of the Fund.

Harold Gores, who is now president of the Educational Facilities Laboratories but who was a recipient of a number of

Fund grants when he was superintendent of schools in Newton, Massachusetts, agrees and adds some comments on the
need for foundation money in stimulating innovation. He
says:

. . . secondary education through the 1940's was a sleeping giant,
unchanged for the most part since the reorganization of 1893. The
progressive education movement never really got in the door of the
American high school, and the junior high school movement failed
to produce schools which were new art forms. The typical junior high
school of the 1930's and 1940's was a miniaturized high school, extending downward to the 7th grade the mixed blessings of the depart-
mentalization, bell schedules, and bands. In the early '50's when the
giant began to stir, grants from the Fund for the Advancement of
Education — the first thinking money most schools ever had — sup-
plied the surplus energy which thinking and reorganization require.
The leverage — amount of change per dollar invested — was fantastically high compared with how much money, federal and philanthropic, it takes today to make any recognizable change in education.

In retrospect, it couldn't have just been FAE's money which helped
the schools to move. As much as the money it was the sense of com-
panionship, the comfort and protection of being in the company of
respected people who believed that change was respectable.

And Willard C. Olson, dean of the School of Education,
University of Michigan, says, "In looking back over the years
of the activities of the Fund, I believe a major contribution
has been the introduction of a spirit of creativity and innovation in education based upon what might be called 'wisdom
research.' "

T. M. Stinnett, during the years of the Fund's activity, was
executive secretary of the National Commission on Teacher
Education and Professional Standards of the National Education Association — an organization that on a number of occasions viewed some of the Fund's programs with alarm. In retrospect, he says:

As you know, I have at certain points been a severe critic of the Fund. Yet, I would be the first to say that, overall, it has made significant contributions to progress in teacher education. I do not question at all that the Fund has had great influence on securing a break away from the extreme concentration upon methodology which most teacher education institutions and state departments of education inherited from the normal schools and teachers colleges. That severance led to a vast strengthening of the liberal preparation of teachers, the telescoping of the professional sequence, and the reduction of education require-ments by state departments of education.

This influence, to which the Carnegie Corporation also contributed heavily, laid the groundwork for the three cooperative conferences (Bowling Green, Kansas, and San Diego) of the National Commission on Teacher Education and Professional Standards. These conferences, as you know, helped materially to create a new climate for critical evaluation of existing teacher education programs, and a new (if not universal and enduring) sense of cooperative fellowship between lib-eral arts and professional education personnel.

Professor Robert N. Bush, director of the Center for Re-search and Development in Teaching at Stanford University, says:

My overall judgment of the Fund is that it was enormously successful. Considering the relatively limited funds available, it is correct to state, to paraphrase an overquoted statement, "never has so little been used so wisely to accomplish so much." It seems to me in retrospect that the staff looked long and deeply into the root problems of American education, selected ones that appeared to them most pressing, and then set out to break the mold by which education in these areas was being conducted and the way in which the problems had been looked at. They also invited radical, unorthodox, new, and even far-out, bizarre, and on first glance perhaps silly approaches to these problems. These they then analyzed, depending heavily upon their judgment and faith in the capacity of the individuals who proposed them, and eventually funded those selected with needed money that would enable them to explore, to try out their ideas. The net effect was to fund some things that did not turn out well, and some that failed miserably. Their batting average, however, appeared to be high, given the hazardous area in which they were working. They did well in terms of their reference, namely, the expenditure of "risk" capital. It exemplified in the best sense what the Foundation in its larger areas was supposed to be following, but which it did not nor could not always do because of more conservative influences at work. . . .

In its promotion of reform in teacher education, in more imaginative uses of teaching staff, and in curricular reform, which were the fields where I was most identified, I believe that they were one, if not the single most leavening force during the years they operated. I believe that the work that the Federal Government is now beginning to support would have been much longer in coming had it not been for the vigorous activities of the Fund.

Mortimer Smith, executive director of the Council for Basic Education and editor of the CBE bulletin says:

Any appraisal I might make of the work of the Fund for the Advancement of Education would have to be based on limited knowledge of its operations and would necessarily be somewhat impressionistic. . . . The record of any foundation, of course, includes hits and misses. Certainly the Fund had its share of both. On the plus side, the first thing that comes to my mind is its record in supporting alternative ways of training teachers. I believe the Fund was a pioneer in supporting programs with stronger liberal arts content, including the MAT programs. . . . I think its support of Advanced Placement and of the John Hay Fellows Program was also on the plus side. . . . To my mind the best thing the Fund ever did was to support the Education Supplement of the *Saturday Review*. For several years this was undoubtedly the most interesting and lively example of educational journalism in the country.

As to my overall judgment of the Fund's effectiveness, my impression is that its success outweighed its failures and that on the whole it was a constructive force in improving American education.

James E. Allen, Jr., commissioner of education for New York State (later U.S. commissioner of education and assistant secretary of HEW) says,

Your letter has been discussed with several members of my staff and the following comments represent a composite of our views:

A major contribution of the Fund was to demonstrate that specially available funds on a grant basis could bring about significant change in education, an approach that has, of course, become the model for many Federal and State programs. The Fund has also made possible the carrying out of projects which could not be undertaken with public monies, perhaps because of lack of public support or because the project initiator was not eligible for public funding. Still another contribution was the provision of funds that could be utilized flexibly and without constraints that limit the ways in which public monies can be expended.

The timeliness of the innovations sponsored by the Fund was mentioned by a number of the respondents. Charles B. Park, who was president of Central Michigan State College at the time of the teacher-aide program, says:

The Fund, in my opinion, appeared on the scene just when some pump-priming was very necessary on the educational scene . . . [it] speeded up a very much needed evaluation in educational methodology, and in so doing, shortened the 50-year gap from proof to practice. The Fund, plus Federal assistance programs, played a very important role in speeding up needed change in many areas of education. The areas of interest and support in Teacher Aides, teacher education, the comprehensive school and others have made a very significant contribution to educational practices nationally. The Fund should not have been discontinued.

And Mr. Park adds:

I would like to conclude by stating that never in a period of Foundation support from 1953 [one of the first programs] for the Bay City, Michigan, Teacher Aide Program through 1970 [a program in Vocational-Technical Education] has the Fund or Foundation dictated the design of the program or insisted on Fund supervision. Central Michigan University has enjoyed one of the most continuous records of support of any institution in the country. Never have we been hog-tied or dictated to regarding the operation of our programs — which have been eminently successful.

The letters that contained the comments quoted above also included many thoughtful criticisms (including some vigorous ones) of Fund policies and activities. A number of these had to do with the relationship of the Fund to professional educators and educational organizations. From President John Fischer:

Because it was willing to try new ventures and because it had to depend ultimately on human judgment, the Fund made some mistakes. There were occasions when, in my view, its treatment of some of the established groups was a bit harsher than necessary. Change might have been brought about on a wider scale and with greater overall benefit to American education if the Fund had recognized the pos-sibilities of working with the establishment to change it, instead of ignoring, circumventing, or fighting it. (This is not to say that I am necessarily opposed to using these latter procedures, but to argue also for the utility of modifying existing mechanisms instead of relying so heavily on the creation of new ones.)

Professor Robert Bush, whose personal relations with Fund officers were excellent, agrees that the Fund might have made a greater effort to work harmoniously with professional edu-cators:

On the debit side of the ledger The Fund, either knowingly or not, I could not judge, seemed to go out of its way, at least in its earlier years, to irritate, if not downright to insult the educationists. Espe-cially, in proudly bringing in advisors and making grants to those who had no prior experience in educational matters, giving the im-pression of strongly preferring those to *anyone* inside the so-called establishment. This was perhaps a calculated strategy. They failed to realize sufficiently, and hence built a tremendous backlog of unnecessary opposition, that there were educators who for long had wanted reform, who were imaginative and creative, and who only lacked funds and a network of support that would enable them to break many of the ineffective, traditional ways. Perhaps it may not have been possible to break the molds of established practice without such brusque, at times almost brutal and seemingly unfeeling attack. But it was my observation that there were many who would have gone along with their programs and would not have opposed them so violently had they been more tempered in their comments, had they not been so extreme as often to seem to throw the baby out with the bath water, and had they not so overclaimed on pet ideas with which they became identified.

They were accused, and not without some justification, of having settled on a few solutions, and being unwilling to look beyond them for new and other ones, and to claim victory before the evidence was in. It seemed to some, especially perhaps to those who had not gotten grants, that all you had to do to become funded was to be vitriolic enough against those who were running the schools and the universities and colleges, especially the educationists. Living in both camps as I was — the recipient of a generous grant and also working in the heart of the educational establishment — I was subject to a wide-ranging barrage of criticism as enumerated above. I think it was much overplayed, but I was able to observe at first hand enough of the irritating behavior to conclude that it was not at all necessary to achieve the ends that the Fund had in mind. I recall a friend of mine who once gave me the advice, "Never insult anyone unintentionally." Surely the Fund people at times seemed to go about unsettling people unintentionally, but I fear that they also too frequently did it intentionally, perhaps from force of habit. In their later years (perhaps they were getting old and conservative too!) they mellowed, so it seemed. At least they seemed to have learned that you can never reform the schools unless you have the genuine leadership of the profession with you.

A number of other educators also commented on the attitude of Fund officers and staff members toward the educa-

tional establishment and some undertook to analyze and interpret it. From Henry Hill:

Over the years there developed in the inner circle of the Fund oper-
ators a kind of egotism and Ford Fund sophistication which did not
especially appeal to me. Perhaps this was not peculiar to this group
but rather is peculiar to all kinds of well-financed programs where
people enjoy a better break in salaries and perquisites over their breth-
ren on the outside and where, to a greater degree than is wise, they
are able to get their own way without too much difficulty. They
become wise custodians of the new sacred ark and speak with authority and some condescension.

And he adds, "The Mount Olympus concept of the Fund attracted some initial and continuing resentment from school
and college leaders who felt that they wanted to do some of
their own thinking or to be in on the Mount Olympus thinking. Some felt threatened by the Fund and many of them did
what they could to block even the most sensible Fund proposals."

Robert Havighurst offers a somewhat different interpretation. After commenting on the high visibility of the Fund
which resulted from the fact that, until 1960, "there were no
rivals of any consequence in the support of educational experimentation," he says:

Related to its visibility was its identification with certain pronounced
positions on the philosophy and conduct of education. Although an
objective examination does not justify the stereotype, yet the stereotype did exist, which described the Fund as a vehicle for the educational attitudes of Robert M. Hutchins. The President of the Fund
was seen and heard as a Hutchins' man. The early grant of $565,000
to support Mortimer Adler's Institute of Philosophical Research
tended to confirm this stereotype. Although Alvin Eurich, the Vice-
President, was more closely identified with educationists through his
work at the University of Minnesota, his later career at Stanford and
his later critical speeches directed at some aspects of the Establish-

ment distanced him from the professional fraternity of education. The outspoken criticisms of Clarence Faust on teacher education as it was generally practiced tended to give the Fund a "negative image" in the eyes of the Establishment of public education. This was heightened by the "Arkansas Purchase," as the critics loved to call it, and they were not about to make allowances for the good intentions of Fund officers or of the Arkansas leaders.

And Havighurst adds:

Certainly the most controversial project was the 1952–56 Teacher Education Project in the State of Arkansas. . . . In his evaluation of the project, Dean Willard Spaulding of the University of Illinois Schools of Education saw many weaknesses in the state, as well as in the conduct of affairs by the Fund, which put more than $3 million into it. There was a good deal of criticism by the educational fraternity of the fact that the Fund did not publish Spaulding's evaluation.

Commenting on the evaluation referred to by Havighurst, Willard Spaulding, in a letter dated March 4, 1969, says:

In evaluating the Arkansas Experiment in Teacher Education, David Krathwohl, my principal associate, and I were desirous of giving primary emphasis to examining the dynamics of its development and operation, secondary emphasis to its programs and products. Our desires were generally unacceptable to both the Fund personnel and Arkansas leaders, none of whom wished to have their behaviors studied for public review. Thus, we did not receive funds for the type of evaluation which we believed would contribute the most understanding to the Fund and to Arkansas as well as lead to greater perception of the interactions of a foundation and its supplicants. Nevertheless we did our best to reflect what we had learned in a mimeographed report. It never received wide distribution for, though it was under contract to a commercial publisher with subsidy from the funds we were allocated, we were not permitted to use those funds. Some data from this report, which by that time were not worthy of much attention, were included in a brief monograph prepared by another investigator. This was produced and distributed by the Fund. The full data are still available in the University of Illinois archives for those wishing to see the original report or to dig deeper into the interviews and history of what we found.

Lindley Stiles says:

With respect to the notable mistakes or failures of the Fund, I think the grossest error has been to refuse to evaluate objectively the programs it has financed. Its leadership was never willing to underwrite an assessment of the advantages of the programs initiated. This is partly understandable because those who invest money rarely are interested in taking the chance of being proved wrong. Nevertheless, I believe the Fund would have made even greater contributions if it had linked with each grant a process of evaluation to test the merits of the program.

But Harold Howe disagrees, saying, "I was always critical of the fact that the Fund had to invest just as much money in evaluating the project in Newton as it did in operating the project. What's more, it seemed to me that the people conducting the evaluation were a kind of pseudoscientific crowd, full of chatter which the ordinary man could not understand, but chatter frequently without much meaning."

Howe also suggests some possible omissions or neglect in the Fund's program:

I am not really competent to judge the failures of the Fund for I have no comprehensive knowledge, without doing a lot of reading to refresh my memory, of its total program. From this uninformed perspective, I would say that at least in its early years the Fund probably did not pay enough attention to the problem of Big Cities. Maybe the documentation will show me wrong about this. It is clear, however, that the Big Cities themselves never really got their important problems on the agenda of their school boards until the last four or five years. I think that the Fund had some effect on their doing this during the latter years but not in the beginning.

Perhaps another shortcoming of the Fund was not to recognize the significance of the preschool or early childhood education movement which has matured so rapidly in very recent years. Am I wrong in thinking that this was not a major portion of the Fund's program? By now, it seems to me, this represents the most hopeful area of educational change and improvement.

T. M. Stinnett's criticisms indicate a change of view over the years regarding Fund programs but a continued dislike for the Fund's tactics:

Let me preface these criticisms with a statement that, I think, tends to substantiate them. That statement is that at several points, and in regard to several innovations sponsored by the Fund, I was vigorously opposed. Now I find myself vigorously embracing and advocating these innovations. Specifically, I refer to the M.A.T. Programs, the use of internships, and the redeployment of the teaching job, through use of the teacher and other aides. Why do I now advocate these though I earlier opposed them? To answer this somewhat oratorical question, I would say (and I have thought this through a thousand times, so to speak) there are three categories in my criticism of the operation of the Fund: First, the approaches and processes were inappropriate. Second, there was too much "hardselling" by Fund officials of the results of experiments on some of these programs. Third, there was the mistaken (so I believe) emphasis on the power of the initiative experiment (or demonstration).

To illustrate the first category, I cite the Arkansas Experiment. The approach to this, the planning by a small committee, and announcement of the plan without prior consultation with anyone else, was, I think, inexcusable. Especially, inexcusable in the light of the sweeping nature of the proposal. For example, the conversion of the two state teachers colleges to liberal arts colleges — colleges whose functions had been fixed by the Legislature, the proposal to drop all undergraduate professional preparation in a state where the average preparation of teachers was scarcely above the two-year college level, and to substitute a five-year program of teacher education, to say the least, was unsound from any standpoint of realism.

But it was the method of planning that set me in opposition to this program. If I had the opportunity to discuss this with you, I would tell you of the background which to this day appeals to me as embodying incredible arrogance. The story is too long to delineate in a letter. I have documents to substantiate the above assertions.

Second — the hard selling — as you may remember, I served on the Advisory Committee of the Bay City Experiment. In the beginning, I was enthusiastic about this venture. What soured me on it was extravagant claims from the Fund (and I have a document to substantiate this) about what had been proved, at a time when the staff at Bay City told me that they were seeking proof, but had none as yet.

Third, the initiative aspect. I felt the Fund made the egregious error of assuming that if Harvard, Chicago, Stanford, and a few other prestigious institutions were given grants to demonstrate an idea, the other colleges and universities would sheep-like follow suit. This did not happen, even though a few did. I believe this assumption is not sound.

In a sense it is painful for me to reconstruct all this. I know I irritated many good people with my opposition, and alienated some of my long-time friends. But I think it was justified, and I still think so after all these years. . . . I now no longer have any vested interest and can view the past quite dispassionately. Finally, I repeat, I now strongly support most of the very things I quarreled with the Fund about. The ideas were often quite sound; it was the process and the approach that aroused my opposition. Incidentally, after a year of controversy the Arkansas plan that developed was all right with all concerned. But the plan was a far cry from the originally announced one.

Willard Olson comments on the cost of Fund-supported projects: "I had a feeling, particularly in the early days of the Fund's work, that the cost of some projects became so high as to militate against generalization without outside aid. Innovation is, of course, always expensive."

From James E. Allen:

On the negative side, it can be said that the Fund did not provide sufficiently for local assumption of support for projects after the termination of the Fund support and that there was not adequate evaluation of the effectiveness of the projects supported. Some of the Fund activities were remote from the activities of operating school systems, and there is some question about the objectivity with which decisions were made with respect to the approval of projects. Financial support seemed to be more available when the project initiator or director was well known to the officers of the Fund.

The early efforts of the Fund to dictate policy to grant recipients was criticized by a number of the respondents. Charles B. Park says:

. . . the Fund made a serious first mistake in designing a program and selling it to the Arkansas colleges. The criticism from this approach was costly, but to the credit of the Fund, they learned from this that they could not and should not dictate programs for funding. . . . I believe the main criticisms, as I see them, were related to the projects they funded. There appeared to be too little interest in good hard scientific evaluation and research, and . . . little concern about providing for the dissemination nationally of the successful proven projects which they supported.

Although most of the respondents applauded the Fund's efforts to encourage innovation, Mortimer Smith thinks the Fund was not sufficiently selective in its support for new approaches to education:

My impression is that at one point the Fund was rather starry-eyed about almost anything that could be called "innovation." I wonder if the Fund didn't put too much faith and money into educational television, especially in the airborne TV programs? Its support in the early days of the National Citizens Commission for the public schools was shortsighted, this being a group committed to not much beyond public relations. In looking over the grants listed in the annual reports of the Fund, it occurs to me that while some of the programs supported might strike out boldly in new directions the grantees were almost invariably either established institutions or new ones backed by solid establishment names. The Fund apparently shared the reluctance of most big foundations to get involved with groups that could possibly be thought of as "off beat" or that could be said to lack "respectability." (Now, of course, the big foundations are more adventuresome, at least when it comes to supporting black-power groups.)

Mr. Smith also observes that the Fund seemed to be more interested in, and better informed about, secondary and higher education than elementary education and thinks it unfortunate that the Fund did not make a greater effort to improve the teaching of reading in the elementary schools.

It would be difficult, if not impossible, to know how to balance these varied criticisms against the Fund's solid record of achievement which is applauded by the same observers. The history of the Fund must include a record of both. While some of the criticisms are of errors or omissions, the majority of them are of the style and attitude of Fund officials, as these were interpreted by professional educators. The fact that some educators were convinced that the Fund gave too little consideration to the views of members of the professional establishment in education, particularly in teacher education, undoubtedly was at times a barrier to effective cooperation, or rather it restricted the number of educators with whom the Fund was able to cooperate. But the basic question in the long run must be, "Did the Fund succeed in its task of advancing American education?" And even the critics agree that the answer to this question is in the affirmative.

OVERVIEW

Sixteen years is a short span in the history of mankind but a very long time in the life of a child. Boys and girls who were in the first grade when the Fund for the Advancement of Education opened its doors were about to graduate from college at the time those doors were closed. In evaluating the achievements of the Fund it is appropriate to ask, "What changes took place in the schools during those years?" and "What part did the Fund play in bringing the changes about?"

Since the Fund looked upon philanthropic money as "risk capital," to be used in trying out new approaches to education rather than as money for the support of building construction, teachers' salaries, or established programs, some risks were to be expected. If all the projects undertaken by or sponsored by the Fund had proved to be successful it would be obvious that the money had been used only for safe purposes — that no real risks had been taken. Consequently the identification of failures among Fund projects does not imply criticism of the officers and directors who chose to take the risks. Risk taking was their job. The proper question to ask in making an evaluation is not, "Were all the projects successful?" but rather, "What was the batting average?"

It seems clear, in retrospect, that some programs were more successful than others. Advanced placement programs were more successful than early admission programs — advanced placement has become a widespread practice while early admission to college still is rare. The MAT program had proven much more acceptable to educators than the Arkansas plan. Closed-circuit television has enjoyed more sustained success than airborne television.

A number of Fund projects, operations, and publications became a clear-cut success which need not be balanced against failures because there were no failures in comparable related ventures. The Ashmore report on school segregation was a significant contribution to the nation's understanding of a vexing problem, and one in which the Fund can take pride. The statistics and projections presented in *Teachers for Tomorrow*, and *Teaching Salaries Then and Now* alerted the nation to the need for higher salaries for teachers and school administrators. The Education Supplement to *Saturday Review* demonstrated the feasibility of a new approach to educational journalism. The teacher-aide plan, though it met with a considerable amount of initial opposition from educators, now is widely accepted as sound. And fellowships provided by the Fund enabled twelve hundred college teachers and one thousand high school teachers to become better prepared for their jobs.

Some projects must be put in the "doubtful" category because of lack of evidence. The half-million-dollar grant to the Institute for Philosophical Research was justified as a proper use of Fund resources on the ground that it would contribute to the clarification of educational philosophy, but there is as yet little evidence that the work of the organization has had much effect on the thinking of educational policy makers. The three-year master's program for college teachers, though soundly conceived, has not been widely accepted.

Although the Fund made grants in support of a wide variety of programs, the main thrust throughout most of its sixteen years was toward the improvement of liberal education at the secondary and higher levels. The advanced placement and early admissions programs were designed to achieve better articulation of liberal education in high school and college. The fellowship programs were designed for teachers of the academic disciplines. The programs in teacher education were designed to prepare teachers of the liberal disciplines in school and college.

This concentration of effort was a natural consequence of the Fund's conviction that excellence in education requires the fullest possible development of each individual's *intellectual* ability. The officers and directors of the Fund did not intend that liberal education of the kind they believed in should be restricted to a single social class or to academically talented students. They were convinced that if proper allowance were made for differences in rates of learning nearly all children could benefit from this kind of education, and it was their earnest hope and belief that education of a truly liberal nature might ultimately be provided for all boys and girls, rich or poor; rural, urban, or suburban; regardless of race or family background. But in their search for models of excellence they were prone to turn to the private liberal arts colleges and to the secondary schools that enroll academically talented students.

Though it was committed to liberal education as an end, the Fund was not insistent on any particular curriculum or program of liberal education. It definitely was not committed to the traditional academic disciplines or to the use of textbooks — some Fund officers would have preferred an interdisciplinary approach making use of the primary sources of scholarship and employing the Socratic method rather than lectures — but in practice most of the grants went to schools and colleges which stressed the academic disciplines, taught separately, because this was the conventional pattern in most of the schools and colleges which were chosen as models. Whatever the curriculum, the Fund was convinced that secondary and higher education should lead to a comprehensive knowledge of the nature of the world and of man and the ability to use that knowledge wisely.

The emphasis on intellectual development through academic learning is clearly demonstrated in the Fund-supported programs in teacher education. Though assistance was given to a variety of programs, the main emphasis in teacher education took the form of support for the fifth-year programs which, in the majority of cases, led to the M.A.T. or A.M.T. degree. Most of the candidates for these programs came from upper-middle-class homes and were graduates of highly selective private colleges. Some of the programs refused to accept candidates from state colleges. Candidates were selected on the basis of their liberal arts background and their desire to teach the academic subjects: mathematics, the sciences, literature, music, history, etc., in the secondary schools. After graduation, because they were in great demand, most of them found

employment in schools located in the more prosperous communities where salaries were high and working conditions
good. Because they were bright, well educated, and highly
motivated, these teachers undoubtedly contributed substantially to the improvement of educational quality in the schools
that employed them.

It is much less clear that the teachers graduating from these
programs had the special talents, interests, understandings, and
skills required of teachers who teach children of limited academic talent or children from less fortunate backgrounds than
their own. They were not selected with such a goal in mind.
Even if their courses in social psychology had given them
some awareness of and sympathy for the special problems of
Negroes, Indians, Mexican-Americans, and the rural poor,
they were likely to find it difficult to understand the outlook
of pupils who lacked their own aspirations and educational
motivations, spoke different variants of the English language,
had different folkways and mores, and saw no point in learning the traditional academic subjects. If it can be assumed that
such pupils require a different kind of teacher, it must be said
that the Fund made a major contribution to one kind of
teacher education (which will always be needed) and only a
minor contribution (mostly after 1962) to another kind of
teacher education for which the need is becoming steadily
more apparent.

In this respect the Fund was a product of its times but
particularly of the time of its origin. In 1951 the demand
throughout the nation was for a more rigorous academic and
intellectual education particularly in the high schools — a demand that reflected a widespread conviction that, during the
era of progressive education, the schools had grown soft and
had come to emphasize social and recreational activities at the
expense of academic learning. But, after 1960, the demand for
academic rigor was less often heard, partly because the na-

tion's attention had been turned toward the problems of the socially and educationally disadvantaged, but partly also because the demand had been met. By 1960 the public high schools, particularly those located in the more affluent towns and suburbs, were far from soft. According to most observers the students in these schools were working harder than ever before. Under great pressure from teachers and parents to qualify themselves for admission to prestigious colleges which had insufficient room for them, they were applying their energies vigorously to the subjects that had been said to be neglected a decade earlier. Thus there was no longer a need for foundation support for programs to raise academic standards. In a sense the Fund was a victim of its own success.

By the time the Fund had become aware of the need to divert its energies into new channels, its staff was becoming a part of the Ford Foundation. The effort to solve the problems of urban schools where demand was not so much for intellectual rigor in the academic disciplines as for compensatory education for the disadvantaged became a foundation effort, even though some parts of that effort were begun by Fund officers.

Because the Fund chose to concentrate its efforts on a small number of problems, it was inevitable that some areas of education would be neglected or left to other agencies. Looking back on the activities of the Fund after his retirement (and after reading a portion of this manuscript), Clarence Faust said:

It may be that we were blind to some important things — to the significance of the beatniks, for instance, and to the implications of the migration of Southern Negroes to Northern cities, or to the young people who were to become society's dropouts. Anyhow our attention was on other matters which then seemed more important or menacing. Maybe we were too academically oriented. But things looked very different to us in the early days of the Fund than they look now in retrospect of the late Sixties. Perhaps we should have been more far-sighted; perhaps we should have been more aware of the major trends in society as a whole; perhaps we should have been less attentive to what educators were worrying about. But in line with what has been called "the problem orientation" of the Foundation and the Fund we were most aware of the day-by-day worries of those in the educational system, so that the feel of the Fund in its earlier days was not quite the feel we would have if we were operating now. The things that concerned us were advancing the educational system, getting public support and an understanding of it, improving teacher education and producing people in education to make better use of their existing resources and to experiment in the areas of articulation of the system.[18]

It would be an easy task for an historian with the benefit of hindsight to expand the list of mistakes, failures, lost causes, and missed opportunities. I agree with Mr. Faust that the Fund might well have been more alert, in the early Fifties, to the educational problems that were bound to result from the mass migration of families from the rural South to the central cities of the North. Any foundation could have made a magnificent contribution to higher education and to the stability of the nation by anticipating the student revolts and protest movements of the Sixties and finding some way of eliminating the need for them. It would be applauded for its foresight if it had predicted, fifteen years ago, that young men and women from affluent upper-middle-class homes would turn their backs on the society that had nourished and protected them, and would become the hippies and flower children of the Sixties. An early investigation of the growing use of psychedelic drugs in high school and college might have had great value. But no single philanthropic organization could do it all, and the Fund was not alone in failing to anticipate the problems that would emerge in the years just ahead.

The Fund's positive achievements were more than enough

[18] Letter to the author dated January 16, 1969; quoted by permission.

to justify its existence. More than any other single organization, it stimulated reform in teacher education. In its many conferences it brought together educators, young and old, who had a vision of better schools and were unfettered by the dogmas and clichés of the past. It encouraged such educators to experiment with better arrangements of time, space, materials, and personnel in the schools and with the various uses of the new educational technologies. It played a major role in the development of team teaching and the use of teacher aides. It stimulated curricular reform by giving assistance to those who were undertaking to update the content of courses in science, mathematics, and other subjects. And throughout its history the Fund played a major role in defending liberal education — the education that makes the most of man as man in contrast to the kind of education that is designed to meet manpower needs — against the many forces that threatened to destroy it in universities, colleges, high schools, and programs of teacher education. This battle has not yet been won — perhaps it can never be completely and finally won — but without the help of the Fund it might have been lost during the years when university professors were placing ever greater emphasis on specialization and the federal government was clamoring for more and more technically skilled manpower to meet the needs of national defense.

The fact that the Fund aroused the animosity of a considerable number of educators in powerful positions is less important than the fact that it gave encouragement and support to other educators who saw a need for substantial changes in education but whose innovative efforts were being blocked by the conventional wisdom of the establishment. Those who were responsible for the Fund can take satisfaction from the fact that many of the ideas and points of view that they espoused against much opposition in the Fifties became popular with educators in the Sixties. The new breed of educators which now is rapidly taking over the positions of power and influence in American education includes many individuals whom the Fund identified in the early Fifties as potential leaders and whom it brought together in conferences and committees. By giving them encouragement and support when they needed it most, the Fund fostered creative approaches to educational reform and helped to break down the barriers to innovation. If it had done no more than that, the Fund for the Advancement of Education would have been a success.

7

A Look Ahead

THE role of foundations in education has been substantially altered, both by the rising costs of education and by the steadily growing commitment of the federal government as well as the various state governments to the support of educational institutions. A nation that undertakes to provide secondary education for all and higher education for more than half of the age-group must rely on public funds for the basic support of its schools and colleges. Consequently, the future task of educational foundations will be, not to provide *support* for even a few schools, but rather to contribute to the improvement of quality in all educational institutions. They will do this by making available the kinds of assistance that governmental agencies are least likely to provide.

Because schools and colleges are, by their very nature, conservative institutions that find it difficult to adapt themselves to social change, there is the constant danger that young people will be prepared to live in the world of the recent past rather than in the world of the future which they must face.

Those educators within the institutions who see the need for change meet almost insurmountable barriers to innovation unless they are given encouragement and support from outside agencies that are committed to the advancement and improvement of education rather than protecting the status quo.

Although the federal government now provides some money for the development of new approaches to education, such funds can be cut off at any time by an economy-minded Congress or administration. Even when money is allocated for "research and development" neither legislators nor taxpayers are prone to accept the use of public funds as "risk capital" to be employed in trying new approaches to education that may or may not prove to be superior to conventional procedures. Philanthropic foundations are in better position than any other agencies to do the things that governmental agencies cannot or are not likely to do.

The unique role of foundations is well described by Alan Pifer, president of the Carnegie Corporation:

Among the vast array of institutions, public and private, profit-making and non-profit, which comprise the fabric of contemporary American society there is none which possesses greater freedom than the foundation. Unlike a business enterprise, it is not subject to the discipline of the market place nor, like public agencies, of the ballot box. It is not dependent on others for funds. It does not have to be responsive to the claims of a membership of alumni, students or faculty. It is not subject to periodic accreditation or licensing or obligatory compliance with a set of traditional professional standards. In short, it enjoys less constraint by the usual forms of accountability to society than does, perhaps, any other type of institution.

As a corollary to this freedom the grant-making foundation possesses uncommitted funds which can, within the limits specific in its charter, be directed by its trustees to whatever philanthropic purposes they think best. These funds are in most cases remarkably free both of stated or implied obligations for their use. No particular cause, group, or institution has a "right" to them. No individual has a special claim on them.

It is these two associated characteristics of the foundation, its freedom and the generally uncommitted nature of its funds — not the size, not its prestige, and not its past reputation — which make it a unique agency in our national life and potentially one of such enormous value. No other has as great liberty, and consequently such an awesome responsibility to diagnose the need for institutional reforms, however controversial these may be, and to help bring them about. The foundation can put itself above the special interests which restrict the vision of most organizations and the parochial concerns of the professions and consider only what is for the common good — tomorrow and on into the distant future.[1]

The Ford Foundation's interest in education did not terminate with the demise of the separate funds. Like many other foundations, large and small, it accepts the improvement of educational institutions as one of its major responsibilities. But the emphasis is changing.

Traditionally, the major emphasis in foundation work has been on higher education, primarily because elementary and secondary education has long been accepted as a public responsibility while, until recently, the majority of college students have been enrolled in private institutions. But this is no longer true. Today nearly 70 per cent of all college and university students are enrolled in institutions classed as "public" while even those institutions that call themselves "private" accept substantial sums from the federal government and in some cases from the states as well. Consequently, the traditional reason for dispensing the major portion of foundation funds to higher institutions is no longer valid. In recognition of this fact, the Ford Foundation now is making a major in-

[1] Carnegie Corporation, *Annual Report,* 1968, pp. 4–5.

vestment in programs designed to improve the quality of education in public institutions from the preschool to the university levels.

A foundation that accepts responsibility for the improvement of education can operate in any one of three ways: it can give its general staff or its senior officers the responsibility for making grants to educational institutions and let these institutions decide for themselves how to use the money; it can establish a separate division, manned by officers and staff members who are qualified to make decisions as to how philanthropic money can best be used for the advancement of education; or it can set up an independent fund or funds with responsibility for education or some special aspect of it. The first alternative is generally considered to be appropriate only for small foundations that cannot afford to maintain specialized staffs.

The Ford Foundation chose the third alternative in 1951 when it established the Fund for the Advancement of Education and the Fund for Adult Education but it soon reversed its decision and began to develop its own Education Division which eventually took over the work of the separate funds. This division, though it operates under the general direction of the president and board of trustees of the Foundation, now enjoys a considerable degree of independence in grant making. Decisions are made, and grants are allocated by a highly qualified professional staff which operates under the direction of an able vice-president of the Foundation. This "Division of Education and Research," which has at its disposal sums much larger than ever were available to the separate funds, now is attacking educational problems along a broad front.

Does such a division make separate funds for education unnecessary? On this there is a sharp difference of opinion. Mr. Hoffman and Mr. Hutchins, who were responsible for the establishment of the separate funds in 1951, still see a clear need for independent funds. The present officers of the Foundation, in contrast, see *no* need for them.

Educators also disagree, but while preparing this report I have discovered that a considerable number of them are convinced that the termination of the work of the Fund for the Advancement of Education has left a vacuum in American education. When writing to distinguished educators to ask for their judgments of the accomplishments of the Fund, and their criticisms of it, I asked one additional question: "Now that the Fund for the Advancement of Education is terminating its existence, do you see a need for a new fund, similarly committed to the advancement and improvement of American education? What could such an independent fund do that the established philanthropic foundations cannot do or are not likely to do?"

Some of the respondents firmly support the present position of the Foundation. Harold Howe II says, "I do not really understand why a separate Fund for the Advancement of Education needs to be created when a Vice-President of the Ford Foundation, with the proper staff, can do the same thing for that organization. He might need a good advisory group for different segments of education, but certainly he can get that kind of help."

Others are uncertain about the need for a new fund. Robert Havighurst says:

Whether there is need for a new Fund for Educational Research and Development is a question which the past experience hardly gives a base for answering. The Federal Government is now putting as much money into educational research and development in one year as the Fund had during its entire life. The Federal Government is supporting as wide a range of programs as the several educational foundations put together.

The argument for an independent educational fund would have to be made on the basis of values it would derive from its independence. This is an interesting thing to think about and evaluate. What kinds of "political" influence affect an "independent" fund, as compared with those that influence a research agency supported by the government? Could an independent fund support basic research more effectively than a government agency or an established foundation? We shall get some evidence on this from the experience of the new basic educational research program administered by the National Academy of Science.

Others, however, see a clear need, not only for private philanthropy but for a separate fund for education. Lindley Stiles says:

I am well aware of the increased appropriations from government to underwrite educational innovations and in some instances basic research. Governmental funds, however, are even more unstable than those from foundations. It is extremely difficult to bring sufficient and consistent pressure on congressmen to sustain a pattern of expansion of governmental resources. In addition, changes in public attitudes caused by such events as the war in Vietnam quickly and easily curtail governmental investments in education. The existence of a Fund might help prime the pump.

James Allen says:

The increasing availability of Federal Funds on a special grant basis has lessened, but not eliminated, the need for private funding to support educational projects. There is a continuing need for funding of projects which cannot or are not likely to be financed by public agencies. It would seem desirable at this time to explore the idea of joint financing of major projects by foundations and public agencies. This would serve the dual purpose of getting a public agency involved in a project and of providing a degree of flexibility in the project which is difficult to arrange with public funds. The philanthropic foundations, within the limits of their charters, their interests, etc., can be helpful, but the advantage of the Fund has been its commitment to the advancement and improvement of American education.

Charles Park agrees, saying:

Very definitely there is a need for a new Fund. This should be so defined and directed as to support the kinds of demonstrations and research programs which will not be supported by Federal grants or other foundations. It seems to me that we have only crossed the threshold and that there must be brain power, desire and willingness to move ahead on a carefully planned national approach to the ever existing needs of education, especially as it relates to the elementary and secondary levels.

Several of the writers expressed doubts that the larger foundations can take the place of separate funds. From Willard Olson:

A fund devoted to education is likely to have a sharper focus and a more cumulative impact than foundations that spread themselves over a variety of purposes. Such a foundation might well have an emphasis on the utilization and dissemination of research findings. I think many agencies — federal and private — will be pushing for reform and social relevance, but I feel that there is a place for inquiry on the foundations of reforms.

And Stiles says:

The advantage of setting up a new fund committed to the advancement and improvement of American education would be linked primarily to its categorical focus. In a broad sense foundations do not have vast amounts of funds to commit to any project. Too many of them tend to spread themselves too thinly over too many fields. This is true, I think, of the Ford Foundation's efforts to try to improve humanity around the globe. There is need to maintain a commitment to improve education that will not happen if foundation trustees are forced to allocate funds here and there to many projects in numerous fields without the guidelines of such an objective. Certainly education ranks at the head of the list of all the fields that need help today. Thus, I strongly concur that foundations such as Ford need to make a commitment and sustain it in the future as the Fund has been able to do in the past.

John Fischer suggests the possibility of several funds with relatively narrow charters:

I can imagine, for example, a fund devoted not to the advancement of "education" but to the improvement of urban elementary and secondary education. Or one might think of a similar group concerned with the advancement of rural schools, or adult education. A particularly urgent need now is for some such specialized focus on issues of structure and governance in higher education, where it is especially important to rely on independent rather than public funding.

Henry Hill also suggests a number of things not being done by the larger foundations that could be done by a new fund:

A new fund might adopt one or more small institutions enrolling 1000 or fewer students, with the idea that in these colleges good teaching would be supreme. Such a purpose need not negate the kind of teaching research which good teachers have always done, but it would eliminate all the tremendous effort put in by our leading universities with things which have nothing whatsoever to do with good teaching.

The new fund might become interested in a school or college which would take as its chief purpose the development of purpose and reasonable achievement among the thousands of average students. The fact that no Ivy League university would understand what I am talking about or have the slightest interest in it seems to indicate some possible proof of the need. If the brightest people are uninterested in doing what has to be done, then the average people must undertake it.

This new fund might do something at least to investigate what good and what harm is being done by the magic gadgets. No one would deny the influence of radio, television, and the mass media in general. Yet if we choose to go back to Socrates, we find that the dialogue and the personal touch were responsible for whatever good came from him. I have viewed a teaching machine as being not much superior to a library book and not as good as a fine teacher.

Somehow or other present disturbances ought to be controlled or guided so that the business of what colleges and universities are supposed to do may go on successfully. A new and independent fund devoted to this or a fund which would put this on the agenda as important might provide the quiet voice of reason and common sense which today would secure an audience.

I would suggest that this new fund concentrate its efforts on not to exceed a half dozen institutions, preferably different kinds of institutions.

The strongest case for a new fund is made by Robert Bush:

The answer to the first part of the question is a resounding YES. What could it do that others won't do? Precisely what the Fund for the Advancement of Education did that others, and particularly its own parent, did not do. Be genuinely risky. Be freewheeling. Help unorthodox people to be heard. Increasingly in an age of impersonality, urbanization, and computerization, this is needed . . . there is need, I think, for some hard-hitting, well-funded, and powerful group to tackle, on the very frontier, some of the root problems which now are different from what they were when the Fund was established. The basic idea underlying the Fund, as I understood it, was and remains sound today. Putting it out of business in a specified period of time was an excellent and indispensable idea. Then a new venture, similar in purpose, but different in structure and personnel can be founded. This is a fundamental part of the process of self-renewal which Gardner so imaginatively delineates as necessary in a democratic society.

One additional advantage of a separate fund for education deserves mention: its board of directors can devote its entire attention to education. The board of a major foundation which accepts comprehensive responsibility for the advancement of human welfare in all its many aspects cannot be expected to give very much attention to any one aspect of the problem, even one as important as education. It can give very little time in board meetings to hearing the presentations of staff members proposing grants for education and often finds it necessary to vote for or against a proposal on the basis of insufficient information or strictly on the recommendation of the president.

In contrast, the board of a separate and independent fund for education can focus its entire attention sharply on educational innovations that give promise of improving the schools and colleges. It can discuss the problems of education at length, hear the proposals of staff members as well as those of the senior officers, and give enough attention to grant applications to know why the officers are rejecting some and endorsing others. It can take time to discuss educational theory and educational trends. It can know what it is doing when it approves or disapproves a grant for a new program in education. A meeting of the board of the Fund for the Advancement of Education often was a prolonged, high-level, philosophical discussion of educational problems, carried on by men and women of broad-ranging backgrounds and exceptional wisdom who were deeply committed to the task of improving the nation's education. These discussions provided the basis for Fund policy and provided guidance for the officers and staff.

A new fund with an equally competent board could fill a very real need if it took care not to duplicate the work of existing foundations. It would begin its work where the Fund for the Advancement of Education left off and build upon the experience of that organization while taking care to avoid its mistakes. Since the board of a specialized fund for education ought to be better qualified than the board of the parent foundation to deal with *educational* problems, it should be completely independent of the foundation once it is established. To assure such independence, the initial grant should be the terminal grant because a fund cannot be truly independent if it must return at regular intervals to ask for more money. The grant should be large enough to support the work of the fund for a specified period — perhaps a decade — and it should be clearly understood from the beginning that at the end of that time the fund would terminate its existence. Perhaps the officers should be promised a pension at the conclusion of the ten-year period in order that they will not spend their last years in search of new employment or trying to find ways of stretching out the lifetime of the fund. A definite, and relatively brief, lifetime is desirable for a fund because even the most innovative and courageous staff is likely to grow complacent as the years pass and even the best organization runs out of steam when it has accomplished its orginal purpose.

A fund of modest size — if it were truly independent of the parent foundation — would be less visible than a major foundation and hence would have less need to be concerned about public relations. It could launch a vigorous attack upon the most pressing educational problems of the day without worrying about its own popularity. Because of its limited life-span it would be less vulnerable to the forces that make for growing rigidity in a permanent institution that must live with its own traditions. Because of its modest size it could maintain an open-door policy and could take the time and trouble to give proper attention to requests for small grants and to imaginative proposals from obscure individuals working in nonprestigious institutions.

The educational problems of the years ahead will differ substantially from those of the recent past but they are not likely to be any less acute. Within the broad spectrum of American education there are more than enough problems for both large foundations and small funds. As we move into the decade of the Seventies, higher education is in such a state of turmoil that major universities are threatened with destruction by their own students. The crisis in urban educational systems has made it obvious that some of the big-city systems are much too large to operate effectively because the multiplying echelons of administrative authority increasingly separate students from those who make policy regarding their education. And yet the forces that oppose decentralization are very powerful. It is increasingly apparent that schooling which begins at the

age of six can never fully compensate for the handicaps of
early deprivation — consequently some kind of educational
experiences must be provided during what have been considered the "preschool" years if equality of educational opportunity is to be achieved.

While the major foundations and the state and federal governments attack such major problems, a smaller fund might
appropriately give its attention to causes that are currently less
fashionable. It might, for example, reject the popular notion
that "disadvantaged" is almost synonymous with "Negro" and
look for ways of providing better education for the millions of
American boys and girls who are seriously disadvantaged —
culturally, economically, and educationally — despite the
fact that they are white, Anglo-Saxon, and Protestant. At a
time when the nation is preoccupied with urban problems, an
imaginative fund might look the other way and discover that
even in 1970 some fifty-four million Americans, including fifteen million children of school age, still live in areas classified
by the Census Bureau as "rural." It would discover that while
some of these children living in very small towns or on farms
have good educational opportunities, many do not, and the
number of those who must go to inferior schools is substantially larger than the number of children living in urban ghettos. By building upon the excellent start made by the Fund for
the Advancement of Education, a new fund could find ways
of providing better education in small schools without requiring children to spend long hours each day on school buses.

At the level of higher education, a new fund might support
a further reexamination of the college curriculum in the light
of the demand of today's students for "relevance." It might
help colleges to find ways of encouraging and rewarding excellence in undergraduate teaching. If it were an operating
agency it might look into the problem of college entrance
standards to determine whether present practices really select

the students who most need a college education and are most likely to profit from it. It might question whether the graduates of the "highly selective" colleges achieve more after graduation because such colleges offer a better education or only because the graduates of such colleges were very bright to begin with. It might question the assumption that the students who make high grades in college are the ones who profit most from what the college has to offer — an assumption clearly implied in the current use of high school grades and College Board scores as selection devices on the ground that they correlate positively with college grades. A new fund might support an effort to discover which of the possible selective devices correlate most highly with various kinds of achievement *after* graduation. It is doubtful that any permanent foundation would dare launch investigations so certain to be unpopular with the colleges and universities that have based their prestige in substantial part on their "highly selective" entrance standards. But it ought to be done because the present practices may very well rest upon erroneous assumptions.

At a time when the major foundations are giving most of their attention to colleges at the two ends of the scale — the most prestigious private colleges and the Negro colleges — a new fund might turn its attention to the colleges in the middle — the less well-endowed private colleges which are struggling for survival and the emerging state colleges which are providing education for an ever larger proportion of the college population. Many of these latter institutions had their origins as teachers colleges or normal schools but they have taken on new responsibilities, often without a clear sense of purpose or suitable models to emulate. Because of their special responsibilities it is not appropriate for them to follow either the private colleges or the major universities. A philanthropic organization might be able to help them develop a better understanding of their unique opportunities.

An educational fund might also give assistance to the universities that have undertaken to break their massive undergraduate student bodies up into smaller units under some version of the "cluster college" plan. Decentralization of authority undoubtedly is the wave of the future, particularly in the state universities and the larger state colleges, but many of the problems yet to be solved require outside support for experimental ventures.

If the new fund had the comprehensive task of advancing *all* education it could also carry on with the problem of providing better educational opportunities for older men and women whose formal schooling has terminated but who still want and need more education of a liberal nature. During the Fifties the Ford Foundation assigned this responsibility to the Fund for Adult Education which made an effective attack on the problem, but new efforts appropriate to the changing times will be necessary in the Seventies.

A new fund should be prepared to deal with new problems, not yet foreseen, but which surely will arise in the years ahead; consequently it should not restrict its activities too strictly to preestablished areas of operation.

The history of the Fund for the Advancement of Education gives evidence of mistakes to be avoided in philanthropic work, but it also gives clear indication of the great potentialities of separate funds. By giving support to imaginative individuals within the teaching profession who without it might have been discouraged by the resistance of their colleagues or beaten down by the opposition of professional organizations, the Fund helped to break down the barriers to reform. By challenging the axioms of the profession, it made innovation respectable. During the first five or six years of its operation, the Fund demonstrated its ability to make a vigorous and effective attack on major educational problems even at a time when the organized profession was highly resistant to change because it was under attack and on the defensive.

A new fund would meet with less resistance to reform because innovation has now become something of a fad, consequently it might use a different approach to educational improvement. But, by providing a continuing, critical examination of educational policies, trends, and developments, it could, like the Fund for the Advancement of Education, "comfort the afflicted and afflict the comfortable." It could carry on the tradition of alerting the profession and the public to promising proposals for meeting the problems that confront us and thereby make its contribution to the continuing advancement of American education.

Appendices
Bibliography

Appendices
Board Members of the Fund

Frank W. Abrams (1951–1967), Chairman of the Board (1951–1952)
  Chairman of the Board, Standard Oil Company (New Jersey)
Frederick B. Adams (1958–1967)
  Director, The Pierpont Morgan Library
Barry Bingham (1951–1954)
  President, The Courier-Journal and Louisville Times Company
Frank H. Bowles (1964–1969)
  Vice-President, The Fund for the Advancement of Education
  (1964–1966), President (1966–1969)
Ralph J. Bunche (1951–1967)
  Director, Division of Trusteeship, United Nations
Josephine Young (Mrs. Everett) Case (1965–1967)
  Author; Chairman of the Board of Trustees, Skidmore College
Joseph N. Charyk (1965–1967)
  President, Communications Satellite Corporation
Charles D. Dickey (1951–1966)
  Director and Vice-President, J. P. Morgan & Company, Inc.
James H. Douglas, Jr. (1951–1967)
  Gardner, Carton and Douglas, Chicago, Illinois
Alvin C. Eurich (1951–1967)
  Vice-President, The Fund for the Advancement of Education
  (1951–1964)
Clarence H. Faust (1951–1967)
  President, The Fund for the Advancement of Education (1951–
  1966)
C. Scott Fletcher (1951–1959)
  President, The Fund for Adult Education
Walter Gifford (1954–1966)
  Honorary Chairman, American Telephone & Telegraph Company
Maurice Heckscher (1957–1967)
  Attorney; Duane, Morris and Heckscher
Mildred McAfee (Mrs. Douglas) Horton (1951–1967)
  Former President, Wellesley College; former Commander of the
  WAVES
Arthur A. Houghton, Jr. (1956–1967)
  President, Steuben Glass, Inc.

Arthur Howe, Jr. (1965–1967)
  President, American Field Service
Roy E. Larsen (1951–1967), Chairman of the Board (1955–1967)
  President, Time Inc.
Walter Lippmann (1951–1965)
  Author and journalist, Washington, D.C.
Ralph E. McGill (1954–1967)
  Editor, the Atlanta *Constitution*
Paul Mellon (1951–1956)
  President, Old Dominion Foundation
Walter P. Paepcke (1951–1959)
  Chairman of the Board, Container Corporation of America
Philip D. Reed (1951–1953)
  Chairman of the Board, General Electric Company
Owen J. Roberts (1951–1955), Chairman of the Board (1952–1955)
  Former Associate Justice, Supreme Court of the United States
James Webb Young (1951–1952)
  Consultant, The Ford Foundation

From April 1967, the Fund's affairs have been handled by a caretaker board and staff made up of the following Ford Foundation personnel: Frank H. Bowles (to October 1969), Howard R. Dressner, G. H. Griffiths, Edward J. Meade, Jr., Marshall A. Robinson and F. Champion Ward.

Officers of the Fund

President

Clarence H. Faust	April 1951–April 1966
Frank H. Bowles	April 1966–October 1969
Edward J. Meade, Jr.	October 1969–present

Vice-President

Alvin C. Eurich	June 1951–April 1965
Frank H. Bowles	April 1965–April 1966
Alan D. Ferguson	April 1966–April 1967
Edward J. Meade, Jr.	April 1967–October 1969
G. H. Griffiths	October 1969–present

Assistant Vice-President

John K. Weiss	June 1951–April 1954

Secretary

Thomas A. Spragens	June 1951–November 1952
O. Meredith Wilson	December 1952–January 1954
Philip Coombs	January 1954–April 1961
Elizabeth Paschal	April 1961–August 1964
John Scanlon	August 1964–April 1967
G. H. Griffiths	April 1967–present

Treasurer

Thomas A. Spragens	June 1951–November 1952
E. L. Young (Acting Treasurer)	December 1952–January 1954
Philip Coombs	January 1954–April 1954
John K. Weiss	April 1954–May 1958
Lester Nelson	May 1958–April 1963
Elizabeth Paschal	April 1963–August 1964
John Scanlon	August 1964–April 1967
G. H. Griffiths	April 1967–present

News Release, April 30, 1967

EDITOR'S NOTE: Conclusion of the program of the Fund for the Advancement of Education was announced and highlights of its activities were summarized in the following news release, the full text of which is reproduced here.

NEW YORK, April 30 — The Directors of the Fund for the Advancement of Education today announced the conclusion of the program the Fund has conducted since it was established by the Ford Foundation in 1951.

Roy E. Larsen, chairman of the Fund's board, said the decision marked the final stage in a transition that has been under way since 1957, when the staff of the Fund and the Foundation's education division became one and the same. The Fund's efforts to advance education have become an integral part of Foundation activities and are being continued by the Foundation, which has provided all of the more than $70 million the Fund has granted to date. The Fund will neither consider new proposals nor make further grants, although administration of existing grants and projects will continue for some months. During this final phase of activity the Fund will prepare and publish a final report and assessment on its work.

"The past sixteen years have been a critical and challenging period for education," said Mr. Larsen. "All aspects of the nation's expanding and profoundly changing educational resources have come under close scrutiny and analysis. In this time, the Fund has sought to encourage practical and effective change in the form of new and better educational practices. It has had the satisfaction of seeing ideas which it assisted on a pilot basis widely adopted in the schools and colleges. Team teaching, use of teacher aides, instructional television, programmed learning, new methods of preparing teachers, cooperative work-study programs, early childhood education, and enrichment of school programs in deprived areas are examples.

"Since the Fund and Foundation began coordinating their activities closely in 1957, the Fund has concentrated on breaking new ground with initial support of promising experiments and developments in education, and the Foundation on amplifying, refining and more broadly demonstrating many of these. Both have also supported activities which were not shared, but the dominant theme has been partnership.

"With the completion of this transition, American society can be confident that the Foundation itself will continue to keep open wide the door and keep strong the hand of support for good ideas to advance education and for the imaginative people to strengthen education."

In a letter to Mr. Larsen, McGeorge Bundy, president of the Ford Foundation, expressed the Foundation's appreciation of "the pioneering and highly effective work of the Fund and its many stimulating contributions to the Foundation's own program in education. The new massiveness and scope of Federal support to education," Mr. Bundy said, "has changed the previous relationship between the Fund and the Foundation, putting the Foundation in the Fund's special role of experimental 'pilot' much more often than in the past. In this role, we know that the Foundation will draw strength from the venturesome and inventive example set by the Fund's directors and staff since 1951."

The Fund will continue to maintain its headquarters at 477 Madison Avenue, New York,* and will carry on its corporate affairs under a new and smaller Board of Directors. In addition to Mr. Larsen, directors serving through the April 24th meeting include:

Mr. Frank W. Abrams	Mr. Alvin C. Eurich
Mr. Frederick B. Adams, Jr.	Mr. Clarence H. Faust
Mr. Frank Bowles	Mr. Maurice Heckscher
Mr. Ralph J. Bunche	Mrs. Douglas Horton
Mrs. Everett Case	Mr. Arthur A. Houghton, Jr.
Mr. Joseph Charyk	Mr. Arthur Howe, Jr.
Mr. James H. Douglas, Jr.	Mr. Ralph McGill

* 320 East 43d Street, New York, since December 1967.

Program Highlights, 1951-67

I. SCHOOL TEACHERS

A. *Teacher Training.* Between 1951 and 1959 some forty colleges, universities, and school systems received Fund grants totaling $9.6 million to experiment with new patterns of teacher training designed to make the profession more attractive to abler candidates, and to improve the quality of instruction in elementary and secondary schools. First in the series was to the University of Arkansas, for the widely noted "Arkansas Experiment." It sought to strengthen liberal studies and general education courses offered to prospective teachers in the state's colleges, and to provide a fifth year of training at the university for college graduates with little or no prior professional preparation.

Though varied in emphasis and content, subsequent grants also stressed broad liberal education, mastery of a subject field, and improved professional preparation. Most were designed specifically to attract liberal-arts graduates to teaching. Colleges and universities were encouraged to work closely with school systems to improve the clinical aspects of teacher training — generally through some form of internship — and to relate clinical experience more directly to studies of teaching theory and technique. Most involved a fifth year of study, many leading to the Master of Arts in Teaching (MAT). The programs were described in a Fund booklet, "New Directions in Teacher Education," and laid the groundwork for the Ford Foundation's subsequent investment of some $30 million in larger and more sustained demonstrations — the so-called breakthrough program.

Although a relatively small number — perhaps as few as 1 per cent — of the nation's current annual teacher crop are produced by programs of this kind, followup studies indicate graduates are widely sought after, display greater assurance and receive greater satisfaction in their teaching, and have more professional staying power, than graduates of conventional teacher-training programs.

B. *Professional Advancement.* To assist teachers in service to deepen their subject knowledge and broaden their general background, the Fund supported two novel forms of in-service training. Between 1952 and 1956 it provided $4.8 million to enable some 1,000 high school teachers to spend a year in liberalizing studies or experience with no immediate teaching responsibilities. And, beginning in 1953, it granted $222,000 for a series of summer institutes at six colleges and universities which brought together teachers from high schools, junior colleges, and four-year colleges to work on problems in a single subject field. Now commonplace in education, and strongly supported by Federal funds, such specialized sessions were then a sharp break with the smorgasbord of unrelated courses offered teachers by conventional summer institutes. Along similar lines, the Ford Foundation since 1958 has granted funds for the John Hay Fellowships, providing a year of advanced study for some 500 high school teachers in the humanities and social sciences.

II. COLLEGE TEACHERS

A. *Faculty Study Fellowships.* At a time when only the most prestigious and prosperous institutions were willing and able to allow instructors of undergraduates to take leave with pay for further advanced study, the Fund in 1951 began awarding individual fellowships for the purpose. By the time the $6.7 million program was concluded in 1956, more than 1,200 "Fund Fellows" from 386 institutions in every state and the District of Columbia had spent an academic year pursuing their specialty and studying promising developments in undergraduate education. In 1965, the Fund sought with grants totaling $550,000 to encourage a limited number of small, independent colleges to establish or expand their own faculty leave programs on a continuing basis.

B. *Graduate Training.* A common problem of young college instructors is that they are plunged into their careers after a period of intense academic specialization which permits little or no opportunity to acquire training or practical experience in the art of teaching. Between 1953 and 1958, the Fund granted $970,000 to eighteen colleges and universities to test the feasibility of providing such experience through internships. Some 300 interns worked under the guidance of experienced teachers, observed effective teaching, and engaged in discussions of curriculum development, course planning, and instruction techniques. The program led to Ford Foundation grants for three-year master's degree programs which included internship experience for college teachers.

In another approach to improve college teaching the Fund granted $1.4 million to ten colleges and universities to experiment with cooperative programs of graduate study, focused on the establishment of a "common core" of work leading to the doctorate and dealing with fundamental problems in the humanities and social sciences.

The Ford Foundation has provided some $52 million for support of graduate education since 1958 through the Woodrow Wilson National Fellowship program, and more recently launched a $41.5 million seven-year program to reform doctoral education in social sciences and humanities at ten leading graduate schools.

III. EDUCATION ADMINISTRATORS

A. *Training Programs.* To lend more realism to the training of administrators, the Fund has granted $1.7 million for experiments which emphasize clinical aspects of administration through internships and workshops, encourage closer cooperation between institutions training administrators and the schools which employ them, and expose administrators in service to a wider range of practical problems and solutions by enabling them to visit selected institutions notable for effective administration. These approaches have received subsequent support from the Ford Foundation, through grants for the National Association of Secondary-School Principals' administrative intern program, and the Washington Internships in Education, which provide clinical experience in public and private educational agencies at the national level for young local administrators.

B. *Leadership Development.* Since opportunities for professional growth tend to be concentrated in areas where educational institutions and resources are most plentiful, the Fund in 1966 appropriated $1.5 million to provide fellowships for teachers from outlying areas, who have displayed leadership potential but who might not otherwise have opportunities for advanced study. Purpose is to help equip fellows upon returning to their communities to take a hand in developing the institutions which employ them. The Leadership Fellows program will be continued and administered by the Ford Foundation after the Fund closes.

IV. TALENTED STUDENTS

A. *Individual Progress.* Partly because it was considered somehow undemocratic, and partly because few schools had resources to implement it, the notion that exceptionally bright pupils should advance at their own speed in school received little effective support until the 1950's. Then, concern over the potential waste of talent through boredom and lost time began to mount. In a series of grants totaling $832,-000 between 1951 and 1961, the Fund assisted a variety of experiments and demonstrations designed to enable bright pupils to avoid the rigid requirements of the academic lockstep. These included early introduction to intensive foreign language and science studies, multiple tracking according to ability, special classes for the able, voluntary summer enrichment programs, and college-level courses in a variety of subjects. Colleges and universities collaborated with individual schools and entire systems in developing these innovations which now are commonly found in progressive systems.

B. *Early Admission and Advanced Placement.* To bridge the gap between high school and college for bright students, the Fund granted $4.9 million to assist testing and demonstration of two strategies now considered proven devices. Twelve colleges were enlisted to test feasibility of admitting without the diploma gifted students who effectively exhausted the resources of their schools by the end of their sophomore or junior year. Between 1951 and 1955, some 1,350 early admission scholars entered cooperating institutions. Their generally good academic, social, and intellectual adjustment was described in the Fund report *They Went to College Early.* The bulk of the funds, however, was used to further refine college-level courses designed for stronger systems able to offer advanced material, develop examinations to verify the levels of knowledge achieved, and encourage colleges and universities to honor the achievement with advanced placement in the subject studied. Twelve high schools and twelve colleges collaborated in the initial advanced placement demonstration. More than 800 colleges now accept students on this basis and such courses are routine at outstanding academic high schools. Since 1955 testing for advanced placement has been continued under administration of the College Entrance Examination Board.

V. CURRICULUM

A. *Better Courses.* In addition to its interest in educating the talented, the Fund shared concern over the quality and content of school curricula generally, which became an intense national issue — especially with regard to mathematics and science — after 1957. In this field, the Fund sought principally — with $3.2 million in grants — to initiate new approaches to more stimulating and challenging courses and to help develop the framework rather than the courses themselves. Thus it assisted the Portland, Oregon, public schools in collaboration with nine Oregon colleges and universities to undertake a comprehensive reevaluation of existing high school courses. Fifty college teachers were enlisted in formulating recommendations on how to present the subject matter in intellectually stimulating ways, maintain continuity through the high school years, and give students greater responsibility for their own progress. A series of early grants to Educational Services, Incorporated (now Education Development Center, Inc.) for the outline of a new social studies sequence based on case studies and original sources, led to support from the Ford Foundation for actual unit design and development of course materials.

Some courses were, however, more directly aided — most notably "Parlons Français," a French course using a full array of audiovisual aids including television, and a new fourth-year high school course to replace the conventional "Problems of American Democracy."

B. *National Assessment.* The Committee on Assessing the Progress of Education, which is engaged in a long-range effort to develop procedures and instruments for measuring the educational attainments of the American people, received Fund grants in 1965 and 1967 totaling $1.1 million. Field trials of testing instruments developed by the Committee are now under way to determine their usefulness in obtaining census-like data on educational attainment as a basis for public policy discussions affecting the nation's educational efforts.

C. *Early Childhood Education.* Although a number of Fund-assisted studies and experiments in elementary curriculum improvement extended to preschool experiences, the first grants directly related to preschool programs were made in 1965, after experience in the national Head Start program suggested a need for further basic research and program development, especially for deprived children. Under a $400,000 appropriation, seven institutions are exploring such facets of early childhood education as the relevance of parent orientation, the role of the mother in preschool programs, adaptability of existing programs for gifted children to the needs of disadvantaged children, and a systems approach — with continual feedback and analysis — to curriculum development.

VI. MORE EFFECTIVE ORGANIZATION FOR TEACHING

A. *Staff Utilization.* The Fund initiated in 1954 what was later to become a widespread movement for more effective use of the time and talent of teachers and other instructional staff through such devices as more efficient scheduling, use of aides to free teachers from nonteaching chores, team and cooperative teaching, variable grouping and flexible pupil scheduling. Between 1954 and 1964 some $6 million was granted for these purposes. In addition to better using the professional capabilities of teachers generally and extending the reach of the most able among them, such arrangements also encourage better subject integration and more responsiveness to individual student needs. They have been adopted widely by forward-looking school systems throughout the country.

B. *Technology*. To complement and assist better deployment of human resources, the Fund also aided efforts to make effective use of new communications technology and other electromechanical aids to education. Most notable was a series of grants, totaling some $5 million, for experiments and demonstrations of television teaching. Begun with a program of fifth-grade American history lessons prepared at Montclair State College in New Jersey, and broadcast by closed-circuit to nearby schools, the grants ultimately assisted experiments with both open- and closed-circuit TV at both school and college levels, and ranging in scale from individual institutions to state, regional, and national levels. Among the best-known projects were Chicago's city-wide junior college program; systemwide instruction in the Hagerstown, Maryland public schools, in Dade County, Florida, and the State of Alabama; *Continental Classroom*, which offered college courses in physics, chemistry, and mathematics nationwide on commercial stations; and the Midwest Program of Airborne Television Instruction, which broadcast videotaped programs to schools and colleges throughout Indiana and parts of five adjacent states. The Fund in 1957 initiated the National Program in the Use of Television in the Public Schools, involving the school systems of three states and a dozen cities across the country, to explore the economic and other advantages of more broad-scale application of instructional television. It, like the Midwest Airborne project and others initiated by the Fund, has received additional support from the Ford Foundation in the course of the Foundation's own $100 million-plus investment in noncommercial television.

Additional funds were granted over the years for smaller-scale experiments in using film, audio tapes, instructional radio, teaching machines, and computers — for scheduling, record keeping, test processing, and reporting. More recently, several school systems have been helped to establish learning laboratories — centers which provide space and facilities for students to become familiar with the variety of materials from which they may learn, and to use them in remedial or independent studies. They also serve as sites for teachers to experiment in the integrated use of various media not available in the classroom.

VII. OVERALL SCHOOL IMPROVEMENT

Many Fund-supported experiments focused primarily on one or another of the foregoing categories of innovation actually combined several of them, and all have been closely related to the context of the institutions and processes in which they were undertaken. But some programs stand out as a separate class — efforts to initiate broad change within a school system or group of systems by using some or all of these concepts in concert. The most extensive such series was undertaken by the National Association of Secondary-School Principals, which between 1955 and 1960 involved, with Fund support, some 100 junior and senior high schools in eleven states in experimental studies of staff utilization. Most represented combined approaches, and many led to further innovation throughout the schools. In another series, Harvard University and the public schools of Newton, Lexington, and Concord, Massachusetts, formed the first formal university-school linkage to initiate teaching experiments, expand them into demonstrations, and finally incorporate them as standard practice in the systems. Known as the School and University Program for Research and Development, it seeks also to spur similar developments throughout the nation. As a result, many similar programs are supported with public funds. A third series dealt with the special problems of rural schools in isolated areas which usually have a hard time attracting and holding teachers, and often are too small as individual units to support the full range of programs and facilities which modern education requires. Groups of schools in the Rocky Mountain area of Colorado, the Catskill area of upstate New York, and in the backwoods of Maine and Vermont, have been involved in programs to supplement their resources through cooperative effort — including correspondence courses, and extensive use of tapes, films, and other technological aids.

School improvement efforts have a direct bearing on the nature of the teacher's job and hence on teacher recruitment and training. They have therefore in many instances been assisted in close relation to teacher training efforts. In the SUPRAD program [School and University Program for Research and Development], for example, participating institutions have also taken part in Fund- or Foundation-supported teacher training programs. Along with teacher training, school improvement ranks highest among Fund interests in continued and expanded support from the Ford Foundation. Curriculum and organization concepts initially supported by the Fund have been prominent features of Foundation-aided school improvement programs. These have included the Great Cities series to improve education in ten of the nation's leading cities; the Gray Areas experiments in Boston, New Haven, Washington, Philadelphia, Oakland, and the State of North Carolina; the Western States Small Schools improvement program, involving schools and the state education departments of Arizona, Colorado, Nevada, New Mexico, and Utah; and of comprehensive improvement programs in urban, suburban, and rural areas in both North and South which have involved some two dozen systems or groups of systems. Projects in Nashville, Atlanta, Durham, New Orleans, and Huntsville, are designed mainly to overcome disadvantages of children from poor families, but their relevance for education of all children is also being tested. The Ford Foundation has granted some $28 million for these purposes.

VIII. IMPROVING UNDERGRADUATE EDUCATION

A. *Cooperative Work-Study.* A growing trend toward post–high school education for more and more young people, growing importance of more advanced preparation for productive adult careers, and the search for ways to expand opportunities in higher education for disadvantaged groups, have all intensified interest in cooperative work-study programs. These permit students to alternate periods of on-campus study with paid off-campus work related to their field of study. Until recently confined largely to engineering schools and a few liberal-arts colleges, these are now being explored and instituted in a wide variety of occupational fields. Having supported in 1960 a study of cooperative education programs which indicated they had value both for institutions and for students, in 1965 the Fund made grants for such programs at seven colleges, junior colleges, and technical institutes for vocational preparation for business and industry. The programs enable students to relate academic studies and career goals more directly and realistically, and in many cases provide a means of helping to finance their education. In the context of its over-all concern with improving vocational and technical education, the Ford Foundation has granted further support to cooperative programs, including technical assistance by the National Commission for Cooperative Education to institutions seeking to establish such programs.

B. *Better Utilization.* Colleges no less than elementary and high schools feel the pressure of rising costs and shortages of both able teachers and modern facilities. Fund assistance to the college-level counterpart of the schools' quest for greater effectiveness and efficiency has included some $740,000 to some forty-one colleges and universities for self-studies to redefine their role in American life. It assisted a nationwide program of experiments in new patterns of college teaching — including independent study for undergraduates, wider use of graduate and undergraduate teaching assistants, greater use of tape, film, and other media, and curriculum reform, under the Committee on Utilization of College Teaching Resources.

C. *Financing.* In a related area, the Fund helped efforts to make long-range financial and development planning a commonplace in colleges and universities, and helped to establish the financing of higher education as a distinct area of study in the field of economics. Altogether, more than $1.7 million was granted to help improve management and planning in individual institutions and in the field generally, including the works of Seymour Harris, Beardsley Ruml, and Sidney Tickton.

IX. EQUALITY OF OPPORTUNITY

In all of the major programs the Fund has supported — teacher education, improved curricula, better use of resources, and efforts to locate and foster talent — it has sought to include educational institutions serving predominantly Negroes, as well as institutions admitting students without regard to race. Because most of these programs have been experimental, grants have tended to go primarily to relatively strong and well-financed institutions capable of carrying the experiments through to a successful conclusion. But an estimated $4.5 million of the total in these fields have gone to predominantly Negro institutions or programs primarily identifiable as directed at improving educational opportunities for Negroes.

In addition, and particularly in recent years as the nation has turned its attention increasingly to eliminating the social and economic barriers to equal educational opportunities, the Fund has sought to enlarge its work with grants totaling an estimated $4 million more directly aimed at these barriers. Among the most notable of these:

— Studies, publications, and conferences on school desegregation starting with the landmark 1954 report *The Negro and the Schools*, by Harry S. Ashmore, editor of the *Arkansas Gazette.* The product of work by some forty-five scholars in the fields of sociology, law, political science, economics, population analysis, and public education drawn mainly from Southern colleges and universities it coincided with, and was a major resource for discussion and planning in the wake of, the Supreme Court's mandate on school desegregation. From 1954 to 1957, the Fund also supported the Southern Education Reporting Service's *Southern School News* as a medium of objective information on school desegregation in the seventeen states directly affected by the Supreme Court decision. After 1957, SERS received support from the Ford Foundation.

— Programs of specialized training for teachers of culturally disadvantaged children and to discover potential college students among those who lack educational opportunity as a result of racial, geographic, and economic factors. It also supported the National Scholarship Service and Fund for Negro Students, to recruit potential Negro college students in segregated high schools in the South and provide scholarships for them to attend integrated colleges. The Fund also supported preparation and distribution of the N.S.S.F.N.S. publication, "Blueprint for Talent Searching." Two notable subsequent programs along these lines supported by the Ford Foundation are "Project Opportunity," sponsored by the Southern Association of Colleges and Schools to identify talented but disadvantaged students in junior high school and assist them to prepare for and enter college; and the National Achievement Scholarships, administered by the National Merit Scholarship Corporation to enable outstanding Negro high school graduates to attend the college or university of their choice.

— A cooperative program between Tougaloo College and Brown University for faculty and student exchange, and to strengthen faculty and curriculum at Tougaloo, as a demonstration of how Negro colleges and major universities may extend each other's educational range. The program was in 1966 extended with a further grant from the Ford Foundation.

— In January 1966, the Fund initiated a program of distributing paperback books in support of an experimental effort to improve the education of disadvantaged students and adults and encourage the reading and ownership of books. Grants totaling nearly $500,000 have been made to fourteen institutions, among them the Southern Association of Schools and Colleges which administers the grant for 108 Negro colleges and Project Opportunity schools.

X. PUBLICATIONS AND INFORMATION

In addition to the publications cited in the foregoing, the Fund for four years supported an education supplement to the *Saturday Review of Literature*, intended to expose major issues in education to a thoughtful readership outside the profession, and has from time to time published, and supported publication by other nonprofit and commercial presses of books and reports designed to expand both lay and professional knowledge of significant issues and developments in the field. Among Fund reports:

Wilbur Schramm, ed., *Four Case Studies in Programmed Instruction,*
     1964
John I. Goodlad, *Changing School Curriculum,* 1966
Julius J. Marke, *Copyright and Intellectual Property,* 1967
B. Ruml and D. Morrison, *Memo to a College Trustee,* 1959
Sidney G. Tickton, *Needed — A Ten Year College Budget,* 1961
——, *Letter to a College President,* 1963
——, *The Year-Round Campus Catches On,* 1963

The Fund has also issued biennial reports of its activities, and the booklet, *Decade of Experiment,* reviewing its first ten years of activity.

Bibliography
Publications of the Fund

Annual Reports for 1951–52, 1952–54, 1954–56, 1957–59, 1959–61, 1961–62, 1962–64.

Better Utilization of College Teaching Resources. A report by the Committee on Utilization of College Teaching Resources. October 1956.

———. A Second Year's Experiments. October 1957.

———. A Summary Report. May 1959.

Bridging the Gap between School and College. Progress report on four related projects supported by the Fund. June 1953.

Buck, Paul H., et al. *The Role of Education in American History.* May 1957.

———. *Education and American History.* 1965.

Decade of Experiment. A ten-year report on the activities of the Fund. 1961.

Dieckhoff, John S. *Tomorrow's Professor.* A report of the College Faculty Internship Program. November 1959.

Donaldson, Robert S. *Fortifying Higher Education.* A story of college self-studies. October 1959.

Four Case Studies in Programed Instruction. A description and evaluation of public school programs with an introduction by Wilbur Schramm. 1964.

Goodlad, John I. *School Curriculum Reform in the U.S.* A compilation of illustrative projects with an analysis of problems and issues, as well as conclusions and recommendations. 1964.

Goodlad, John I.; Stoephasius, Renata von; and Klein, Frances, M. *The Changing School Curriculum.* 1966.

Marke, Julius J. *Copyright and Intellectual Property.* 1967.

Meany, John W. *Televised College Courses.* A report about the College Faculty Released Time Program for television instruction. 1962.

Murphy, Judith and Gross, Ronald. *Learning by Television.* 1966.

Paschal, Elizabeth. *Encouraging the Excellent.* A report on special programs for gifted and talented children. 1960.

Ruml, Beardsley, and Tickton, Sidney G. *Teaching Salaries Then and Now.* A fifty-year comparison with other occupations and industries. October 1955.

Schramm, Wilbur. *Programmed Instruction.* Current developments and a brief review of research. 1962.

Stoddard, Alexander J. *Schools for Tomorrow: An Educator's Blueprint.* 1957.

Strothmann, F. W. *The Graduate School Today and Tomorrow: Reflections for the Profession's Consideration.* A report written on behalf of the Committee of Fifteen. December 1955.

Teachers for Tomorrow. A study of teacher shortage and anticipated teacher needs. 1955.

Teaching by Television. A report from the Ford Foundation and the Fund for the Advancement of Education. May 1959.

They Went to College Early. A report on the early admission in college program. April 1957.

Tickton, Sidney G. *Letter to a College President.* A statistical report on the need for long-term planning. 1963.

———. *Teaching Salaries Then and Now: A Second Look.* 1961.

———. *A Ten-Year College Budget.* 1961.

———. *The Year-Round Campus Catches On.* An inventory of developments at thirty-five colleges and universities. 1963.

Woodring, Paul. *New Directions in Teacher Education.* August 1957.

A Selected List of
Fund-supported Publications

Adler, Mortimer. *The Idea of Freedom*. New York: Doubleday, 1958.

Ashmore, Harry S. *The Negro and the Schools*. Chapel Hill: University of North Carolina Press, 1954.

Barber, C. L. *The New College Plan*. Amherst: Amherst College, 1958.

Brickell, Henry M. *Commissioner's 1961 Catalogue of Educational Change*. Albany: State Education Department, 1961.

———. *Organizing New York State for Educational Change*. Albany: State Education Department, 1961.

Bushnell, Don D., and Allen, Dwight W. *The Computer in American Education*. New York: Wiley, 1967.

California and Western Cost and Statistical Study for the Year 1954–55. Berkeley: University of California Press, 1960.

Carmichael, Omer, and James, Weldon. *The Louisville Story*. New York: Simon & Schuster, 1957.

Committee for New College. *Student Reactions to Study Facilities*. Amherst: Amherst College, 1960.

Committee on Assessing the Progress of Education. *How Much Are Students Learning?* New York: Carnegie Corporation and Fund for the Advancement of Education, 1969.

Committee on Government and Higher Education. *The Campus and the State*. Baltimore: Johns Hopkins Press, 1959.

———. *The Efficiency of Freedom*. Baltimore: Johns Hopkins Press, 1959.

Cruickshank, William M., and Haring, Norris G. *A Demonstration: Assistants for Teachers of Exceptional Children*. Syracuse: University of Syracuse Press, 1957.

Erickson, Clifford G., and Chausow, Hyman M. *Chicago City Jr. College Experiment in Offering College Courses for Credit via Open-Circuit TV*. Chicago: Chicago Public Schools, 1958–1960.

Ford, Charles E., and Roy, Edgar L., Jr. *The Renewal of Catholic Higher Education.* Washington: National Catholic Educational Assoc., 1968.

Fraser, Dorothy M. *Deciding What to Teach.* Washington: National Education Association, 1963.

The Gifted Child in Portland. Portland: Portland Public Schools, 1959.

Goodman, Samuel M. *The Puerto Rican Study, 1953–1957.* New York: Board of Education, 1958.

Gow, James S., Jr. *Curriculum Development through School and University Collaboration: The Pittsburgh Curriculum Continuity Demonstration.* Pittsburgh: University of Pittsburgh Press.

Harris, Seymour E., ed. *Higher Education in the U.S.: The Economic Problems.* Cambridge: Harvard University Press, 1960.

Ilg, Frances L., and Ames, Louise Bates. *School Readiness: Behavior Tests Used at the Gesell Institute.* New York: Harper & Row, 1964.

Jamer, Margaret T. *School Volunteers.* New York: Public Education Association, 1961.

Keezer, Dexter, ed. *Financing Higher Education, 1960–70.* New York: McGraw-Hill, 1959.

Kinney, Lucien B. *Certification in Education.* Englewood Cliffs, N.J.: Prentice-Hall, 1964.

Maryland Commission on Interracial Problems. *Desegregation in the Baltimore Schools.* 1955.

McGrath, Earl J., ed. *Universal Higher Education.* New York: McGraw-Hill, 1966.

Modley, Rudolf. *The Challenge of Symbology.* New York: Art Directors Club of New York, 1959.

Morse, Arthur D. *Schools of Tomorrow, Today!* New York: Doubleday, 1960.

National Association of Secondary-School Principals. "New Horizons in Staff Utilization." *The Bulletin,* January, 1959.

———. "Exploring Improved Teaching Patterns," *The Bulletin,* January, 1959.

———. *New Horizons for Secondary-School Teachers.* Washington: National Association of Secondary-School Principals, 1957.

————. "Progressing Toward Better Schools," *The Bulletin*, January, 1960.

————. "Seeking Improved Learning Opportunities," *The Bulletin*, January, 1961.

————. "Locus of Change," *The Bulletin*, January, 1962.

National Committee for Support of the Public Schools. *Education in the States*. Washington: 1967.

————. *Leadership for Education*. Washington: 1967.

National Education Association Project on the Instructional Program of the Public Schools. *Schools for the Sixties*. New York: Mc-Graw-Hill, 1963.

National Federation of college and University Business Officers Association. *A Study of Income and Expenditures in Sixty Colleges 1953–54*. New York: 1955.

————. *A Second Look at the Sixty-College Study, 1957–58*. New York: 1960.

New Horizons in Learning. Titusville, Fla.: Brevard County Board of Public Instruction, 1960.

The Norwalk Plan — A Two-Year Study. Norwalk, Conn.: 1960.

Norwalk School Improvement Program, 1962–1963. Norwalk, Conn.: Norwalk Board of Education, 1963.

Parker, Charles F., ed. *Emergence of a Concept*. Prescott, Ariz.: Prescott College, 1965.

Pierce, Truman M., with Kincheloe, James B.; Moore, R. Edgar; Drewry, Galen N.; and Carmichael, Bennie E. *White and Negro Schools in the South: An Analysis of Biracial Education*. Englewood Cliffs, N.J.. Prentice-Hall, 1955.

Plaut, Richard L. *Blueprint for Talent Searching: America's Hidden Manpower*. New York: National Scholarship Service and Fund for Negro Students, 1957.

Ruml, Beardsley, and Morrison, Donald H. *Memo to a College Trustee*. New York: McGraw-Hill, 1959.

Shaplin, Judson T., and Olds, Henry F., eds. *Team Teaching*. New York: Harper & Row, 1964.

Shoemaker, Don, ed. *With All Deliberate Speed: Segregation-Desegregation in Southern Schools*. New York: Harper, 1957.

Smith, Elmer R., et al. *Teacher Education; A Reappraisal.* New York: Harper & Row, 1962.

Southern Education Reporting Service. *Southern Schools — Progress and Problems.* Nashville: Nashville, Tennessee, Book Co., 1959.

Swanson, Ernst W., and Griffin, John A. *Public Education in the South Today and Tomorrow.* Chapel Hill: University of North Carolina Press, 1955.

Trump, J. Lloyd. *An Exciting Profession: New Horizons for Secondary School Teachers.* Washington: National Association of Secondary-School Principals, 1957.

——. *Image of the Future.* Washington: National Association of Secondary-School Principals, 1958.

——. *New Directions to Quality Education.* Washington: National Association of Secondary-School Principals, 1959.

Trump, J. Lloyd, and Baynham, Dorsey. *Focus on Change — Guide to Better Schools.* Chicago: Rand-McNally, 1961.

Trump, J. Lloyd, and Karasik, Lois. *The Present Is Prologue.* Washington: National Association of Secondary-School Principals.

Trytten, M. H. L. *The Baccalaureate Origins of Doctorates in the Arts, Humanities, and Social Sciences.* Washington: National Research Council, 1956.

Tyler, Ralph W., and Mills, Annice. *Report on Cooperative Education.* New York: Thomas Alva Edison Foundation, 1961.

Washington County Closed Circuit TV. Hagerstown, Md.: Hagerstown Board of Education.

Wey, Herbert, and Corey, John. *Action Patterns in School Desegregation — A Guidebook.* Bloomington, Ill.: Phi Delta Kappa, Inc., 1959.

Woodring, Paul, and Scanlon, John J., eds. *American Education Today.* New York: McGraw-Hill, 1963.

Yale-Fairfield Study of Elementary Teaching. *Report for 1954–1955.* New Haven, 1956.

——. *Teacher-Assistants.* New Haven, 1959.

Index

A.B. degree, 94, 122, 224–225
Abrams, Frank, viii, 34, 47, 48, 115; as chairman of Fund board, 44–46; on selectivity, 114
Academic scholars. *See* Colleges
Academy for Educational Development, 56, 58
Achievement testing, 139, 141, 156, 168–171
Adams, Frederick B., 49
Adler, Mortimer, 64, 166–167, 230, 252
Administrators, school: Fund policy, 71; and parental demands, 80–81; and certification laws, 124; training of, 165–166; and Assessment Program, 170–171; salaries, 189; grants for, 216; as Fund advisors, 232–233. *See also* Educators, professional
Admissions, early: Fund programs, 152–155, 157; grants for, 216; evaluated, 259, 260
Adolescent subculture, 5–6, 8
Adult education, 20–21. *See also* Fund for Adult Education
Advanced placement: Fund programs, 152, 155–156; grants for, 216, 217; evaluated, 248, 259, 260
Advisory committees, 58, 59–61, 199, 232–233; and Briggs affair, 238, 239, 241
Allen, James E., Jr., quoted, 248–249, 256–257, 272
American Association of Colleges for Teacher Education, 128
American Association of School Administrators, 169, 170
American Council Book Award, 198
American Federation of Teachers, 220
Anderson, Robert, 235
Andover (Phillips Academy), 197
Annual reports, Fund: 1951–1952, 57, 65–66, 114–115; 1952–1954, 57, 69, 164; 1954–1956, 57, 70; 1957–1959, 57–58, 70, 206–211; 1959–1961, 58, 71; 1961–1962, 58, 71; 1962–1964, 71
Antioch College, 167
Arithmetic. *See* Mathematics
Arkansas, University of, 36, 230; and Fund program, 126–27, 129, 226, 227
Arkansas Gazette, 175
Arkansas program, 125–130, 218, 229, 230; compared to MAT programs, 132; evaluated, 236–237, 245, 255, 256, 257, 259

Armed services: education in, as Fund goal, 29, 69–70, 116; desegregated, 107
Armsey, James W., 57–58
Art, 88, 97, 146
Ashmore, Harry, *The Negro and the Schools*, x, 174–177, 196, 259
Aspen, Colorado, 49, 200
Aspen Institute for Humanistic Studies, 52, 56
Assessment Program, National, xi, xiii, 168–171
Audio-visual aids, 161, 162, 165. *See also* Educational Television
Automation, and dropouts, 100

B.A. in Ed. degree, 122
Baltimore, Maryland, 97, 111–112
Barnard College, 134
"Battle of the Books," 55
Baxter, John, 142
Bay City, Michigan, 40, 60; teacher aide program in, ix, 147, 230, 249, 256
Bell, Bernard Iddings, 83
Berkeley, University of California at, 7, 229
Bestor, Arthur, 83, 124
Better Schools (NCCPS), 159
Better Utilization of College Teaching Resources (FAE), 191
Bingham, Barry, 48, 49, 50
Biology courses, 87, 162, 173
Bixler, Paul, 17
Blacks, 112. *See also* Negroes
Board of Directors, Fund: competence, 32–33, 276; members, 43–49, 195; and Hutchins, 64–

65; structure, 50–52; and Fund policies, 68–72, 114–115, 119–120, 205, 206, 237; Briggs on, 239. *See also* specific programs
Books: paperback, 7, 158; "Battle of the Books," 55; textbooks, 82, 92, 107, 261
Bowles, Frank, 56, 76
Braddon, Natalie, 62
Braucher, Joan, 56, 62
Breakthrough programs, 78, 135–137, 229
Bridging the Gap between School and College (FAE), 191
Briggs, Paul, ix
Briggs, Thomas, 238–242
Brish, William, 140
Brown, Courtney C., 239
Brown, Dyke, 17
Brown University, 227
B.S. in Ed. degree, 122
Budget of the Fund, 115, 211–217
Buildings, school: Fund policy on, 68, 115; improved, 204
Bunche, Ralph, 48, 50, 51
Bundy, McGeorge, 77–78
Burbank, Luther, 14
Bush, Robert, 199; quoted, 235, 247–248, 250–251, 275
Business, and education, Abrams on, 44–45

Cahn, Frances, 57
Carleton College, 134, 135
Carmichael, Oliver, 60, 164; *Graduate Education Today*, 198
Carmichael, Omer, *The Louisville Story*, 196
Carnegie, Andrew, 13, 14, 15

Carnegie Corporation, xi, xii, 92, 168, 213, 234, 247, 268
Carnegie Foundation for the Advancement of Teaching, 60
Carr, William, 169
Carroll, Thomas H., 17
Case, Josephine Young (Mrs. Everett), 49
Cass, James, 181
Center for Advanced Study in the Behavioral Sciences, Palo Alto, 53, 168, 199, 200, 201
Central Michigan University, 147, 230, 250
Certificate of Incorporation, Fund, 172
Certification of teachers, 119–125 *passim*; debate over, 94–96; and teacher shortage, 101; Arkansas program, 127; and mature women, 133
Chall, Jeanne, *Learning to Read: The Great Debate*, 92–93
Chalmers, Gordon Keith, 84
Changing School Curriculum, The (Goodlad et al.), 192
Charlotte News, 178
Charyk, Joseph, 49
Chemistry courses, 142, 162, 173
Chicago, Illinois, 112
Chicago, University of, 36–37, 51, 53, 62, 63, 153, 230
Cities: population shifts in, 4–5, 79, 111–112, 264; school systems, 146, 192–193, 277; schools, and Fund programs, 159, 244, 254, 263; teachers' salaries, 189
Citizens' committees, 80, 98. *See also* National Citizens Committee

Civil rights. *See* Segregation
Civil Rights Commission, 112
Class sizes, 101, 149, 151, 220–224
Classrooms: shortage of, 101, 192, 193; self-contained, 135, 146, 148, 150, 203
Cleveland, Ohio, ix, 108, 112
Coles, Thelma, 61, 181
College Entrance Examination Board, 154, 156, 158
College Faculty Internship Program, 165, 191
Colleges: student unrest in, 7; Study Report on, 20, 22; policy making in, 31–32; Hutchins' influence on, 62–63; in 1950's, 82; admissions policies, 88–89, 105, 152–155; enrollments, 100–101, 102, 187, 204; salaries, 104; teachers at, shortage, 105–106, 164; and Negroes, 109, 157–158; and Fund grants, 115–116, 216, 217, 228–229, 256, 261; faculty fellowship programs, 117–119, 216, 245; and teacher training, 120–136, 164–166, 224–226, 260; and educational TV, 140–141, 142; advanced placement, 155–156; and high school curriculum, 163; work-study programs, 167; and Education Supplement, 184; Ruml's report on, 197–198; and Fund advisors, 232; private and public, 269–270; and new fund, 277–280. *See also* Teachers' Colleges; *specific entries*
Colorado, 147, 160
Colorado State College, 229
Cominsky, Jack, 180, 183

Communism: fear of subversion by, 82, 84; educational goals of, 209–210

Compact of the States, xi

Compton, Karl, 16

Conant, James B., viii, 46, 131, 160

Conferences: sponsored by Fund, 199, 201, 232. *See also specific entries*

Congress, United States, 268; NDEA, 98–99, 206, 207–208; Reese Committee, 240–241. *See also* Federal government

Connecticut, 126

Constitution, United States: and religion in public schools, 96, 97; and federal aid to education, 98; and desegregation, 107, 175

Consultants to Fund, 59–61. *See also* Advisory committees

Continental Classroom (TV program), 142, 162

Coombs, Philip, 53–54, 143, 186

Cornell University, 227

Cornog, William H., 239

Correspondence courses, 161

Cousins, Norman, 180, 181, 183, 185

"Cultural imperatives," 152

Culturally disadvantaged, 156–159, 262, 263, 278

Curriculum: and Fund goals, ix–x, 22, 69–72, 195; debate over, 85–88; and advanced placement, 156; and Negro schools, 157; Fund efforts to improve, 160–163, 203, 204, 216

Dabney, Virginius, 178

Decade of Experiment (FAE), 161, 193–196

Defense, United States Department of, 70

Defiance, Iowa, 35

Delaware, 110

Democracy, education for: study committee on, 18–19, 20; and educational philosophy, 65–67, 209; and Fund policy, 71–72

Denver, Colorado, 192

Desegregation. *See* Segregation

Desegregation in the Baltimore Schools, 196

Detroit, Michigan, 14, 112

DeVane, William C., 17

Dewey, John, 120, 179–180

Dickey, Charles D., 48, 49

Dieckhoff, John, *Tomorrow's Professor*, 191

Dillard University, 157–158

District of Columbia, 110, 176

Dodds, Harold Willis, 84

Donaldson, Robert S., *Fortifying Higher Education*, 191

Douglas, Jr., James H., 48

Drake University, 35

Dual Progress Plan, 151–152

Dugdale, Dorothy Mitchell, 61

Duke Endowment, 213

"Eastern Establishment," 50

Edison, Thomas A., 14

Education, United States Office of, 101, 168, 187, 200

Education Division, Ford Foundation: and Fund staff, 9, 57,

58, 60, 64, 73–78, 211, 214; present operation of, 270

Education Supplement. See *Saturday Review*

Education Writers Association Award, 185

Educational Development Center, Inc., 163

Educational Forum, 169

Educational opportunity, equalization of, as Fund goal, 69. *See also* Culturally disadvantaged

Educational philosophy: Study Report on, 18–23; and Fund goals, 65–68, 69, 116, 119, 195, 204–211, 218; and criticism of public schools, 83–84, 95–96; and academic scholars, 86–87; conflicts over teacher training, 120–125, 128; courses in, 136, 224–225; Adler's research, 166–167, 260. *See also* Educators, professional

Educational Policies Commission, 192

Educational Press Association Award, 185

Educational Services, Inc., 163

Educational television, 41, 71, 78, 136, 162, 203, 204; evaluated, x, 219, 237, 257, 259; Fund projects, 137–146; Stoddard report, 193; grants for, 216; and class sizes, 220, 221, 222

Educational Testing Service, x, 154

Educators, professional: and college programs, 7; conflict with Fund, 56, 119–125, 127–131, 183, 218–219, 224–226, 234; and Hutchins, 62–63; and public schools in 1950's, 81–92; and certification, 94–95; and revenues, 98; and TV, 138, 144; and teacher aides, 148–149; and early admissions, 153; and assessment program, 170–171; and research, 173, 236, 237; integrity of, 235; and Briggs affair, 238–242; and evaluation of Fund, 242–258 *passim*; new leadership, 265–266

Elementary schools: teaching reading, 91–93, 258; teacher preparation, 94, 102, 119–125, 129, 132–133, 187; enrollment, 99, 186, 204; salaries, 103–104, 189–190; women teachers, 104–105; TV in, 141; classrooms, 146; class sizes, 149, 222–224; team teaching, 149–152; and Fund advisors, 232. *See also* Public schools

Elicker, Paul, 153

Encouraging the Excellent (Paschal), 191

English, courses in, 85, 152

Ethridge, Mark, 110

Eurich, Alvin, viii, 54, 180, 199; life of, 33–35, 37, 40–41, 50, 51, 56; role in Fund, 41–43, 48, 52, 57–63 *passim*, 200, 252; and Ford Foundation, 73, 74, 75; and Arkansas program, 125, 126; and educational TV, 137, 145–146; and research, 174, 237; *Reforming American Education,* 219–220; on class size, 221; on methodology, 225; and

Eurich, Alvin (*cont.*)
 decisions on grants, 230, 231, 234
Evangelical church, 34
Evangelical Theological Seminary (Naperville), 35
"Executive staff," Fund, 57
Exeter, Phillips, Academy, 197
Experimental Study of the Utilization of the Staff in the Secondary School, Commission on, 151
"Exploratory Committee on Assessing the Progress of Education," 168, 170

Faculty Fellowships, Committee on, 117–118, 216, 245. *See also* Fellowship programs
Fairfield, Connecticut, 147
Faust, Clarence H., viii, 54, 56, 62, 238, 245; role in Fund, 30, 33–34, 38–40, 41–49 *passim*, 52, 57, 186, 253; life of, 34–37, 50, 51, 153; and Hutchins, 63–64; on educational philosophy, 65–66, 206–211; and Ford Foundation, 73, 74, 75, 76; and grant making, 115, 116, 230, 231; evaluates Fund, 194, 263–264
Federal government: aid to education, 78, 98–99, 106; and innovation, 248, 249, 267–268, 271, 272
Fellowship programs, 117–119, 157, 161, 216, 248, 260
Fifteen, Committee of, 191
Fifth-year programs, 125–134, 164. *See also* Master of Arts in Teaching degree

Fischer, John H., quoted, 243, 250, 274
Fisk University, 157
Flesch, Rudolph, *Why Johnny Can't Read*, xi, 90, 91
Fletcher, C. Scott, 48, 49
Flexner, Abraham, 34, 38, 125–126, 234
Ford, Benson, 14
Ford, Edsel, 14, 15
Ford, Mrs. Edsel, 14
Ford, Henry, 13–15
Ford, Mrs. Henry, 14
Ford, Henry, II, 14, 16
Ford, Mrs. Josephine, 14
Ford, William, 14
Ford Foundation, 33, 72, 252, 264, 280; and start of Fund, 10–12, 26–30, 68; Ford family and, 14–16; Study Report, 15–25, 26–28, 67–68, 73, 202–203; and Fund staff, 39–40, 44, 45, 52, 53, 56–62 *passim*; and Hutchins, 62–65; and end of Fund, 72–78, 240–241; and breakthrough program, 78, 135–137, 229; grants to Fund, 115; and educational TV, 138, 142–144; and city schools, 159, 244–245, 263; Leadership Fellows Program, 161; and curriculum changes, 163; masters' program, 164; vocational training, 167; and SERS, 178; administrative costs, 213; current projects, 269–270, 273. *See also* Education Division; Fund for Adult Education
Ford Motor Company, 15
Fortifying Higher Education (Donaldson), 191

Foundations: role of, xii–xiii, 38, 75–76, 171; history of, 12–15; boards of, 50, 52; and public school reforms, 81, 83, 98; and educational controversies of 1950's, 90; and faculty mobility, 106; joint funding, 167; problems of assessing results of, 202–203; overhead, 212–213, 214; and private colleges, 217; selection of advisors for, 232–233; relations with grant recipients, 234, 235; and Reese Committee, 240; need for new independent fund, 267–281

Fowler, Burton, 60
Franklin, Benjamin, 208
Froebel, Friedrich Wilhelm, 120
Fuller, Harry J., 83
Fund for Adult Education, 28, 56, 138, 270, 280; coordinated with Fund, 49, 64; terminated, 73
Fund for the Republic, 73

Gaither, Rowan, 16, 17, 73
Gardner, John, viii
Gary, Indiana, 108
General Education in School and College, 197
Germany, 162
G.I. Bill, 98, 100, 118
Giannini, Bernadette, 60
Gifford, Walter, 49
Goodlad, John, 199; School Curriculum Reform in the United States, 192; The Changing School Curriculum, 192
Gores, Harold, quoted, 245–246
Gould, Lawrence, 245

Graduate School Today and Tomorrow, The (Strothmann), 191
Graduate schools. See Master of Arts in Teaching degree; Ph.D. degrees; Universities
Grammar, 85, 87
Grant making: Study Committee on, 25; and educational philosophy, 67, 68; and Fund goals, 71, 114–171 passim, 172; major categories, 215–217; and charges of favoritism, 229–231; and dictating policy, 257. See also specific programs
"Great Books" approach, 64
Great Books of the Western World, 166
Greenfield Village, 14
Griffiths, G. H., 56–57
Griswold, Whitney, 84, 219
Gross, Ronald, 56, 58; and J. Murphy, Learning by Television, 141, 142–143, 144, 145–146, 192
Gross national product, 5, 170

Hagerstown, Maryland, 139–140
Hammer, Philip, 175
Hampton Institute, 157–158
Hardy, Gladys Chang, 61
Harrison, Marjorie, 62
Hartford Foundation, John A., 213
Harvard University, 51, 171; MAT program, 131–132, 226–227; Fund grants to, 157, 197, 198–199
Havighurst, Robert, quoted, 244–245, 252–253, 271–272

Head Start, xii, 163
Heald, Henry, 57, 73, 75
Heathers, Glen, 152
Hechinger, Fred, 85
Hekscher, Maurice, 49
Henry Ford Hospital, 14
Henry Ford Museum, 14
Herbart, Johann Friedrich, 120
High schools: preparing teachers for, 42, 94–96, 102, 118–125, 129, 130–132, 136, 216; Lester Nelson and, 55; curriculum, 85–89, 161–163, 203, 244, 261; enrollment, 99–100, 186–187, 204; class sizes, 101, 151, 222; salaries, 104, 189, 190; women teachers at, 104; and segregation, 110–111, 158; and educational TV, 141, 142, 143; and team teaching, 151; and early college admissions, 153–155; and advanced placement, 156; Conant report on, 160; and Fund advisors, 232; Fund programs evaluated, 245, 246, 258, 262–263
Hill, Henry, quoted, 244, 252, 274–275
History courses, 88
Hoffman, Paul, viii, 72, 73, 270; and founding of Fund, 28, 34, 43, 172
Homemaking courses, 88
Horton, Mildred McAfee (Mrs. Douglas), 48, 51
Houghton, Jr., Arthur A., 49
Howe, Arthur, 49
Howe, Harold, II, quoted, 201, 245, 254–255, 271
Huff, Ronayne, 62

Hutchins, Robert Maynard, 72, 73, 172, 230, 240, 270; and founding of Fund, 28, 34, 43; and Faust, 37; role at Fund, 62–65, 252; and Arkansas program, 128

Illinois, University of, 253, 254
Images of the Future (Trump), 151n
Immigrants, and role of schools, 208
Indians, 106–107, 262
Institute for Philosophical Research, 166–167, 230, 252, 260
Internships for teachers, 224, 255; Arkansas program, 126, 127, 130; other programs, 132–133, 136, 244; for college instructors, 164, 165
Iowa, 147
Ivy League colleges, 50, 51, 105, 226, 228; Negroes in, 108–109

James, Weldon, *The Louisville Story*, 196
James, William, 120
Jennings, Frank, 181–182
Johns Hopkins University, 227
Johnson, Charles Spurgeon, 221
Johnson, Lyndon, 99, 108
Jones, Lewis Webster, 126, 129
Jones, T. Duckett, 17
Josephs, Devereux, viii
Journals of education, 180. *See also specific names*
Junior high schools, 246

Kaufman, Bel, *Up the Down Staircase*, 184

Kellogg Foundation, 213
Kentucky, 110
Keppel, Francis, v-vi, xi, 131
Khrushchev, Nikita, 209
King, Jonathan, 57
Klein, Frances M., *The Changing School Curriculum* (with von Stoephasius and Goodlad), 192
Korean War, 3, 70
Krathwohl, David, 253
Krell, Eleanor Slaybaugh, 61, 181
Kronenberg, Arthur, 126
Kuesel, Arnold J., 57

Land Grant College Act of 1861, 98
Languages, 87, 88, 162, 163, 203
Larsen, Roy E., 46–47, 48, 51, 77
Lauristsen, Charles C., 17
Lawrenceville School, 197
Leadership Fellows Program, 161
Learning by Television (Murphy and Gross), 192
Letter to a College President (Tickton), 191
Let's Talk Sense About Our Schools (Woodring), vii
Liberal education: Hutchins on, 62–64; Study Report on, 67–68; and Fund policy, 71, 260–261, 265; for teachers, 94, 224–225; and faculty fellowships, 117; and teacher training, 122–124, 134; and Arkansas program, 126–130 *passim*; problems of 1950's, 197–198. *See also* Master of Arts in Teaching degree
Libraries, school, 55, 82
Life magazine, 85

Lilly Endowment, 213
Lippmann, Walter, quoted, 47–48, 67, 205
Literature courses, 88
Local government, and school costs, 98–99
Los Angeles, California, 192
Louisville *Courier Journal*, 49
Louisville Story, The (Carmichael and James), 196
Loyalty oaths, 82
Luce publications, 46
Lynch, Roberta, 62
Lynd, Albert, 83

MacDonald, Dwight, 236
McGill, Ralph, 49, 50
McGuffey, William, 14
McKnight, C. A., 178
McLuhan, Marshall, 219
McNeely, Janet Moreland, 62
McPeak, William, 17
Mademoiselle, 61
Magazines: and TV, 7; articles on schools in 1950's, 179–180
Maine, 161
Maine, University of, 40
Mann, Horace, 208
Marquis, Donald, 17
Martus, Marjorie, 61
Maryland, 110
Maryland Commission on Interracial Problems, 196
Massachusetts, 108
Master of Arts in Teaching degree (MAT, AMT), ix, 131–133, 216; evaluated, 226–229, 244, 248, 255, 259, 261
MAT. *See* Master of Arts in Teaching degree

Mathematics, 85–88 *passim*, 142, 152, 162, 203, 265

Meade, Jr., Edward J., 58

M.Ed. degree, 132

Medical schools, Flexner report on, 125, 126, 234

Medical services, use of personnel, 221

Mellon, Paul, 48

Mellon family foundations, 49

Mexican-Americans, 262

Midwest Program of Airborne Television Instruction, 143–144

Minnesota, 147

Minnesota, University of, 40, 53, 252

Minority groups, and educational opportunity, 20, 70, 71. *See also* Culturally disadvantaged

Missouri, 110

Montclair State Teachers College, N.J., 138

Morehouse College, 157

Morgan State College, 157

Morrison, Donald, 197–198

MPATI. *See* Midwest Program of Airborne Television Instruction

Multiversities, 222

Municipal colleges, 121

Murphy, Judith, 56; and R. Gross, *Learning by Television*, 141, 142–143, 144, 145–146, 192; *Decade of Experiment*, 193–196

Music, 97, 146, 152

Nance, Arlene Mensher, 62

National Academy of Science, 272

National Assessment Program, xi, xiii, 168–171

National Association of Secondary-School Principals, 151, 153

National Citizens Commission (Council) for the Public Schools, vii, viii, ix, 46, 47, 51, 181, 257; goals of, vii, viii; Fund grants to, ix, 159, 216

National Defense Education Act, 98–99, 206, 207–208

National Education Association, 83, 101, 148, 169, 200; National Commission on Teacher Education and Professional Standards, 246, 247

National Endowment for the Humanities, 61

National Program in the use of Television in the Public Schools, 142–143

National Scholarship Service and Fund for Negro Students, 158

Needed: A Ten-Year College Budget (Tickton), 191

Negroes: move to cities, 4, 263; equal opportunities for, 70, 106–113, 156–159, 216, 262; Ashmore Report, 174–177; and new fund, 278, 279

Nelson, Lester, 54–56, 57, 58, 60, 199

Neo-scholasticism, 167

New Directions in Teacher Education (FAE), 191

New Orleans, Louisiana, 158

New York, State University of, 34, 41, 54

New York City, 34, 41, 64

New York State, 160

New York State Board of Regents, 96–97

Newark, New Jersey, 111

Newton, Massachusetts, 246, 254

Nobel Prize, x, 142

Normal schools. *See* Teachers colleges

North Central College, Naperville, Illinois, 34, 35, 40

Northwestern University, 40, 51

Oakland, California, 112

Odegard, Peter H., 17

Officers of Fund: Study Report on, 24–25; policies, 32, 65–72, 120, 205, 206; described, 52–56, 195; salaries, 211, 212; Briggs on, 239, 240. *See also* Educational philosophy; *specific programs*

Official Register of the Graduate School of Education for 1936–7 (Harvard), 131

Olds, Jr., Henry F., *Team Teaching*, 150–151, 198–199

Olson, Willard C., quoted, 246, 256, 273

Oregon, State Department of Education, 229

Pace, Robert, 199

Paepcke, Walter P., 48, 49, 50

Park, Charles B., quoted, 249, 257, 273

Parochial schools, 96, 111

Pasadena, California, 34, 41, 64

Paschal, Elizabeth, 54, 56, 57, 199; *Encouraging the Excellent*, 191

Peabody Institute, 227

Peer group, and early admission, 155

Pennsylvania, 97

Pennsylvania State University, 141

Pestalozzi, Johann Heinrich, 120

Ph.D. degrees, 22, 103, 106, 164, 187

Philadelphia, 64, 112, 192

Philanthropic funds. *See* Foundations

Phillips Academy. *See* Andover

Philosophy. *See* Educational philosophy

Phonics, teaching of, 90–94

Physical education courses, 88, 146

Physics courses, 142, 162, 173

Pifer, Alan, quoted, 268–269

Population: growth, 3–4, 33, 204; shifts, 4–5, 79, 111–112, 264; postwar baby boom and school enrollment, 99, 100, 118, 185–186

Portland, Oregon, 61, 163, 230

Preschool programs, xii, 163, 254–255, 278

Price, Don K., 17

Princeton University, 197

Principals, 95, 118, 153, 155, 189. *See also* Administrators, school

Private schools, 50, 51, 105, 111, 160. *See also* Colleges

"Problems of American Democracy," 163

Progressive education, 83, 87–89, 209, 246, 262

Progressive Education Association, 60, 89

Project Opportunity Schools, 158

Psychology courses, 87, 136, 173
PTA, 80
Public Affairs Committee, 177
Public schools: criticized, 8, 79–90; religion in, 96; costs of, 97–99; and desegregation, 109–112; Fund grants for, 159, 217; "breakthrough program," 135–137; shifting role of, 208; teacher training for, 226, 227–228. *See also* Cities; Elementary schools; High schools; Rural schools; Teachers
Puerto Ricans, 5
Puerto Rico Department of Education, 229
Pupil-teacher ratio. *See* Class sizes; Teachers
Purdue, Indiana, 143
Purks, Harris, 199

Rae, Patricia Norris, 62
Rafferty, Max, 89
Reading: teaching of, xi, 86, 90–94, 174, 258; and impact of TV, 6–7; conference on, 232
Recreation and public schools, 86, 88, 97, 110
Reed, Philip D., 48, 49
Reese Committee, 240–241
Reforming American Education (Eurich), 219–220
Rehmus, Paul, 60–61, 199, 230, 239
Religion, in public schools, 86, 96–97
Research: and Fund staff, 61; professors prefer, 106; meaning of, and Fund projects, 30, 173–174; Fund grants for, 236–237; and

need for new fund, 273, 274. *See also specific programs*
Richmond Times Dispatch, 178
Roberts, Owen J., 46, 47, 49, 51, 176
Rockefeller, John D., 13, 15
Rockefeller Foundation, 115, 213
Roper Survey, 85
Rousseau, Jean-Jacques, 120
Ruml, Beardsley: *Teaching Salaries Then and Now,* 188–189, 191; *Memo to a College Trustee,* 197–198
Rural schools, 143, 160–161, 262, 278
Russia. *See* Soviet Union

St. Louis, Missouri, 112
St. Louis University, 158
San Francisco, California, 166
Satellites, 98, 144, 162, 206
Saturday Review, 85, 107; Education Supplement, 56, 61, 178–185, 248, 259
Scanlon, John, 56, 57, 145, 181, 186
Scarsdale, New York, 55
"Scatteration giving," 38, 115, 231
Scholarships, 29, 45, 105, 153
Scholastic Aptitude Test, 158
School and College Study of General Education, 197
School and Society, 129, 238, 239, 240
School Bell Award, 185
School boards, local, 22, 80, 97, 104, 159
School Curriculum Reform in the U.S. (Goodlad), 192
School Improvement Program, 58

Schools for Tomorrow, an Educator's Blueprint (Stoddard), 192
Science courses, 139, 152, 162, 163, 203, 265
Sciences: emphasis on, 98–99, 162, 206; research and, 173
Secondary schools. *See* High Schools
Segregation, 4, 106–113, 156, 158; publications on, x, 174–178, 196–197, 259
Seminars for teacher training, 224
Sex, courses in, 86
Shaplin, Judson T., *Team Teaching*, 150–151, 198–199
Sherman, Frances, 62
Shoemaker, Don, *With All Deliberate Speed,* 196
Sloan Foundation, 213
Smith, Elmer, *Teacher Education: A Reappraisal,* 199
Smith, Mortimer, 83, 248, 257–258
Smith Hughes Act of 1917, 98
Social life. *See* Recreation and public schools
Social sciences, 152, 173
Sociology, 87
Soderlund, Dorothy, 62
Southern Association of Schools and Colleges, 158
Southern Education Reporting Service (SERS), 177–178, 196
Southern Regional Council, 177
Southern School News, x, 178
Soviet Union, 98, 162, 206, 208–210
Spaulding, Francis T., 17, 23n
Spaulding, Susan, 57
Spaulding, Willard, 253–254

Specialization, 21–22, 62
Spelling, 85
Spragens, Thomas A., 53
Sputnik I, 98, 162, 206
Staff of Fund: members of, 51–62, 195; absorbed by Ford Foundation, 73–75; salaries, 211, 212. *See also* Officers of Fund
Stanford University, 37, 40, 41, 62, 252
State governments: and school costs, 98, 99; departments of education, 83, 123–124
State School Officers, Council of, 169
Stiles, Lindley J., quoted, 243–244, 254, 272, 273
Stinnett, T. M., quoted, 246–247, 255–256
Stoddard, Alexander J., 60; *Schools for Tomorrow,* 192–193
Stoddard, George, 151–152
Stoephasius, Renata von, 58; *The Changing School Curriculum,* 192; *Decade of Experiment,* 193–196
Strothmann, F. W., *The Graduate School Today and Tomorrow,* 191
Study Committee Report, 15–25, 26–28, 67–68, 73, 202–203
Suburban schools, 4, 79–80, 88
Superintendents, 118, 189. *See also* Administrators, school
Supervision and Curriculum Development, Association of, 169
Supreme Court, United States, 46, 108; on school desegregation, x, 109–111, 174–178 *passim*; and

Supreme Court (*cont.*)
religion in public schools, 96–97
Swarthmore College, 134
Synopticon, 166

Taconic Foundation, xii
Tax rates, 97
Teacher aides, 71, 161, 193, 265; Bay City project, ix, 147, 230, 249, 256; effectiveness of, 147–149, 249, 255, 259; and class sizes, 220, 221, 222
Teacher education: Study Report on, 22, 67; Hoffman on, 28, 29; Eurich on, 41–42, 225; Hutchins on, 62–63; improvement of, as Fund goal, 69–71, 116; 196; controversy of 1950's, 83, 94; improvements in, 102, 203, 204; Fund programs for, 117–137, 157–158, 162–166, 198–199, 216; Fund programs evaluated, 224–229, 243–264 *passim*
Teachers: shortage of, 33, 99, 101–102, 134, 142, 164, 186, 187, 193, 195; and McCarthy period, 82; and teaching reading, 91; certification of, 94–96, 101, 119–125 *passim*, 127, 133; salaries, 97, 102, 103–104, 131, 188–190, 198, 222; increase in, 102, 118; men-women ratio, 104–105; and educational TV, 137–145 *passim*; articles by, 184; teacher-pupil ratio, 192–193, 198, 221–222; and class sizes, 219–224; recruitment of, 228; as Fund advisors, 232–233. *See also*
Teacher aides; Teacher education; Team teaching
Teachers colleges, 94, 120–122, 128, 226, 279. *See also* Educational philosophy; Teacher education
Teachers for Tomorrow, 186, 187, 221, 259
Teaching by Television (Murphy and Gross), 192
Teaching machines, 136, 219
Teaching Salaries Then and Now, (Tickton and Ruml), 186, 188–190, 191, 259
Teaching Salaries Then and Now: A Second Look (Tickton), 190, 191
Team teaching, 136, 195, 203, 265; development of, 149–152; Harvard study of, 198–199; and class size, 221, 222
Team Teaching (Shaplin and Olds), 150–151, 198–199
Technologies. *See* Sciences
Television, 6–7, 33. *See also* Educational television
Temple University, 227
Texas, 110
Texas, University of, 109
Textbooks. *See* Books
They Went to College Early (FAE), 154, 191
Thompson, Margery, 62
Thornton, Dorothy, 62
Three-year Master's degree program, 164–165
Tickton, Sidney, 56, 58, 60; *Teaching Salaries Then and Now,* 186, 188–190, 191, 259; *Teaching Salaries Then and Now: A*

Second Look, 191; *Needed: A Ten-Year College Budget,* 191; *Letter to a College President,* 191; *The Year-Round Campus Catches On,* 191
Time, Inc., 46–47
Tomorrow's Professor (Dieckhoff), 191
Toulson, Margaret, 62
Trump, Lloyd, 151
Tyler, Ralph, 168, 170, 199, 239

Ungraded classes, 136
United States Riot Commission Report, 112
Universities: graduate schools, 22, 103, 106, 164, 187; schools of education, 83, 91, 120–121, 136, 164–165, 219; and purpose of education, 86; salaries, 104, 189, 190; and team teaching, 150; class sizes, 222; grants to, 226–230; present problems, 277, 280. *See also* Colleges
Utah, 147
Utilization of College Teaching Resources, Committee on, 165, 191

Vanderbilt University, 227
Vermont, 161
Veterans' education, 20, 98, 100, 118
Vietnam war, 3, 7
Virgin Islands, 157
Vocabulary, children's, 91
Vocational training: Fund policy on, 72, 160; demands for, 80, 85; in public schools, 86, 88, 97; federal aid for, 98
Voice of America, 177

Volunteer assistants in schools, 147

Walsh, Clifford, 62
Walton, John, 199
Washington, D.C., 111
Washington County, Maryland, 139–140
Weaver, Warren, quoted, 212–213
Webster, Noah, 14
Weiss, John K., 54
West Virginia, 110
Western Washington State College, 181
White, Harvey, 142
White House Conference on Education of 1965, 169
Why Johnny Can't Read (Flesch), xi, 90, 91
Williams, Wendell, 62
Williamsburg, Virginia, 200
Wilson, O. Meredith, 53
Wilson College, 134
Wisconsin, University of, 229, 244
Women teachers, 102, 104–105, 133
Woodring, Paul, 56, 181, 182–183, 199; *Let's Talk Sense About Our Schools,* vii
Work-study programs, cooperative, 167
Wright Brothers, 14

Yale University, 197, 219, 227
Year-Round Campus Catches On, The (Tickton), 191
Yeshiva University, 227
Young, James Webb, 48, 49, 50, 51